Motorbooks International

Authentic Restoration Guides

HOW TO RESTORE YOUR
BMW MOTORCYCLE
TWINS 1950-1969

Roland Slabon

First published in 1994 by Motorbooks International Publishers & Wholesalers, PO Box 2, 729 Prospect Avenue, Osceola, WI 54020 USA

© Roland Slabon, 1994

Motorbooks International books are also available at discounts in bulk quantity for industrial or sales-promotional use. For details write to Special Sales Manager at the Publisher's address

Library of Congress Cataloging-in-Publication Data Available

ISBN 0-87938-933-8

On the front cover: The quintessential BWM twin? A very handsome 1967 R60/2. The Earles-forked machines make particularly good sidecar haulers. *Jeff Dean*

Printed and bound in the United States of America

Contents

Acknowledgments

This book is dedicated to all those motorcycle enthusiasts I have had the unique privilege to meet over the past two decades, years filled with the pleasure of restoring, riding, and writing about vintage BMW motorcycles.

Most soon became good friends and joined me as members of Vintage BMW Motorcycle Owners, Ltd., and among us we shared a mutual passion for BMW motorcycles. All helped add to my knowledge of these unique machines by gifting me with their experiences.

A virtual encyclopedia of advice, ideas, and suggestions has been woven into the pages of this book and should be credited to friends and fellow enthusiasts Armen Amirian, Duane Ausherman, Robert Beeman, Bruno Canale, Jo Groeger, Joel Hansen, Jonathan Hayt, Bill Kuhlman, Vern Mitchell, Oak Okleshen, Harold Sharon, Ted Strobl, Craig Trottier, and Pete von Sneidern. Many of their suggestions are on these pages, to be shared with you.

Additionally, special thanks go to those whose many photos were added to my collection, among them Tracy Baker, Oscar Fricke, John and Marie Lacko, and Rich Sheckler.

Finally, my gratitude to a special few, whose encouragement and assistance helped make this book possible. They are Bob Henig; Ed Korn; Larry Sparber; Robert Hellman, Editor of *On the Level*; and Craig Vechorik, Technical Editor of my own *Vintage BMW Bulletin*. Particular thanks go to Richard Kahn of Butler & Smith, and Hans Fleichmann, formerly of the BMW Archives in Munich, who provided me with many priceless historical photos and technical literature which I am privileged to share with you.

If enthusiasm can be measured by the depth and breadth of such friendship and fellowship, then this book can truly be considered the enthusiasts' guide to the enjoyment and restoration of vintage and classic BMW motorcycles.

Roland Slabon
Exeter, New Hampshire USA
July 1994

Introduction

Many books have been written detailing the history of the Bavarian Motor Works and the cars and motorcycles bearing the blue and white roundel. All give the reader a fine overview of what has rolled out of the gates at Munich, Spandau, and Eisenach. Some concern themselves with BMW's myriad racing successes, the number and variety of which are now legend. Some delve with almost clinical precision into the details of engine design and corporate manufacturing policy. A few are intended to give the reader a modicum of knowledge about the models actually produced, or how to make a wise decision when contemplating the purchase of either a vintage, classic, or contemporary car or motorcycle.

None, however, seem to address themselves to informing the enthusiast on just how to go about selecting, finding, and restoring a vintage machine. Shop manuals and reprints of instruction books are not enough when it comes to resurrecting and correctly restoring a thoroughbred such as the BMW.

A workshop manual, no matter how comprehensive, can only cover the technical details, yet no restoration effort should be contemplated without access to at least one good one. However, when it comes to the fine nuances that separate a quality, correct, and authentic restoration from a simple conscientious rebuild, there is nothing that can guide the enthusiast better than experience, knowledge, and the assistance of experts. The BMW, for all its conservative traditions and a seemingly constant production plan, nevertheless underwent countless detail changes that can overwhelm and confound both novice and expert alike.

This book is directed to both such enthusiasts. The expert will find it reinforcing, and will use it as a checklist for future restorations. The novice will find it invaluable not only as a road map and project plan, but also as a guide to which of the sixteen different postwar BMW twin-cylinder classics he might consider. Details requiring the assistance of skilled machinists, employing tools rarely found in the average workshop, have been omitted. Complex technical operations such as crank rebuilding and cylinder reboring are best left to qualified machine shops, and will not be included in the scope of this book. This book will attempt to address all the subtle details that go into a restoration, that are only learned over the years, and will supplement them with technical data and directives previously available only to dealers and repair shops.

Over twenty years of enthusiasm are brought to you on the pages of this book, coupled with the advice and knowledge gained from experts and other vintage BMW collectors and restorers. Its audience is the BMW enthusiast, whether he is embarking on his first restoration or completing his tenth, whether he is planning his first purchase, or readying his newly restored machine for its first showing. Armed with the knowledge, guidelines, and assistance presented here, both novice and expert will be able to rebuild, restore, ride, and thoroughly enjoy one of BMW's most enduring and exciting artifacts, the 1950–1969 vintage and classic BMW twin.

Chapter 1

Historical Perspective

The history of BMW spans more than three quarters of a century; and began in the years just prior to World War I. At that time, two small concerns—an aircraft company and an engine manufacturer—were operating in the outskirts of Munich. Had it not been for the outbreak of war, it is possible the two might never have combined to form the company that eventually became Bavarian Motor Works.

The first of the two firms was Rapp Motoreren Werke, founded in 1913, which built aircraft engines under license from Austro Daimler. During the war, its aircraft engines rivaled those of Daimler and Benz and powered the Fokkers of Richthofen's Flying Circus.

The second company was Otto Flugzeugwerke, founded by Nikolaus Otto. Otto left the firm

An early 1917 advertisement for the aviation engines of the newly incorporated Bavarian Motor Works. In the background are the national flags of Imperial Germany and the Austro-Hungarian Empire, BMW's two major clients. *BMW Archives*

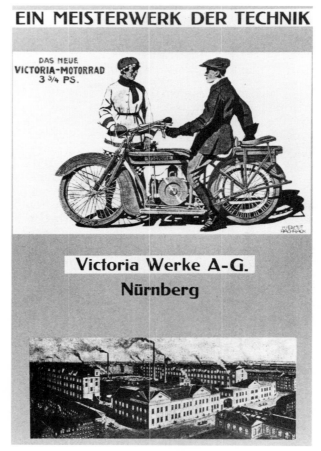

A 1922 press photo from the Victoria Works of Nuremberg, extolling their popular 3.75 PS model KR2 propelled by a proprietary BMW M2B15 engine. *Oscar Fricke*

in 1916, and on July 21, 1917, Rapp Motoreren Werke engineers Franz-Josef Popp and Max Friz reincorporated the firm as the Bavarian Aircraft Works. At war's end, the firm was dissolved and all aircraft production ceased.

In 1922, Popp and Friz moved into the old Otto factory with financial backing from the Austrian financier Castiglioni. The Bavarian Motor Works was reincorporated and limited production of stationary engines and other mechanical equipment was begun. Throughout the 1920s and 1930s, BMW excelled in the production of aircraft engines, setting numerous altitude and endurance records. The company began producing a small car under license, then sports and touring cars of its own design. Despite these aviation and automotive successes it was motorcycle production that brought in most of the much needed revenue. Prior to World War II, motorcycles accounted for the majority of BMW production at both the Munich and Eisenach factories.

By the early 1920s, a number of German motorcycle manufacturers were using the BMW opposed twin M2B15 side-valve engine, all in a fore-to-aft configuration with chain or belt drive to the rear wheel.

The popularity of BMW's M2B15 engine convinced engineer Friz that he could design and sell a truly new concept powered by the tried and accepted powerplant. After a hurried but successful design effort, Friz and BMW introduced their new motorcycle at the 1923 Paris Show. The revolutionary BMW R32 featured a 493cc, 6.5hp, 2-cylinder side-valve motor mounted transversely in the frame. The engine was coupled to an automotive-style transmission, with final drive to the rear

Two other German brands whose manufacturers found the BMW engine ideally suited to their needs were the 1924 "RS" and the "Bayerland." As clever as these concepts were, none could match BMW's tour de force, the 1923 R32. *Oscar Fricke*

Another view of the Victoria KR2, just one of the many German motorcycles using the BMW side-valve engine in the early 1920s.

wheel by a geared Cardan shaft. The R32 concept was such a success, and was met with such enthusiasm, that BMW has kept to basically the same design for the past seventy years!

From those historic beginnings, BMW motorcycle production can be broken down into four prewar phases, ending with the destruction of all manufacturing facilities in 1945. Production was allowed to resume in 1948, and through 1969 two more distinct phases can be seen. After 1970, production of motorcycles was transferred to Spandau, a suburb of what was then West Berlin, and BMW entered the modern age. It used more innovative designs, electronic ignition, upgraded suspension and chassis systems, and even three- and four-cylinder in-line engines. As of 1994, BMW offered its first chain-driven motorcycle, with an Austrian single-cylinder motor mated to a chassis of Italian design. While the first R32 of 1923 may have been revolutionary, it is innovation nurtured by evolution that has kept BMW in the forefront of motorcycle design.

The famous shot of BMW's early assembly line at its former aircraft shops at Oberwiesenfeld near Munich. Being completed, and not yet fitted with their distinctive tank badges, are several 1923 versions of the R32, which in its early production run had non-detachable heads and no front brake. *BMW Archives*

An improved version R32, upgraded with an optional lighting set, horn, and front brake. Rear braking, such as it was, was accomplished with a "dummy rim" device and foot pedal, a common practice with many manufacturers. *BMW Archives*

8

Prewar Production Phases

BMW's first era of pre-World War II motorcycle production encompasses 1923 through 1929. During those years, all the machines, both singles and twins, had brazed tubular steel frames, primitive (by later standards) rigid front forks with leaf spring front suspension (similar to that employed by Indian in the U.S.). Engines were side-valve or overhead valve twins, in capacities of 500 and 750cc. One single-cylinder OHV machine of 250cc was also offered. Drive to the rigidly mounted rear wheel was by Cardan shaft. Rudimentary front brakes were eventually supplemented with a contracting-drum brake on the driveshaft coupling at the transmission. As basic as these machines were, they represented the best in German engineering at the time, and many were raced with considerable success in England and throughout Europe.

By the end of 1929, even these excellent designs were hard pressed by competitors, forcing BMW to again astound the world, this time with an innovative pressed-steel girder frame and pressed-steel front end, still retaining leaf springs. Upgraded versions of the earlier engines were employed in side-valve and overhead valve twin-cylinder designs of 750cc. Single-cylinder machines were offered in OHV versions of 200, 250, 300, 350, and 400cc capacity. The pressed-steel frame, leaf spring fork era ended officially in 1936, when the last of the 400cc R4 singles were produced.

However, even with such detail design

Die eleganteste und zuverlässigste deutsche Beiwagen-Maschine

BAYERISCHE MOTOREN WERKE
AKTIEN-GESELLSCHAFT + MÜNCHEN

A nice advertisement of the mid-1920s, showing what was probably an R42 of 1926–1928 and a BMW proprietary sidecar. *BMW Archives*

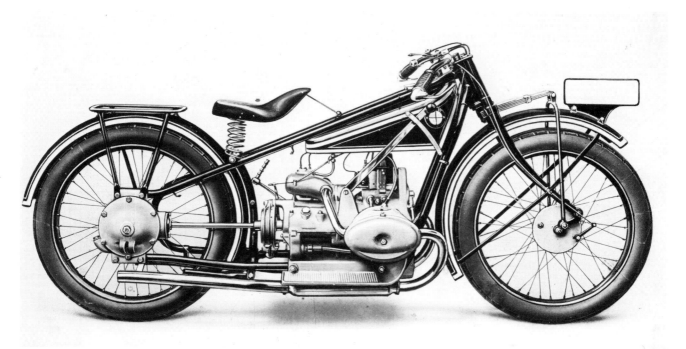

The second overhead valve BMW twin, the 18hp 500cc R47 of 1927-1928 was treated to a refinement of the earlier R32 frame, and also enjoyed a substantial front brake and rear driveshaft brake. Lighting was still an option. *BMW Archives*

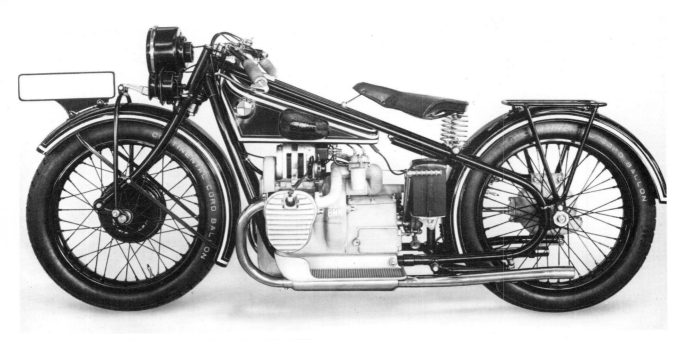

One of the last of the first series machines, this 18hp 750cc SV R62 typified the brazed tube, leaf sprung BMWs of the mid-1920s. *BMW Archives*

Typical of all second series designs was this 33hp 750cc R16 of 1932–1934, with its massive pressed-steel frame and pressed-steel fork blades. In spite of the bridge girder look of these chassis members, the R16 and its stablemates weighed in at a reasonable 363lb. *BMW Archives*

changes, BMW saw the need for further improvements, in particular in the area of handling, a traditional BMW shortcoming. In 1935, the telescopic fork era began with the introduction of the R12 and R17, both pressed-steel framed machines of 750cc capacity, the former having a side-valve motor, the latter a high-performance overhead valve design. With the world's first production oil-damped telescopics, plus interchangeable wheels, internal expanding drum brakes front and rear, and distinctive Art Deco styling, the BMW R12 and R17 models were eagerly sought after in most of the Western world. A number of these machines made their way to the U.S. before the war, and the R12 was such a successful design that over 36,000 were produced through 1940, primarily for the military and for sale to the armies of other countries, notably the Netherlands.

The third prewar production era ended in 1940, but not before the beginning of the fourth and final prewar phase. In 1936, concurrently with the introduction of the R12 and R17, BMW introduced what is now considered to be the first modern BMW, the double-loop tube frame R5. It had the same forks as the R12/R17 series, and a rear drive rigidly mounted in the frame, but the 500cc overhead valve engine was of a totally new design, as was the transmission, which now had a foot-shifter

as well as the traditional hand-shift lever. The double-loop conical section frame carried a stylish teardrop tank and a sprung solo saddle, design cues that were to be continued with only minor refinements all the way until 1954.

Other engines of 600 and 750cc followed, again in side-valve and overhead valve configurations. By 1937, the rigid rear end had been replaced by vertical plunger shafts and coil springs, a direct carryover from BMWs successful racing models. Overhead valve singles of 200cc and 250cc capacity were also produced, as well as a complex 750cc ohv twin, the R75, for military use. This machine included such innovations as torsion bar suspension for the sidecar wheel; locking and limited slip differential; eight forward and two reverse speeds, in high and low ranges; hydraulic brakes to the rear wheel; and even a sidecar heated by recycling exhaust gas. By 1945, production of all but a few of the R75s had ceased; the factories at Munich and Eisenach lay in ruins, with what remained of the latter in Russian hands.

Postwar Production

After the war, the Allied Occupation authorities prohibited all German motorcycle production until 1948. That year, BMW was allowed to reintroduce the prewar single-cylinder R23, now re-

The third series and the final refinement of the pressed-steel frame era. This model was the world's first production motorcycle to have oil-damped telescopics. The first of these machines was the 1935–1940 R12, a 750cc side-valve machine, whose conservative 18hp were offset by its wonderful Art Deco sculptured fenders. *BMW Archives*

The fourth series of prewar BMW production design was ushered in with the 500cc OHV R5 in 1936–37. Among its novel features, which were to remain basically unchanged into the mid-1950s, were telescopic forks, a streamlined teardrop tank, and a double-loop frame of an excellent, oval-section design providing great strength and light weight. Owners of pre-1955 BMWs can look to the R5 as the ancestor of their own machines. The solid rear axle of the R5 was soon replaced with sliding plungers on the R51 that followed in 1937–1940. *Rich Sheckler*

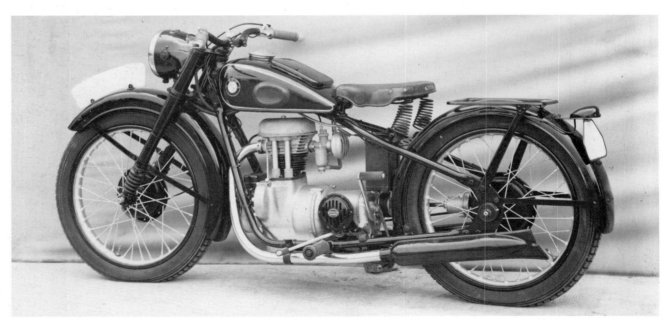

Even the diminutive BMW singles shared the good looks and engineering advances of the R5, as can be seen in this 10hp 250cc R23 of 1938–1941. *BMW Archives*

The last refinement of the fourth series frames was this 22hp R71 of 1938–1939, which was also built in small numbers at the request of the military as late as 1941. Clearly shown are the excellent rear plungers and the flexible driveshaft, linked to the various components by a rubber coupling and a universal joint. If you take away the 750cc side-valve engine, you'll have basically a 1950–1954 BMW twin, so advanced was the design. *BMW Archives*

A 1952 R67/2, last of the postwar twins to still retain the earlier metal fork covers. Compare the styling cues of this machine with the earlier R71 and even the 1936 R5, and you'll understand just how advanced the mid-1930s BMW twins really were.

named the R24, but basically the same 250cc overhead valve single of 1938–1941. A twin was added to the line in 1950, the R51/2, which was nothing more than a slightly updated version of the 1937–1940 R51. Nonetheless, these new BMWs sold amazingly well, and by 1951 two all new engine designs were released, soon to be followed by the first true 100mph twin, the R68. The first of the postwar production phases ended in 1954, after more than 32,000 twins had been sold. Of these, the overhead valve 500cc R51/2 and R51/3 were the most popular, followed by the 600cc R67 series and the R68. An updated version of the R24, the R25, offered rear suspension and was built in several variations, with over 108,000 being sold between 1950 and 1954.

The last of the two classic postwar production eras began in 1955 and continued until 1969, when the first of the new /5 series finally replaced a school of design that had its beginnings with the R5 of 1936. The first of the "new" twins was the R50, a 500cc OHV machine fitted with Earles forks and a double-loop tubular frame, adjustable rear shock absorbers, and a swing-arm rear suspension. Engines were basically unchanged from 1951, and the R50 was soon followed by a 600cc variant, the R60. The "sports" R68 was replaced by the R69, and by 1961, BMW was cashing in on its sporting successes on the sidecar circuit by introducing what today are called supersports bikes, the R50S and R69S. Upgrades to the earlier R50 and R60 engines resulted in the R50/2 and R60/2, and by 1968 even the ubiquitous Earles forks were replaced by modern US-telescopics. Singles slowly fell out of favor, and although the R26 and R27 (Earles fork descendants of the R25 series) accounted for nearly 50,000 additional sales, the small one-cylinder machines were dropped in 1967.

By 1969, enthusiasm for the decidedly old-fashioned and increasingly expensive leading-link twins had nearly evaporated. BMW noted the growing popularity of fast sports machines from England, Italy, and Japan as a sign of things to come in the seventies. The new /5 series which, with the exception of the US-forks from 1968, were of a totally new design, effectively ended BMW's postwar classic era.

The end of the plunger era gave us this 1954 R67/2, which gained full-width brakes and rubber fork gaiters, the new headlamp with covered key slide, and a marginally larger dual lens taillamp. With the exception of the 1950 R51/2 and the R68, all front fenders wore this type of pinstriping. *BMW Archives*

From 1955–1968, most of the BMW twins available in the U.S. looked like this one, with a one-piece bench seat, raised handlebars, and small standard tank. All were striped the same, and the only way to tell them apart was by the shape and number of valve cover fins. *K. Attenberger*

By 1969, the postwar classic era came to a close, and this R50US is typical of all the US-fork machines. Unique to these models were the elaborate front fender cum fork brace and massive aluminum lower fork legs. This particular model is also fitted with a headlight guard, crashbars, sidestand, bar end signals, and Denfeld solo saddle. *Guy de la Rupelle*

The last of the Earles fork machines, this 1968 R69S displayed the characteristic bulge in the front cover to clear the vibration damper and the Hella bar-end signals, not so affectionately called "ox eyes" in Germany. *BMW Archives*

Chapter 2

Choosing Your Mount

If you've already found your BMW, I assume you put some thought into the purchase and, after many long hours of soul searching and deliberation, bought the one you knew would suit you best. But, if you're like the rest of us, you probably bought the first thing that caught your eye—the one that wasn't too overpriced or that was too good of a deal to pass up.

Did you make the right choice? Only time, and the balance remaining in your bank account, will tell. At least the hard part is done.

However, you might not have been as lucky as you think. Even though the BMW you've dragged or ridden home seems to be just what you were looking for, will it really be the best one for you? There are a number of things you might not have considered, and a number of wrong decisions you might have made, which could spell disaster somewhere down the road.

The following points to consider are as important for the current owner of a BMW to review as they are for those new to the game. While most of the 1950–1969 BMW twins may look alike to the novice, there is a world of difference between the various models, and even within different years of production of the same model. An R69 is not the same as an R69S, nor is an R50 anything like an R50 US. The engine in an R50/2 or R60/2 may look identical to the engine in an R67/3, but you're in for an expensive lesson if you think anything other than the heads, valve covers, or oil pan are interchangeable.

For those about to start their search, narrow your field of view. To blindly chase after every BMW that is advertised can be both time consuming and expensive, especially if you end up buying what later turns out to be not at all the BMW you wanted. For those who have completed their search, or those about to start the restoration of a BMW, let's go over the rules of the game.

Never buy an incomplete motorcycle unless you need it only for spare parts or have the needed parts stockpiled, ready to be installed. Not only will you not be able to ride the incomplete motorcycle, but you will also spend countless hours locating the missing parts, time that could be spent riding and enjoying your purchase.

Next, before you buy decide just what it is you want. Do you want a BMW that is exotic, unusual, unique, and so rare that you'll never see another one parked next to you at a show? All well and good, but if it's that rare, and that unique, just how rare do you think any missing parts will be? Do you want to own a non-functioning museum piece or something you can ride? No matter that decades down the road it will become a museum piece. Think about the present.

Which to Choose?

To the uninitiated, the variety of postwar BMW twin-cylinder models may appear somewhat limited and unexciting. Compared to their British and American contemporaries, there is very little to tell them apart or to aid one in the determination of age or production series.

With only a little study and a sharp eye for detail, however, a very complex family tree emerges. The twins' styling roots are with the R5 of 1936–1937, and their engineering heritage goes all the way back to the first overhead valve twins of 1925. Quite often, a prewar twin has been mistaken for a 1955–1969 model, or vice versa; it's still common, even in today's climate of vintage motorcycle fever, to find judges unable to tell one from another, even though forty years may separate the two. Rather than being a detriment, this actually is of some benefit to the average enthusiast, who may have no desire, or who cannot afford to accumulate a large collection of motorcycles. If it is charisma or crowd appeal you are after, a nicely maintained postwar BMW can be as interesting and enjoyable as any of the more rare prewar twins, and at a considerable savings in cost.

If you're determined to own and ride a prewar twin, or if you happen to stumble across one in your search for the ideal postwar model, here are some guidelines to follow. All prewar BMWs are worth owning, if only for their relative rarity. Granted, as

You won't have to go to darkest Africa to find some forgotten BMW these days; there are still many good examples to be found right in your own backyard. BMWs have been imported into the U.S. through an extensive dealer network since the early 1950s, and many of the older models are still in use today. Shown is one model that never quite got to US shores, ending up instead with a Steib sidecar. Here missionaries in 1951 raft across an African river. *BMW Archives*

investments alone they're certainly worth a second look, but if it's a bike that you want to enjoy riding, there are certain caveats worth remembering.

The first is age. Anything built before World War II is now over fifty years old, and no matter how well a BMW was designed, assembled, and maintained, it's now on its second half century, and years of use and deterioration will leave you with a less than reliable mount. Short of a total rebuild, which may require the manufacture of many scarce and extraordinarily expensive parts, your prewar BMW will not be as reliable, as safe, or as fast as any of the postwar twins. If you have the money to undertake such a task, the time to hunt for scarce parts (few of which will be found in this country), and the patience to ride your completed restoration slowly and infrequently—at considerable risk to yourself—then give a prewar machine a try.

But, if you want to enjoy a postwar BMW, which to the casual passerby may look like a prewar machine, then I suggest any of the 1950–1969 twins. These machines are still reliable, are capable of maintaining safe highway speeds, and can stop in time when the need arises. Replacement parts and even an extra parts machine are readily available.

Here are the choices open to you. From 1950 through 1969, BMW built and sold in relatively limited numbers (when compared to other brands) five basic types of twin-cylinder machines:
• a touring 500
• a sports 500
• another touring 500 (a prewar holdover)
• a touring 600 (which was also useful for sidecar work)
• a sports 600

BMW changed fork design three times in those nineteen years, going from telescopics to leading link and back to telescopics again. Rear suspension went from sliding plungers in the 1950 to 1954 years to a rear swingarm with two shocks from 1955 to 1969. Horsepower went from a meager twenty-four in the 1950 R51/2 to a more than adequate forty-two in the 1969 R69US.

Some of these machines, regardless of condition, are so desirable today that they command prices nearly eight times what they cost when new. Others are common and still relatively underpriced, true bargains in today's overheated collector bike market. All are a pleasure to look at, yet not all

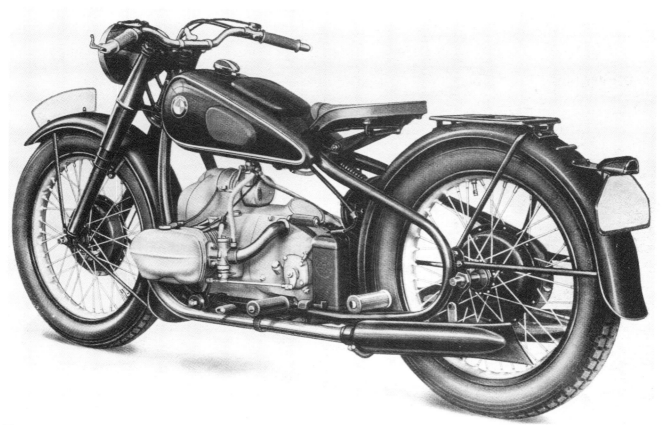

The one that started it all, the 1937 R5, with a frame, fork, and engine layout that was to influence BMW styling all the way to 1954. Allowing for minor evolutionary changes to tank and fender shapes, this BMW could be mistaken for a model from the 1950s. *BMW Archives*

Typical of the plunger framed BMWs of both the 1930s and 1950s, this R51 of 1937–1940 already had the brakes, wheels, and forks that the 1950–1953 machines enjoyed. Clearly seen here is the driveshaft and its aluminum dome covering the universal joint, and the famous auxiliary hand-shift lever, source of much comment and confusion. *BMW Archives*

The prototype 1950 R51/2, clearly little more than a re-introduced prewar R51. Only the split valve covers and the chimney vane air cleaner scoop permitted onlookers to tell them apart. Although this is the new 1950 model, it's shown here with 1in handlebars and reversed control levers, as well as a prewar taillamp and license plate bracket. The tank emblems and gas cap are also prewar. Few 1950 R51/2s were delivered with these prewar accouterments. *BMW Archives*

are capable of providing the same pleasure when it comes to restoring and riding.

The Plunger Twins

With the exception of the 1950 R51/2, all 1950–1969 BMW twins had magneto ignition, a single gear-driven camshaft, and pushrod-operated overhead valves. The other models that appeared after World War II and were the first to be imported in any great number alongside the R51/2 were the R51/3, the R67 (and its variants the R67/2 and R67/3), and the high-performance R68. All became available in late 1950 and early 1951, and all ceased being produced in 1954, though the R67/2 and R67/3 still appeared in sales catalogs until 1955, when they were finally superseded by the R60 and R69 models. There are some exceptions to this, of course, and 1955 year models of these earlier series have been documented, but these are due to the factory choosing to use up what parts were available.

Early production models of all 1950–1954 twins had half-hub iron brake drums, but by 1954 all models had full-width alloy drums. All 1951– 1954 twins have similar engine cases (a design externally identical to the 1955–1969 twins), improved transmissions with a neutral switch, and air cleaner canisters mounted on top of the transmission case.

All 1950–1954 twins also have "wing-nut" steering dampers, an exposed driveshaft, plunger rear suspension, an auxiliary hand-shift lever on the transmission, telescopic forks, small capacity teardrop profile tanks, solo saddles, 19in steel or alloy wheels, small taillights and, with the exception of the R68, deeply valanced elephant ear front fenders. There are, of course, other exceptions to these rules, for one could order a 1950–1954 BMW from the factory with a number of optional accessories, such as larger Hoske or Meier tanks, narrow "Schorsch Meier" bench seats, large Hella taillamp, as well as factory-installed BMW Spezial sidecars and attendant sidecar gearing. A few limited-production ISDT replica R68 models were also built for trials use, as were specially prepared racers based upon the production R51/3 and R67 series.

Just because the BMW you're looking at doesn't look anything at all like what is in the factory

The R68 came in various flavors, each to suit the taste of the owner. This 1954 model, identified by its full width brakes and alloy rims, sports a large Hoske tank and, again, an incorrect version of the pillion saddle. If you're really sharp, you'll note the remains of a folding AKIPP stand, s-bend pipes, and the correct 1954 transitional headlamp with covered key slide.

photos or picture books, don't pass it up. In 1973, I literally threw away a number of parts which "looked wrong" on the first vintage R51/2 I bought, only to find out later that I had discarded (or sold too cheaply) a special-order Hoske 10gal tank, an R68 front fender, an AKIPP sidestand, and a rare ventilated "racing" front brake!

The R51/2: Prewar Holdover

The R51/2, the first true postwar production twin, was a 500cc tourer with twin chain-driven camshafts and coil ignition that shared engine, transmission, and other minor styling and engineering details with its 1937–1940 R51 cousin. It's nice, with its small tank, swoopy "bell" front fender, metal fork covers, fishtail mufflers, and hand shift lever attached to the transmission case. Its split valve covers, exposed generator, and chimney vane air cleaner intake set it off from all subsequent models. To the untutored, it could be mistaken for a prewar BMW, which is exactly what it is. To be sure, a few minor changes were made, but for all intents and purposes, it is really a 1939 R51. The "/2" suffix says as much: It is the second version of the same prewar R51.

The R51/2's forks were simple oil-filled telescopics devoid of any dual damping. Correctly restored or rare original examples will have the metal covers over the fork tubes, though it was common to replace damaged forks with the improved 1951–1954 double-damped versions that had rubber fork gaiters.

Although a properly maintained R51/2 is a good choice, both for ease of restoration, parts availability, performance, and overall visual appeal, there is a dark side to this picture. Parts are nearly impossible to find, and nothing from a later model will interchange. No comprehensive workshop manual exists, not even in German. The engine had twin camshafts driven by a chain and sprockets which, to the mechanic unfamiliar with this model, will prove to be perplexing at the very least. Worst of all, the ignition is by coil, not magneto, which means you will need to have a fresh battery in the machine at all times. Finding a source for the old-style, black, 6-volt 8-amp hour batteries these days can be a quest in itself. Also, correctly restored examples of the R51/2 will not even have a stoplight filament in their single tiny taillight bulb, and the pin striping on the front fender edge will be a bit awkward compared to later models. Still, it is a nice, unusual machine—very rare and worth buying if you find one. But for serious riding, or ease of restoration, it is better to look to the 1951–1969 models.

The R51/3 and R67: The First Modern Twins

The first of the modern twins was the R51/3, which, as you've gathered by now, should be the third version of the same 500cc R51 series. But, it's

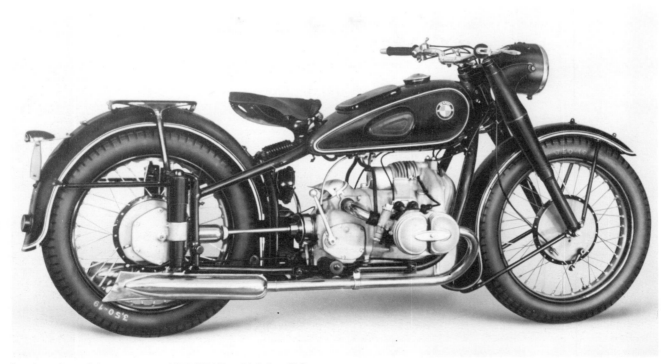

Another view of the prototype 1950 R51/2, which is still fitted with a narrow prewar R51 front fender. *BMW Archives*

The first of the postwar BMWs you might encounter is this R51/2, a 24hp twin of 500cc. Although the photo is correct in the depiction of the R51/2 front fender striping scheme, it should be pointed out that the gas cap and emblems are from a prewar R51. Airbrushed out of the picture is the external rear fender wiring harness. The R51/2 is instantly recognized by its split valve cover and generator with finned clamp mounted on top of the engine. *BMW Archives*

A model that's often found is one of the 1951–1954 twins, such as this 1952 R67/2. Note that it still has the early metal fork covers, but has the 1953 upgrade to the exhaust system, complete with s-bend adapters and "salami" mufflers. The unique two-color wheel rims are seen here as well. *Rich Sheckler*

A nice period shot of an R51/2 with BMW Spezial sidecar. Finding something as original as this these days is every enthusiast's dream. The sidecar has the correct unvalanced fender for 1950, and the R51/2 is recognized by the manual ignition timing lever just visible through the windshield. *Halbert Speer*

not as simple as that. True, the frame, forks, wheels, and tank looked the same, but the engine and transmission were entirely new. Nothing from the R51/2 engine will work in the R51/3. Gone is the twin camshaft arrangement and coil ignition, now replaced by a single gear-driven cam and a magneto. The engine block was different, and so were the cylinders and heads. Even the oil pan from an R51/2 will not fit an R51/3.

Horsepower remained at 24ps. ("ps" relates to the German DIN horsepower measurement. It is slightly conservative compared to the American SAE rating. Add about 5 percent to arrive at an approximate SAE figure.) The wiring was cleaned up a bit, as was the pin striping. Both the R51/3 and the 600cc R67 are ideal machines if you want a plunger frame, telescopic fork pre-1955 BMW. The rather rakish styling doesn't hurt, either, nor does that exotic looking "bell" front fender. Unfortunately, the pretty metal fork covers of the R51/2 would soon be replaced with rubber "gaiters," which to some aren't as desirable. If you want better stopping power, hold out for one of the late-1953 or 1954 models, which had larger brakes. The earlier R51/2s had nice looking but smaller half hub iron drums. A number of engine and electrical parts from the 1955–1969 R50 and R60 series will also

A happy owner and his 1952 R67/2. Although little more than two years separate this from the prototype R51/2, the improvement in looks is quite evident. *Rich Scheckler Photo.*

interchange, which makes finding spares a bit less of a gamble.

Without checking serial number lists found at the back of this book, you can recognize a 500cc R51/3 by inspecting its iron cylinder fins, which have a rounded profile. This holds true for all 500cc twins built through 1969. The R67 series have a pronounced point to their fin profile, which again was carried forward on the 600cc twins through 1969. Both the R51/3 and the R67 series have the same six-fin valve covers, and all share the same cylinder heads. In fact, heads and valve covers are visually identical to those found on the 1955–1969 R50 and R60 series!

The Sports R68: 1952–1954

Early in 1952, the first sports model since the 750cc R17 of 1936 was presented to an anxious motoring public. It borrowed a bit from both the prewar and postwar Rennsports in styling, and was touted as a true 100mph machine. The R68, as it was called, had a 600cc motor somewhat similar to that found in the R67/2, but with its own unique barrels and heads, larger carburetors, and a narrow unvalanced racing type front fender. Frame, forks, transmission, and rear drive were essentially the same as on the R51/3 and R67 series. Han-

dlebars were low, in the European fashion, and had their own unique risers.

Of all the pre-1955 twins, the R68 is the most desirable today, mainly due to its performance and to the fact that only 1,453 were produced in the years 1952 through 1954. By late 1953, the R68 also received the larger full hub brakes and alloy rims, but for many the early versions with their small steel drums are the most desirable. A few R68 models were available with special order, high, curving two-into-one exhaust systems, primarily for ISDT competition. Numerous examples were set up for racing, which the factory sponsored to some extent by providing such items as vented brakes, special tanks, and large, finned aluminum drums.

The sports R68 is easily spotted by its larger, uniquely shaped twin-fin valve covers, larger cylinder heads, finned exhaust pipe rings, narrow front fender, and manual spark control lever on the handlebar clutch control casting. An R68, if correctly restored, will have a flat, swinging passenger pillion pad attached at its front to the frame of the rider's rubber solo saddle. Between the rear pad and the taillight should be a chrome grab handle. None of the R68 models were ever fitted with pressed-steel pillion racks, although many owners have fit-

The ultimate plunger frame postwar twin is the R68, seen here in its final 1954 version, with full width alloy drums, aluminum wheel rims, and the latest series Knecht air cleaner. Also fitted by 1954 to all models was a precursor to the Ear- les fork headlight bucket, complete with triangular indicator lights and chrome and plastic key slide. Unique to the R68 were the flat "swinging pillion" saddle and chrome grab handle, as well as the narrow width front fender. *BMW Archives*

Another 1952 model, this time a 100mph sports R68. Of the pre-1955 machines, only the R68 had a narrow, unvalanced front fender. Correct on the rear fender is the chrome grab handle, but the stamped steel pillion rack and rubber saddle should only be fitted to the R51 and R67 series of 1951–1954.

ted them later.

Of any of the 1950–1954 twins, an R68 will cost the most, but happily the engine was continued for another five years in the Earles fork R69, so many parts are still available. If you find an R68, and if you can afford the price, buy it. Even incomplete R68 machines should be given a second look, since so many of the parts from the more common R51/3 and R67 can be used to finish the project.

The Earles and US-Fork Twins

Now that we've summed up what's available among the 1950–1954 BMW twins, let's see what the far larger 1955–1969 BMW world has to offer.

Over 65,000 of the "new" BMW twins were built in 1955–1969, compared to a little over 32,000 during 1950–1954. Statistically, more of the 1955–1969 series should still be around, either as running machines or as non-runners awaiting restoration. Until recently, the factory still stocked spare parts for these models as well. After a brief hiatus, when no spares were available except out of dead or forgotten stocks, replacement parts are now being remanufactured by several authorized firms in Germany. The number of private concerns

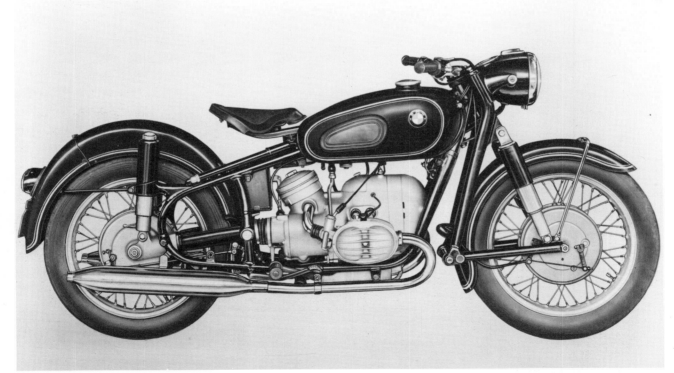

In 1955, BMW astounded the enthusiast with the radically changed Earles fork R50, which replaced the plunger frame R51/3. Although the engine was the same, everything else was different, except for the little Eber taillamp. The driveshaft was now enclosed in a rear swingarm, and the motorcycle had a pair of automotive-type shocks at each end. The

Earles leading link fork, borrowed from BMW's world champion sidecar racers, provided a smooth and comfortable ride. Twin leading-shoe front brakes were now standard on all models, as were 18in rims on both wheels. *BMW Archives*

First of the 1955–1969 Earles fork twins was this R50, with its totally redesigned swingarm frame, new tank, and larger rear fender. Wheels were now 18in in diameter, and the solo saddle was now sprung with a rubber suspension block rather than a single coil spring. This model along with the R60 and their /2 variants are the most plentiful BMWs to be found today, and the easiest to restore. Both are ideal machines for the novice restorer and collector. *BMW Archives*

Another Earles fork twin of the 1955–1960 era was the R69, which shared the engine of the R68 that preceded it. Even the least astute of BMW enthusiasts can tell it apart form the R69S, once the telltale cable for the manual magneto control is spotted where it goes into the engine case. The two fin valve covers were another hallmark of both the R68, R69, R69S, and R50S models. This R69 is also fitted with a swinging pillion, but by this time the chrome grab handle was a seldom seen optional accessory. *BMW Archives*

in the U.S. making anything from electrical parts to seats, fenders, and exhaust systems is growing daily.

If you want a good "first" BMW to start on, any of the 1955–1969 twins is an ideal starting point. A good "entry level" twin would be an R50 or R50/2, with the R60 series, then the R69, R69S, and R50S following in order of complexity and initial purchase cost.

The First Series Earles Fork Twins: 1955–1960

In 1955, BMW abandoned the telescopic forks and plunger rear suspension and borrowed some ideas from its successful leading-link front fork Rennsport models. The result was the R50 and R69. There was no 600cc touring machine available in 1955, so the factory continued to list the R67/2 and R67/3 as their 600cc solo and sidecar machines respectively. By 1956, the 600cc R60, sharing the same frame and forks as the R50 and R69, was added to the line, and the last remaining R67/2 and /3s were quietly dropped.

All that the 1955–1960 machines had in common with their 1951–1954 predecessors were the engines, which were a direct continuation of the R51/3, R67/2, and R68. Parts such as pistons still interchanged, as did carburetors. Transmissions did not, however, and although a 1951–1954 engine will fit perfectly into a 1955–1969 frame, and vice versa, you must use the transmission that was originally installed in the machine. If you don't, you will be in for an expensive surprise, because the transmission output shaft on the 1955–1969 models rotates in the opposite direction of those used from 1951 to 1954!

There's really no great advantage to buying a 1955–1960 R50 or R60. They look virtually identical to the 1961–1969 Earles fork models, yet they do not share the improvements that the 1961–1969 twins enjoyed. Prices consequently run somewhat less for the 1955–1960 twins. They're also bound to have had more use, and abuse, than the newer twins. An exception is the sports R69 (which is a bit more desirable than the touring R50 and R60).

Typical of most American market BMWs, this late-1960s R60/2 has the long bench seat, high US handlebars, bar-end signals, and the large Hella taillight in use since late 1955. The bulge on the front cover was to accommodate the vibration damper on the S models, and after a while all BMW twins were shipped in with the same cover. *Wagner International Photos*

By 1964, the last of the Steibs rolled out of the factory at Nuremberg, to be fitted to BMWs such as this R60/2. All Steibs mounted to BMW motorcycles at the factory were trimmed with BMW emblems and had no characteristic "co-bra" handle that other Steib sidecars used. BMW renamed the Steib TR500, like this one the Spezial in their catalog, and fitted a hydraulic brake as standard. *BMW Archives*

Note that we have not called these the "R50/2" or "R60/2" models. That's a common misconception, which has given rise to the misappellation that everyone persists in using these days. Not all the 1955–1969 twins were "slash twos." That designation was only used after 1961.

The First Slash-Twos: 1961

By 1961 BMW incorporated a number of major internal changes to their bread and butter touring models, the R50 and R60. The changes were primarily to the engine, which now was listed as the /2 version in the parts lists and service bulletins. Since the changes were not cosmetic but done for reasons of reliability and performance, any 1961–1969 machine would be the best choice for the rider and restorer. Parts are still readily available, either as new-old-stock or of current re-manufacture. BMW has even authorized certain firms in Germany to remanufacture some of the major components.

Again, the R50/2 and R60/2 series were the touring models, and the R69 was upgraded and renamed the R69S. To set it apart from earlier versions, BMW soon affixed a small plated "R69S" name tag to the rear fender. The R69S "sports" is desirable, as it provides the best performance, while the R50/2 and R60/2 touring models offer the best reliability and have the additional advantage of running well on regular octane fuel. As a negative, the R69S requires a little more owner attention, as it has a rubber mounted vibration damper on the front of the crankshaft, something the R69 did not possess. It also has a hydraulic steering damper, easily identified by a little red dot on the adjustment knob, something not fitted to the touring models.

The Sports R50S

Another sports model, the R50S, briefly made an appearance in 1961, but for a variety of reasons it only lasted one year. BMW had miscalculated the motorcycle market in the 1960s and had not anticipated the appearance of mass-produced, inexpensive motorcycles from Japan. Most would outperform the R50S or the R69S. All would cost at least a third less than the $1,536 that BMW dealers were asking for the R69S. The high-performance British 500cc singles and twins that the R50S was to compete with soon either faded from the scene, or outperformed the R50S from the outset. Used Norton Internationals, BSA Gold Stars, or Velocettes gave their owners much more for their money, and one even had an overhead camshaft, while the BMW was still limited to pushrod actuated valves.

The Slash-Two Misnomer

Before we get too bogged down with series tags, let's discuss the term "slash two" (or more commonly "/2"), which seems to permeate any discussion of postwar BMWs, be they 1955–1969 or earlier twins. It's become common, but incorrect usage, to call all Earles-fork Twins "slash-twos." The suffix "/2" does not appear in any of the owner's manuals, nor does it appear stamped on the steering head ID plate on any of the 1961–1969 models.

To be proper and correct, any number appearing after the slash pertains to a variation of the same series, with the first version of any series being neither "/0" nor "/1." When you look at the designation of the first postwar twins, this designation becomes obvious. The R51/2 was the second version, or upgrade, of the prewar R51. The R67 (without any slash) was a logical follow-on to its prewar predecessor the R66. The R67/2 and R67/3 were variants of the original R67. The R68 was the next logical number after the R67.

It's all so very Teutonically simple, isn't it? So where did we go wrong when it came to describing the 1955–1969 twins? The obvious culprits are those Earles forks that, along with the new double-loop swingarm frame, set the post-1955 twins apart from all previous models. When the 1950–1954 plunger-frame twins were phased out in 1955, the first new models were the 500cc R50, along with the R69 (which shared the high-performance engine of the R68). The engine of the R50 was the same as the one in the R51/3 of 1954. In 1956 the old R67 series was replaced with the R60, which again retained the same engine as the R67 series.

All remained the same until 1961, when major internal engine changes (and some minor detail upgrades) forced the factory to differentiate between the models by appending the "/2" identifier to parts lists and shop manuals. To further confuse the issue, in 1961 BMW also came out with the R50S, which had a high-performance version of the new R50/2 engine, but neither the factory nor any owners would ever in their right mind refer to it as an "R50S/2." Similarly, the R69S, which replaced the R69 in 1961, should never be referred to using the "/2" label.

By 1968 most of the Earles forks twins were coming into the U.S. with the radically new (for BMW) US telescopics, which did little to improve the looks of the 1955–1969 twins, but did much to improve the controversial handling of the Earles forks models. Although everyone seems to persist in calling all post-1955 twins "slash-twos," perhaps only the US-fork models can safely be described using that moniker, for indeed only their engines are truly of the second series of post-1955 twin production. For purposes of clarity, all future discussion of post-1954 twins will refer to the 1955–1960 models by their true designation (R50, R60, R69), by their 1961–1969 designation (R50/2, R60/2, R69S, R50S), or by their final series nomenclature (R50US, R60US, R69US).

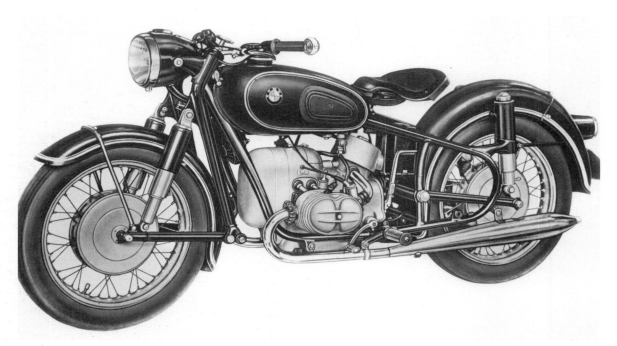

In 1961, a sports R50S was added to the line. Although it looked just like all the other models, its short, twin-fin valve covers differentiated it from the R69S. Although at 35hp the sports 500 gave a good account of itself, real or perceived crankshaft deficiencies ended its production run after only one year and 1,634 units. *BMW Archives*

The Old Reliables: The R50/2 and R60/2

While the R50S was a high revving 500cc twin, it never was the success on the track that BMW had anticipated. The crankshaft was prone to vibration problems, and for sheer high speed performance, the R69S was a much better choice. Today, an R50S may still be a risky proposition, especially if it has had less than adequate care. If looks alone are a deciding factor, an R50/2 or R60/2 looks almost the same, so why choose an R50S? Again, an R50S will cost more to buy and restore, because only 1,634 were built in 1961, its only year of production. If you want an Earles fork machine as your first ride, or your first restoration, chose the R50/2 for its reliability and understressed motor, or the R60/2 for a little more power, or as the ideal mount for hauling a sidecar.

Last of the Line: The US-Fork Models

By 1968, BMW had nearly completed development of the "new" /5 series, which were to premier in Europe in late 1969. Among the many new features that would soon set the motorcycling world on

its ear were a set of steel and aluminum telescopic forks. What better way to give the world a taste of things to come, and to test them out in the all-important US market, than to fit them to the current Earles fork models? In late 1968 BMW announced a series of "US" models to be known as the R50US, R60US, and R69US, which could be had with the "new and improved" front telescopic forks.

The reaction was less than overwhelming. Purists, especially those who hauled a sidecar with their BMWs, considered them faddish. Other manufacturers thought them too heavy and overengineered, particularly their massive forged-aluminum fork sliders. A few unfortunate owners and the BMW factory, to its chagrin, soon learned that the US forked models were not capable of handling the stresses induced by hauling a sidecar. A Service Bulletin was immediately issued warning dealers not to allow the attachment of sidecars, and the factory hastily deleted the sidecar mounts from the frame, a feature that had been common to all BMWs since the mid-1930s.

Occasionally, one still sees an all-original US

The newest pre-1970 BMW the American enthusiast will encounter today is the US-fork model, such as this R69US. Again, the valve covers give it away, as do the extra-wide dual seat, large tank, and high US handlebars. The tele-

scopic forks were continued virtually unchanged in the 1970 /5 series that followed and use hydraulic fluid instead of the motor oil used in the 1950–54 machines. *K. Attenberger*

model with its non-characteristic sidecar mounts, but more often than not someone sometime along the way probably replaced a set of damaged US forks with the earlier Earles forks, which interchange quite easily. To many, the US-forked models are not as photogenic as the Earles versions. They certainly do not have the charisma associated with the latter, and for that reason US-fork models command a somewhat lesser price. Still, handling is good for the era and you can't go wrong buying one, as parts are readily available.

A Spotter's Guide

As a quick aid to identification, the R50, R50US, R50S, and R50/2 series have round iron cylinder fins; the R60, R60US, and R60/2 series have pointed fins; and the R69 has a manual ignition control cable entering the timing chest, finned exhaust clamps, and two-fin valve covers. The engines in the R69S and R69US look like those in the R69, with the manual ignition control deleted. The R50S has two-fin valve covers and finned exhaust rings. For all series built after 1961, the frames have small reinforcing gussets on the downtubes by the battery carrier. Early R69S models had no "R69S" emblem on the rear fender, while few if any of the R50S ever carried their own rear fender emblem.

A Quick Summary

You are faced with many choices. If you already own some of the other BMWs, then adding a pre-1955 model to your collection would be a plus, as their numbers are decreasing daily. Handling and overall feel of all the 1950–1969 models is about the same, although you do seem to sit a bit closer to the ground with a pre-1955 machine. The unusual tendency of having the Earles fork rise, rather than lower, when using the front brakes hard is something one soon gets used to.

The 500cc R50, R50/2, and R50US are the easiest to start due to their low compression ratio and ability to run on low-octane fuel. The R60 and R60/2 are best for sidecar work, and the R69US, most often fitted without sidecar lugs on its frame, is a good choice for a high-speed tourer. If it's performance you want, get an "S" model or an R69. If it's reliability you're after, get an R50/2 or R60/2. For sheer beauty, the R51/3, R67, R67/2, or R67/3 have no equal. For rarity (and high purchase cost), there's the R68 and R50S. Even the R51/2 would not be a bad choice, if you're willing to accept the risk of not finding certain replacement parts or manuals, and don't mind the annoyance of a coil ignition setup.

The R50S, produced only in 1961, is rapidly becoming a most desirable model, if only for its

More often seen in the U.S. than overseas, the R69S proved to be the top performer, with 42hp and a vibration damped crankshaft. This example has the US-handlebars, the larger non-choke air cleaner, the standard narrow bench seat, and the round coffee can Hella taillamp. Below the tank one can clearly see the hydraulic steering damper, also unique to the "S" models. *BMW Archives*

scarcity. As a sidecar machine, its high revving engine is ill suited, but as a 500cc sports tourer it is unsurpassed.

You really can't go wrong with any of them. The severely abused or badly neglected ones will be so obviously bad that you'll probably shy away from them instinctively. Over restored examples may not be to your particular taste. Finding one having just the right combination of condition and price will be your biggest challenge. Once you've found one, the fun begins. Arming yourself with some of the facts and remembering some of the caveats will increase the odds that your choice will be a good one.

Sold alongside the "S" models after 1961 were the R50/2 and R60/2, which outwardly looked very similar. Seen here is a 1967 R60/2 with smaller choke-type air cleaner, bench seat, US-bars, and the new 1966 sans serif tank emblems in use after 1966. *K. Attenberger*

By 1969, all BMWs exported to the U.S. had the new US-telescopic front forks. This R50US has in addition the optional larger sport tank with top mounted tool box. *BMW Archives*

Chapter 3

The Search, the Inspection, and the Offer

You've done some reading and examined the state of your finances—you're now ready to go out and buy that BMW you've always wanted. All you have to do is get the classified section of the paper, find a BMW for sale, or maybe visit a dealer, right? Wrong! Nothing will get you into trouble quicker than to blindly answer a few ads. Your local dealer probably will want to sell you a new bike. If he has one of the 1950–1969 twins, he'll either put such a high price on it that you won't be able to afford it or he'll want to keep it for himself. Still, visiting a dealer is a reasonable place to start. At least

a dealer will have gone through the machine and will possibly guarantee it for at least thirty days.

Getting "buyer's remorse" won't be of much help to you when you try to return a machine too hastily purchased from a private party. Most states allow you seventy-two hours to change your mind, but if you buy a motorcycle privately on a Friday, and the seller takes off that night for two weeks in Aruba, that seventy-two hour grace period won't mean much.

Before buying a BMW motorcycle, the first thing you should do is meet up with some other

The best place to find BMWs is at the events where enthusiasts gather. Even if there are no machines for sale, there are bound to be fellow enthusiasts who can give you some leads. *Tracy Baker*

owners of older models, if you haven't done so already. Nothing will please an owner of an older BMW more than being asked questions about his machine, especially by someone full of enthusiasm who just happens to be searching for one "just like it." Your newfound friend will probably know of at least one other person who has a BMW to sell, or he may just add you to the list of all those who have wanted to buy his machine at one time or another.

If there are no local clubs, there's bound to be a motorcycle or old car flea market or swap meet in your area. Walk through the parking lot and look for old machines. Leave notes if you have to.

We've all heard stories of estate sales, bank foreclosures, even old BMWs found abandoned and neglected at police auctions. They're not as fanciful as you think. I found a nice BMW, albeit a 1972 R60/5, at an auction at the U.S. Customs House in Boston some years ago.

I'm not saying you should become a dump picker, or start canvassing the police impounds, but there are more places to find an old motorcycle than you might imagine. However, the best sources, once you've exhausted the classifieds and stopped haunting your local dealer's showroom, are one of the several major BMW clubs, all of which publish excellent newsletters or magazines containing screened classifieds. By this I don't mean all the bikes are somehow guaranteed, or that you might not end up with a lemon. It's just that all the clubs require the sellers to be members, which means he or she is probably known to at least several others among the readership. This does screen out those whose major source of income is derived by selling used or abused BMWs to the unwary.

Spotting the Good, and Avoiding the Bad and the Ugly

Now that you're armed with a fistful of logic and reason, how will you know if the BMW you're looking at is going to turn out all right? The impression the seller makes will have much to do with it. If he or she can't give you a good reason for selling it, look elsewhere. Ask about the machine's history, any work recently done, and any work still needed. If the seller appears to have no knowledge of his BMW, other than the price he's asking, continue your search. Virtually all BMW owners, once they've been bitten by the bug, are lifelong enthusiasts. Most will only be selling their motorcycle under conditions of extreme duress. If the seller tells you he's "tired of the bike," there's got to be a reason.

The impression the motorcycle makes is al-

Lined up at a vintage BMW meet for all to admire are these two R69S Earles fork beauties, both fitted with VDO tachometers, solo saddles, and two variations of the Albert mirror. The one at left also has the extra capacity finned aluminum oil pan.

most as important. You can overlook dents, dings, and scratches. Even rusty exhaust systems, the bane of most older BMWs, should not turn you away. Bent rims, cut tires, badly scuffed valve covers, and unexplained oil leaks should be a warning of chronic neglect and abuse. Again, look elsewhere, unless the price is so low that you can afford to put all the money you've saved into the repairs you'll soon have to make. If you have the patience, and the money, keep looking until you find a near perfect, all-original machine that requires no further work. In the long run, you'll be money ahead. All things being equal, an unrestored, original BMW will almost always prevail over a similar, yet fully restored machine at any show, if the judges have even a modicum of good sense.

Things to look at closely, even before you ask the seller to start the machine, are such often overlooked areas as wheel spokes and wiring. Bent, rusted, or missing spokes will mean an expensive wheel rebuild. Taped or patched wiring will mean a new harness, and could pose a fire hazard if neglected. The battery should be a German black case model, but in all likelihood it may be a plastic Japanese retrofit. Budget about $50 for a new bat-

If you've already found your BMW, there's always the opportunity to find some needed parts. At this recent US vintage meet, among the rare items to be seen are a complete tachometer setup, a Meier and a Heinrich tank, plus two "elephant ear" 1951–1954 front fenders.

An early R67, with metal fork covers and correct (and probably original) fender and tank striping. Unfortunately, the picture is marred somewhat by the late-1960s leather bags, which are of the wrong era for the bike and mounted too far back, probably to clear the rear plungers. The nonstandard generic mufflers should be replaced with the proper finned ones for 1951.

tery. Chrome plated items, although few in number on a BMW, will mean expensive replating if the chrome is pitted or peeling. Tires will likely need to be replaced, but good German ones are again available in the older 18in or 19in sizes. An exhaust system, even an aftermarket reproduction one, will run into hundreds of dollars. The headlight shell should have its plastic and chrome key slide or, if a 1950–1953 version, just a round hole. A scraped or dented headlight rim or scuffed valve covers means the machine has been dropped at least once. Look for additional accident signs such as bent or scraped foot pegs.

While few nonstandard parts will work on a BMW, it's best to check before you buy. If anything looks out of place, ask why. Japanese or British carburetors won't work too well on a BMW, but people have tried worse. If that odd tank just doesn't look right, check the pictures in Chapter 8 or Chapter 18 of this book. If it's not a Heinrich or a Hoske, or one of the large BMW 6.5gal tanks, it might be a plastic reproduction, which should be avoided. Seats are easy to damage, and even easier to replace with something nonstandard. Finding the correct seat for a BMW could cost $200 to $500.

In its long life in the hands of numerous prior owners, that BMW you're looking at may have been used for something other than solo riding. Check for sidecar mounts still attached to the front engine bolt or to the bracket welded below the tank. Examine the rear welded-on ball for worn paint. Check the fenders for stray holes that might have held old saddle bags. If the front fender on an Earles fork machine has a round ding just under the headlight rim, it means that either the front shocks are badly worn, or that the bike hit a pothole or curbstone with such force that the swingarm flexed enough to allow the fender to hit the headlight.

Check the toolbox for the tool roll and the tools. Replacing missing tools will leave you with little change from a $100 bill. An original owner's manual would be nice to have, but if it's missing, reprints are available. See if the fork lock key fits the tool box lid. The two should be the same. If not, either the tank has been replaced or the machine has undergone a rebuild. At the very least, some prior owner lost the keys and had to buy a new lock. If the tire pump is missing, it will only cost you $10 to replace.

After you've looked over the machine, ask the seller to start it. If the BMW can't be started, there had better be a good reason. Be suspicious of any seller who has difficulty with the starting drill.

While you're at it, inspect the serrations on

Two opportunities not to be missed, should they be for sale, are either of these two pre-1955 machines. In the foreground, a 1950 R51/2, correct in every detail. Behind it is a

1954 R67/2 with large Hoske tank and Schorsch Meier bench seat. *Rich Sheckler*

the kick start lever. If they're worn off, it means the machine has been kicked into life more times than you'd care to know. If the kick lever is brand new while the rest of the bike is ragged and worn, it could mean the machine has suffered a recent accident or the lever was so worn down that the owner had to replace it. In any case, if there's something absolutely brand new on the machine, and the seller doesn't use it as a selling point, be suspicious.

Check the ID plate behind the headlight. The plate is held on with two screws, so it might have been removed or swapped. Blanks are available, but an original one is better. Finally, verify that the engine numbers and the frame numbers agree. All BMWs built from 1950 on had matching engine and frame numbers. Both the numbers on the frame and engine should be "boxed in" with two little BMW roundels. Late in 1968, BMW ran out of six-digit numbers and started to prefix them with a single "1," again boxed in with the BMW logos.

If the machine starts, ask the seller to let it idle for a while. Not long enough to cook the pistons, but long enough to get the oil warm and circulating. The valves should quiet down after the machine warms up. No unusual scraping, whirring, or slapping noises should be heard. Inspect the

Where contacts pay off. This 1950 R51/2 found a new owner in Massachusetts, when its owner in Oklahoma contacted the Vintage BMW Club asking if anyone would be interested in buying his machine. The two parties were put in touch with each other and a deal was made.

An all original, unrestored 1952 R67/2. It's seen here proudly displayed at a Vintage Club ride.

headlight. Is the speedometer face faded, or does it have water stains near the bottom? If so, the machine has either been left out a lot or it fell down hard enough at one time or another to break the speedometer face seal. Is the speedometer too new for the rest of the machine? Again, this could mean that it, and possibly the headlight, have recently been replaced, probably due to an accident. The red generator light should be on at idle, but should go off when the throttle is turned a bit. If the light stays on, it could be something as simple as worn brushes, or something much worse. The horn may or may not work at idle, especially if the battery is weak. Even with a dead battery, all 1951–1969 BMW twins should be able to start. Pull in the clutch lever. If you hear scraping noises, it might mean a bad clutch. If you're lucky, it's just a sign of dry clutch rod bearings, an easy repair.

Look under the machine at the engine oil pan. If the pan is of the original stamped tin variety, check where the pan meets the engine block. Overzealous tightening of the bolts holding on the pan will cause severe warping and leakage. Some owners try to correct this by doubling up on the cork gasket, or by using a liquid gasket compound.

It's a sure sign of abuse. If the oil pan is of the aftermarket finned aluminum type, check for broken fins. While you're down there, inspect the feet of the center stand, and the stand retracting rod on the left leg. The rod can break off if the bike goes down, and worn feet indicate many years of hard use.

Let the owner ride the machine while you watch. Do the wheels wobble? Again, this will mean a wheel rebuild. As the seller shifts the gears, anything other than the normal clunking noise is reason for suspicion. While BMW did have noisy shifting transmissions, the units themselves were virtually bulletproof, so any strange noises should be a warning.

Oil leaks should be minimal. Some sweating is allowed, of course, but leaks at every seam and joint spell trouble. Do the carburetors start to drip when the engine is stopped and the fuel tap remains on? This means worn float needles and seats, or sunk floats, all simple items to remedy, but still time consuming. If the seller didn't spring for these simple parts, it could indicate a world of invisible neglect. While the machine is up on its stand, try rocking the rear wheel with the transmission in gear. Any free play other than that

Typical of most BMW clubs, the members enjoy a weekend ride, like these enthusiasts in the late 1960s with their Earles fork machines. It's at outings like this where you stand the best chance of making new friends and of finding that elusive BMW you've been searching for.

If you wanted a new BMW in the 1960s, a number of American tour groups sponsored trips to the BMW factory in Munich, where you could take delivery of your BMW and ride it around Germany before shipping it home. Seen here in this 1969 photo are some proud new owners being escorted from the factory grounds by the local Munich "Polizei." Note that the American models have the high US-handlebars, while the white police machines have the low European ones. *Richard Kahn, Butler & Smith, Inc.*

caused by the meshing of transmission and rear end gears is a sign of wear. At the least, the output flange bolts under the rubber boot (on 1955–1969 models) may be loose. At the worst, the rear wheel splines will need to be replaced, which could mean a whole new rear wheel or a splined rear hub for the rear drive case. Both are expensive. The universal joint in the swing arm could also be worn, but this is hard to check without tearing into everything. It's not inappropriate, however, to ask the seller to remove the rear wheel to check the splines. It's also a good way to see if the rear fender hinge is

rusted solid. If the seller won't agree to pull the wheel, look elsewhere.

Finally, ask to ride the machine. Some sellers might balk at this, especially if they don't know you. We've all heard horror stories of "buyers" never coming back from their test ride! If the seller offers to give you a ride as his passenger instead, that should give you a good idea how the machine handles. In any case, if the machine can't start, or if the seller can't ride it around for you, either insist on a price adjustment, or look elsewhere. If you do get to ride it, try all the gears and use the brakes both singly and together. The machine should stop in a straight line, without any shuddering or grabbing. If the brakes squeal, ask to look at the brake linings.

Cutting a Deal

If you're ready to make the deal, ask if there's anything else that goes with the bike. Unless coached, some sellers might forget that there's still a shop manual in the basement, and a few extra factory tools in the tool box. It never hurts to ask. If there are any accessories lying about, such as fairings, saddlebags, or a spare fender or tank, you might have to pay extra to get them. Still, it's better to get them now than to have to look for them later. It's up to you to decide whether you really need them, however.

What should you pay for the BMW of your dreams? Prepare yourself by reading all the classified ads in the BMW club magazines. If the machine is priced too high, you might be able to negotiate a better price by quoting the asking prices of similar models.

Remember that prices vary according to geographical area. Prices in the East and West are usually the highest. The most reasonable asking prices are found in the Midwest or South. Prices in Canada are usually stated in Canadian dollars; the actual price in U.S. dollars would be much lower.

Safe at Home

Once your machine is home, get it inside as soon as you can. Don't add to the neglect it may already have suffered by leaving it outside under a piece of plastic. Now is also the time to go through everything in detail and make a list of the defects. Keep the list handy when you visit a dealer, or attend a BMW event.

Now is also the time to decide where you proceed to next. Will you plan a complete restoration or ride the bike for a while? If the machine is good to begin with, why suffer the expense of a complete tear down? As they say, "If it ain't broke, don't fix it." Why add to your already considerable cash outlay by spending more on painting and plating? Besides, by extended use, you might discover some hidden defects.

No matter what road you take, however, you've got the bike home, so now is the time to see just how much you can do yourself, and just how much you will have to farm out to specialists.

Chapter 4

Setting Up Shop

No matter which of the 1950–1969 BMW twins you've settled on, having a place to work on it is essential. It's not necessary to have a complete professional workshop, or to acquire every possible factory tool and shop manual. However, a few minimum requirements are essential.

Many BMW owners choose to work on their own machines; many more are competent enough to undertake even the most complex rebuilds. If you're like the majority, however, you know just enough to stay out of trouble, but not enough to solve everything beyond a minor problem. It's to you that this book is addressed. Complex and potentially risky tasks like crankshaft rebuilds, cylinder reboring, and transmission overhauls are best left to professionals. This book is aimed at the enthusiast, the BMW rider, owner, and collector who wants to maintain a machine in running order or to repair or restore as much as is possible before calling on experts.

It can be rewarding to do your own work. Not only does it force you to learn more about your BMW, it can also save you money in the long run. Many of the simple tasks required to repair or rebuild your motorcycle can be done by even the least skilled enthusiast. It's not necessary nor is it cost effective to pay a mechanic's high hourly rate for simple disassembly and cleaning tasks that you could do at home.

Before starting any task, arm yourself with knowledge and the proper tools. Skill isn't really necessary in the beginning. That will be acquired over time. Mistakes are usually only made once. This book will help you recognize some of the common mistakes and avoid making them. It is not be a substitute for a comprehensive workshop manual, nor will it attempt to guide you through the major and complex steps required to do a full restoration, which should be handled by professional mechanics. It will, however, point out some of the shortcuts, and show you some of the fixes that are not mentioned in any manual, fixes that professionals have learned during their long careers as BMW motorcycle mechanics.

Tools for the Enthusiast

When it comes to working on your BMW, it does not matter whether you're a semi-skilled amateur or a master mechanic—you need to have a good set of tools. This does not mean that you need every tool in the book or every one of the suggested BMW factory tools. First, the cash investment to acquire each one would be prohibitive. Second, you'll seldom need to use the tools more than once, unless you make your livelihood restoring old BMWs. However, quality tools are a must.

Trying to do more than your tools are capable of is a sure ticket to disaster. Don't rely solely on the tools that came in your BMW tool roll. Other than the few specialized pin and hook wrenches that you'll need to remove exhaust nuts and swingarms bearings, you're better off with store bought wrenches and sockets.

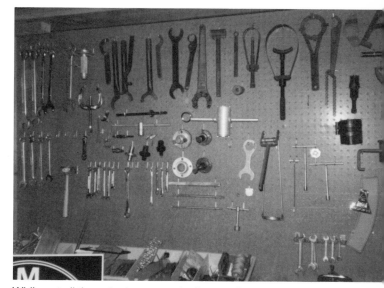

While not all these tools are required, a number seen in this enthusiast's basement workshop will make your job much easier. The hook wrenches in the top row are useful in removing exhaust rings, and the finned gripper is used for the exhaust clamps on the R68, R69, and other "S" models.

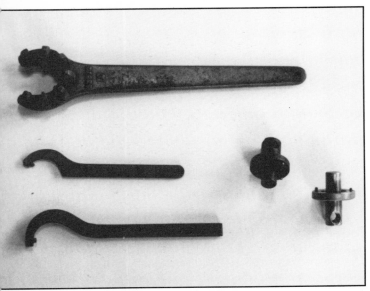

An example of the minimum set of shop tools needed to make your job much easier. The lethal looking club at the top is tool No. 338/2, for the R68, R69, and R69S exhaust nuts. Below it, hook wrenches Heyco No. 4550 and Matra No. 338/1, and a pair of wheel bearing extractors, Matra No. 517.

The absolute minimum to have at hand are a good set of box and open end wrenches in metric sizes of 6mm to 19mm. A quality set of sockets in 1/4, 3/8, and 1/2in drive, again in the same sizes, are also recommended. The sizes you'll need the most will be 10, 13, 14, and 17mm, so get a few extras in each size.

Among the absolute minimum of recommended specialized tools are a gear puller, a bearing puller, a piston ring compressor, a wrist pin extractor, and a valve spring compressor. Many of these can be rented rather than bought. Drifts and punches can be purchased as the need arises. For wheel work, use a spoke wrench and pin wrench, BMW tool 517, for the 1950–1954 wheels. These same wrenches also fit the wheel bearings on the 1955–1969 versions. Another must-have tool is number 519/1, for removing Earles fork swingarm bearings. This tool will save you hours of frustration. Some of the more specialized tools can be built if you have the skill and the equipment; if not, arm yourself with a set of factory tool drawings and visit your local machinist. Better still, contact specialists like Ed Korn, Vintage BMW Club member (see appendix for listing), who has been making excellent copies of original factory tools for years. A list of the minimum essential tools that BMW recommended for its dealers appears at the end of this book.

A few damage-reducing items are worth considering. A leather mallet and a copper, brass, or lead faced hammer are good for loosening frozen parts or reassembling press fit items. An 8oz weight is best, though heavier ones can be used if you're careful. A small propane torch to heat parts is also useful, otherwise warming in the kitchen stove will do.

As tempting as it might also be to wash your parts in the sink or dishwasher, invest in a gallon can of degreaser, such as "Gunk." Another good way to clean dirty parts is to use kerosene, acetone, or any type of paint thinner or paint remover, but as with all hazardous substances, these should be used with caution. Diesel fuel or automatic transmission fluid are both good soaking agents for freeing frozen parts or loosening stuck pistons and rings. Commercially available penetrating oils, like WD-40 are also useful but costly if used to excess. Disposable rags, available from auto parts suppliers, are handier than old undergarments. In any case, never keep used, dirty, and oily rags in your workshop unless they're in an Underwriters Laboratory approved anticombustion container.

A few power tools can make your job easier. An air compressor is handy, not only for pumping up tires, but also for blowing out clogged oil passages, cleaning parts, and painting. If you have the skill necessary to run a blaster, stick to walnut shell media. Bead or abrasive grit may contaminate engine parts with tiny particles of residue. If you plan to weld, a small MIG welder is recommended. You can

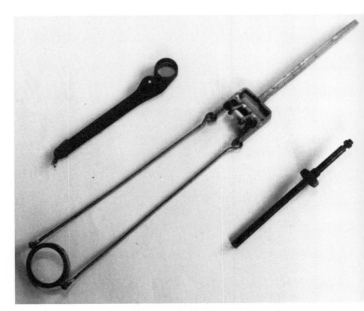

If you're going to do serious and effective work on the suspension members of a 1955–68 Earles fork machine, you'll be wise to buy or borrow these three tools. On the left, Dowidat No. 31 for unscrewing the hydraulic shocks from their bases. In the middle BMW's own shock assembly compression device, and to the right, the Matra No. 519/1 pilot pin, needed to drive out and replace the Earles fork swing arm shaft.

recover your investment in a welder quickly if the BMW you're restoring has many random holes waiting to be filled in its fenders, tank, or other parts. Frame repairs are best left to professionals, however.

Among the smaller tools, a handheld electric drill is useful, but not essential. A good machinist's vise with padded jaws is also useful.

If you have the space, build a nice heavy workbench, out of wood or metal. Three different plans are detailed near the end of this chapter, one from the *British Motorcycling Manual*, 11th edition (1949), the other from BMW Factory Drawing V5043, and finally one from the former Ducati Club of California. The latter, also doubles as a roll on work stand, eliminating the need to find the space and money for a hydraulic lift. Whichever one you use, cover the working surface with a sheet of tin or heavy gauge aluminum. Stainless steel is best, if you can afford a piece. A handy source for all sorts of sheet metal is your local appliance dump.

Finally, possibly the best thing for both your BMW and your back is a hydraulic or pneumatic lift, like the ones you've seen in the motorcycle shops. A new one will set you back close to a $1,000 but used ones do occasionally turn up. Watch the classifieds for auction notices or "Going Out of Business" sales, especially at firms that deal in industrial equipment. A fine hydraulic motorcycle lift is an early Italian-made Grazia. Don't use a hydraulic lift as a substitute for a workbench, however. The lift is not particularly stable, and besides, you'll want to carry some of the work to another area, either to set it safely aside, or to work on it with other tools.

Building a Work Stand

A work stand is essential if you want to do work on your BMW, and if you want to end the day without a sore back. Several commercial stands are available, either hydraulic or pneumatic, if you have the money. If you're lucky perhaps you can catch a dealer just at the time he is planning to replace all his aging hydraulic stands with more modern pneumatics.

If you have the skill, time, and lumber, a serviceable wooden work stand can be constructed. I suggest using the BMW factory plan number V5043, which is reproduced in this chapter, or the design mentioned earlier from the *British Motorcycling Manual*, 11th edition (1949). While no detail description of this stand exists other than the following rendering, you can see that it's made from heavy lumber, is 2 feet high, and has a 6.5ftx2.5ft work surface. The length of the ramp is left to the builder's own choosing, but the method of folding it up is rather ingenious and may require some thought on your part before you proceed.

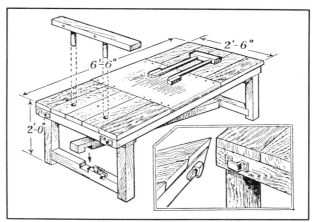

A robust, collapsible bike stand featured in the 11th edition of *The Motorcycling Manual. Roland Slabon collection*

The best described plans are courtesy of a California Ducati Club newsletter of about ten years ago. The materials list consists of a sheet of 3/4in plywood and boards in 2ftx4ft and 2ftx6ft size. If you're like most of us, you've probably got enough scraps around to cut your cash outlay to zero. My only modification would be to avoid painting the top when done, since once oil gets on a painted surface everything gets slippery. Cover it all with sheet tin, aluminum, or, if the budget can stand it, a nice sheet of aluminum diamond plate.

A Place to Work

Now that you've collected some of the tools you'll require, all you need is a work space. A quiet, secluded area would be ideal, preferably away from the house, but close enough to allow easy and frequent access. Avoid those kit-style tin tool sheds. They're poorly ventilated, impossible to secure, usually too low to stand in, unsightly, and prone to rust both inside and out. The corrosion damage they'll do to your BMW will make grown men cry.

One workshop solution is to purchase a surplus ocean-going cargo container and have it dropped in your backyard. They're built like a bank vault, can be locked securely, and can be ventilated effectively.

If you're doing your work in the basement, having one that's at grade, with a walk out door wide enough to accommodate your motorcycle is the best. There's nothing worse than horsing the motorcycle up and down narrow basement stairs. Again, proper ventilation and attention to fire hazards are necessary. An area at the back of your garage is probably a better solution, and it also allows easy access to the motorcycle.

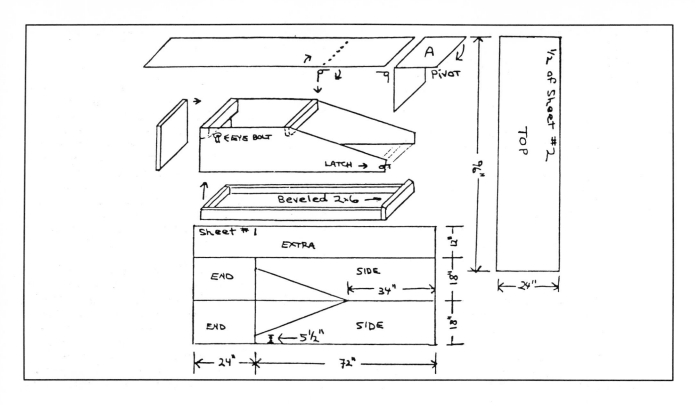

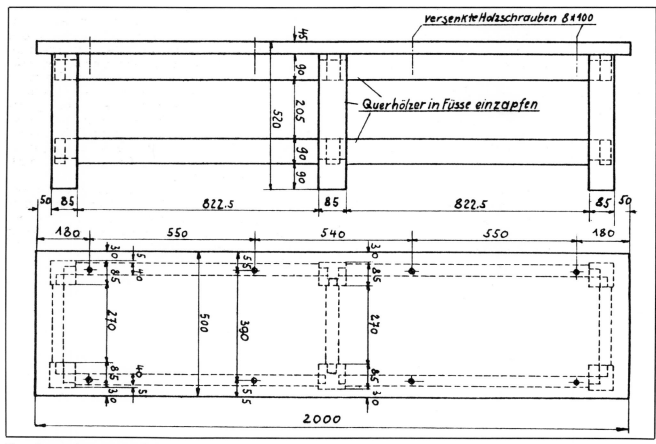

Plans for another motorcycle work stand.

Knowing Where to Start and When to Quit

Where does your project begin, and just how much should you be doing? Remember, we're not talking a total rebuild here, complete with new crank, rods, and fresh paint, chrome, and striping. Again, those tasks are best farmed out to professionals. However, your BMW may require such extensive work, and what you can do yourself can greatly speed things along and save you considerable expense. It's much better to bring just the crankshaft to a specialist than the whole engine. It's much easier to carry in your transmission, than to wheel in the whole bike. Fenders can be brought singly to the stripper, welder, painter, and pinstriper. Gas tanks can be removed, flushed, and cleaned before being sent off to a shop to have their dents repaired.

All that you can do yourself will save you money. It might even be fun. At the very least, you'll learn more about BMW motorcycles than the average owner and rider, and you'll probably soon know as much as most mechanics. If it's a 1950–1969 BMW you're working on, you'll probably know more about it when you're done than most BMW dealers—many of them weren't even around when your model was new. The sense of satisfaction and pride of accomplishment you will get from doing something as simple as changing a tire, replacing your generator brushes, or adjusting your carburetors cannot be measured.

The first thing any project requires is a plan. If you need only the valves reground or the cylinder heads rebuilt, stick to doing just that. Unless the motor requires it, don't do anything more. You'll run the risk of losing parts, causing more damage, and turning a simple top end job into a major overhaul. If you're sending out the wheels to be rebuilt, think about what else can be done while they're gone.

Read the manuals you've accumulated and discuss the proposed work with experienced friends. Arm yourself with knowledge, tools, and the repair parts you need and stick to your plan. Before you know it, that neglected BMW will begin to shine like a new machine, and all the work and planning will start to pay off.

Tool Lists and Drawings

While it would be great to have every special tool that BMW recommends for its dealers, the cost is just too prohibitive. Besides, the chances that you'll need all of them are slim, unless you plan to give up your day job to repair BMW motorcycles.

At the very least, you'll want to supplement your own collection of mechanics tools with a few special items. Remember, a BMW is built to close tolerances, with many things pressed, shrunk, or threaded together. Tools that may work well on your Buick or your Briggs and Stratton, won't do much for helping you get your BMW running again.

Rather than list all the tools you could ever hope to need, or burden you with all the drawings that BMW has provided for making your own tools, I have included in an appendix a select number of tool drawings and charts. If you need to see more drawings, or want someone to make the tools, a comprehensive set of drawings is available from me, or through other sources listed in the appendix. Tools can be made up for you by Vintage BMW member Ed Korn.

A number of tools are generic in nature, such as valve spring compressors, cylinder hones, piston ring compressors, and wrist pin extractors, and can be found at your local auto parts store. The bare minimum you'll need are some large hook wrenches, the four-pin tool to remove the wheel bearing caps, some extractors to help you remove the magneto rotor and generator armature, and the special tool to help remove the 1955–1969 front and rear swingarm bearings. Beyond that, you'll be considering specialized drifts and pullers for working on your transmission and rear drive, some of which are also described in the appendix.

Remember, it's not the tool that does the job, it's the person wielding it. If you haven't done your homework and at least read your shop or owner's manuals, no amount of special factory tools will help you restore your BMW.

Chapter 5

Conquering the Beast

The BMW motorcycle you've chosen is basically a simple design that has been refined over the years. Some of these refinements are seen in improved brakes, engines, and higher performance figures. Many are mere cosmetic changes or styling improvements. If you have not yet purchased the machine you've settled on, I hope the caveats below won't discourage you from buying an older machine. Like all things mechanical, nothing is designed to last forever and even a BMW, well engineered as it is, will eventually wear out.

Just how badly worn a machine is will be up to the prospective buyer to discover. Most owners either will not know about hidden problems or will be too prudent to mention them for fear of ruining a sale. Most of the major, life-threatening problems, such as cracked frames, bent wheels, and unsafe tires, will be obvious to all but the most nearsight-

Yes, you can still find them like this, complete with sidecar, ready for the restorer's hand. This 1954 R68 and BMW Spezial were recently found in this condition. After some sheet metal work, some paint, plating, and striping, this BMW will look like new. *Marie Lacko*

ed prospective buyer. If something doesn't look right, look again and, if necessary, pass up the machine.

To the Bare Bones

If your new purchase requires total disassembly, don't despair. Unless your project BMW has been dropped off a cliff or run over by a truck, virtually anything can be fixed, given enough time and money. I once bought a running 1939 BMW R12, a 750cc side-valve ex-Wehrmacht model, which not only had a bullet hole in one of its cylinder heads, but also had a section of frame cut off by a hacksaw and a cracked steering head that flexed 1/8in each time a bump was hit! It was almost unsafe to ride, but it started on the second kick, on stale gas transferred from a farm tractor via a Coke bottle. When it came time to restore the machine, all that was really required was extensive work with a welding torch, and replacement of both fenders with more desirable civilian versions. Nothing is impossible if the machine still has a bit of a heartbeat left.

Occasionally, you may have to combine two machines to come up with one good one. While this means that one machine will be forever lost, it does save yet one more BMW that otherwise might never have run again.

In the simplest case, you've located an almost complete older BMW for your restoration project. After you get the machine home, try to fire it up to see just how well it runs. Unexplained noises may or may not be a cause for alarm. If you can determine that the problems are minor, such as piston wear or cylinder defects, start there. Removal of cylinders and heads is straightforward and spelled out in the following chapters. If the engine has to be removed from the frame, that is also a simple task, requiring less than an hour's effort and possibly the help of a friend. Remove the heads and cylinders first to cut down on the weight and make the job easier.

You can remove the transmissions, as well as the rear drive and rear end, without disturbing the engine. Wheels come off with the motorcycle on the center stand. Fenders can best be removed after the wheels have been pulled because some of the bolts are impossible to get at otherwise. Naturally, sheet metal work, painting, and plating cannot be done while the parts are still attached to the machine. Disassemble your BMW in stages, photograph the project as you go, and everything will go well.

Keeping Track

Most restorations or repairs will take weeks and months. Some have been known to take years. Don't rely upon memory alone to help you put things back together, or to tell you where all the parts have been stored. Take copious notes as you go. Better to note how a part fits than to reinstall it incorrectly and ruin all your work.

Plastic, zip-lock bags in various sizes are ideal for storing small parts and protecting delicate assemblies, such as electrical components. Stockpile small boxes, preferably white cardboard ones. These can hold the various items and are easy to write on. The little tins with the snap-on lid that gourmet coffees come in are ideal for this purpose, and provide a dust and moisture proof seal.

Reserve a space on your shelf in the workshop for all the components, and don't get them mixed up with parts from other projects, in particular other BMW parts. Most BMW parts look similar, yet will not work in machines other than the ones from which they came. During the 1950–1969 era, pistons could be of the three-, four-, or five-ring variety, with different heights and wrist pin locations. Heads came in three of four different styles, and in both long and short reach spark plug versions. The tapered ends on crank and camshafts varied between models, so that generator armatures and magneto rotors will not interchange. Avoid mixing things up at the beginning, and you won't mix them up at the end.

Getting Help

Investigate the local shops in your area that do specialized work such as welding, polishing, and plating. Read the ads in the journals devoted to the hobby, such as *Hemmings Motor News*. Ads in the major BMW club magazines, such as *BMW Owners News* (published by the BMW Motorcycle Owners of America) or *On the Level* (published by the BMW Riders Association) will prove invaluable in helping you find not only firms that specialize in plating and painting, but also those that provide parts. While the biggest ads don't necessarily mean these firms do the best work, it does indicate a certain commitment. Big ads cost money, and unless a business is making money by serving a large number of customers, it won't be featuring big ads for long. Investigate the service section of the *Vintage BMW Bulletin* (published by the Vintage BMW Motorcycle Owners Club), which lists most of the major firms and individuals catering primarily to the restoration of pre-1970 BMWs. Inquire also at your local BMW dealer.

Find out where your friends had their work done. If their plating or striping looks as good as in the factory photos, the firms that did the work may be the firms for you. If in doubt, send one item, such as a fender or a handlebar, to be either painted or plated. If the company is poorly managed, and the parts get lost, at least you will not have lost everything.

Once you've found a good shop, cultivate it. Try to get as much done as quickly as possible, as your own time and your finances allow. Even good shops have a habit of being there one day and gone the next. Check on your work often, even if you've sent it halfway across the country.

Pitfalls and Problems

Although you've purchased all the workshop manuals available for your model, as well as a parts book, and you've got your owner's manual and some BMW club publications to guide you, nothing can prepare you for what will come next. There will be hundreds of unanswered questions and problems never addressed by even the best of publications.

Just how does that engine really come apart? How will you ever get the engine back in the frame without damaging the paint? How do you know if a prior owner used the correct recommended parts, when there are so many possible wrong choices? What were the things the BMW factory only told the dealers and mechanics, that aren't mentioned anywhere in the workshop manuals? Why did BMW change a part for no particular reason during the model run, and how will not using that part affect your machine? Should regular or Hypoid oil be used in the gearbox or rear drive? Why can't hy-draulic fluid be used in the pre-1955 forks? Can later BMW parts be used on earlier machines? What sort of aftermarket parts not made by BMW can be used in your particular model. Can American made bearings and seals be used? Are German tires that fit the older models still being made?

As discouraging as all this may sound, especially to the BMW owner about to start on his first restoration, the road ahead is not completely full of pitfalls. BMW, in true Teutonic fashion, went to great lengths to document every little engineering change and sent out specific service bulletins to all its dealers as these changes were incorporated in production models. Most of the changes were of a minor nature, such as alternative wheel spokes, changes in tire recommendations, and fuel and lubrication specifications. All, however, served to improve the BMW and keep it running more reliably.

Some of the bulletins addressed manufacturing oversights, such as improperly installed pistons, defective cylinder head castings, and problematic bearings. Before you panic and start thinking that your BMW is about to disintegrate into thousands of defective little fragments, remember that your pre-1970 machine initially came from a BMW dealer, and that it has in all likelihood been

Even the last of the line, BMW's US-fork models, like this 1969 R60US, can be resurrected and made to shine like the day they came off the boat.

This is how it used to be done. A shipment of new Earles forks BMWs, being off loaded at JFK International Airport in New York in the late 1960s. If today's enthusiasts could have seen how their beloved machines arrived, strapped to a pallet with shock cords, most would have raised their stress levels to new heights. *Richard Kahn, Butler & Smith, Inc.*

back to a BMW dealer at least once in the hands of its former owners, at which time many of the factory warnings would have been addressed.

For example, a common malady in the late 1960s was a run of defective cylinder heads, wherein the steel spark plug insert would eventually loosen, leak, or blow out entirely. BMW immediately altered the casting, thickening the area where the spark plug hole was, and tapped a threaded hole of greater length which had no steel insert. The heads were marked "LK" (which stood for *Lange Kerze*, or long-reach plugs), and BMW told all the dealers to install only the newer heads whenever a customer required one. It's now been nearly thirty years since those original heads gave problems. Those that haven't been replaced will probably work fine for another thirty. All the bad ones have probably been melted down by now. If your BMW still has the older, short reach heads, they would have to have been built in the 1966–1968 era for you to have any concern. Older machines didn't have that problem. Fortunately, heads can be interchanged over a wide number of models, and used heads are plentiful at flea markets and in used parts dealers' stocks. Knowing about such problems gives you some advance notice of what might happen to your machine if you neglect it.

As you embark on your restoration, keep these factors in mind. BMW never abandoned its dealers or its customers. The reputation of the factory was of as great concern as the reliability of its products. BMW continued stocking spare parts for ten years after the end of a model run, and is now again licensing private firms to remanufacture parts for the older machines. The growing interest in both the U.S., Germany, and elsewhere in the world for vintage and classic BMWs had much to do with this. BMW gradually began to realize that the best advertising of all for its motorcycles is seeing the older ones still running on the roads or on display at shows. The growth of BMW clubs devoted solely to the preservation, enjoyment, and use of these older machines has provided the impetus for both the BMW factory, private firms, and enthusiasts to view these older machines as artifacts to be preserved, and as enduring legacies of BMW long manufacturing heritage.

Chapter 6

Frames, Forks, and Suspension

From 1950 through 1969, BMW maintained essentially the same double-loop frame design, with the engine bolted into the frame at the bottom, either telescopic or leading link front suspension, and coil spring and plunger or swingarm rear suspension. The overall layout, with transverse engine, shaft drive, black paint, and white striping, was so conservative in execution, and the changes so subtle, that over the years people began to think that BMWs never changed, and that all models

All plunger frames looked like this, seen here on a 1951 R67. They followed the prewar design first laid down by the 1936 R5, with the innovative rear suspension members of the 1937–1940 R51 added. The frames were robust and fitted with sidecar mounts on the right side. This photo also provides an excellent view of the size and location of striping on fenders and tanks. *BMW Archives*

A nice frontal view of a 1952 R67/2, showing the sheet metal covers over oil filled front fork tubes. This particular machine is fitted with an extra large Hoske tank. *Michael Gross*

were pretty much the same.

Unfortunately for the restorer, such is not the case. In reality, none of the frame and suspension parts from the 1950–1954 machines will fit the 1955–1969 designs. This is to the good, for it does spare us custom abominations bolted up from several models of different eras. However, it does foster some confusion, since wheels appear to be similar, and axles look so much alike that the wrong ones are often purchased for the wrong machine.

Fortunately, as BMW improved the frame and suspension over the years, the changes were documented in both service bulletins and shop manuals still available for the 1951–1969 models. Nevertheless, there are some things to watch out for which could get the unsuspecting owner and restorer into trouble.

Early Frames 1950–1954

The frame on the 1950 R51/2 was a carryover from the prewar R51, and as such had a few of the earlier model's defects. It was a double-loop, conical steel tube frame, with a horizontal center tube under the main spine. Sidecar mounts were incorpo-

rated on the frame's right side, and a lug with a ball was permanently welded to the right rear plunger brace. The frame carried a set of oil-filled telescopic forks at the front, mounted in uncaged ball bearings at the steering head. Rear suspension was by sliding plungers and coil springs, with the former lubricated via grease nipples.

The engine was solidly bolted into the frame by two long bolts passing transversely through the block. The frontmost bolt also served as an attachment for the lower sidecar mounting ball, as needed. There was no upper support for the engine. The fork lock was removable, and dropped through the fork's top into a catch welded to the steering head. If yours is missing, it's still listed under BMW part number 32 32 9 016 005. It's transferable from machine to machine, so this part number will apply to any 1950–1954 BMW. In fact, the same lock fits most BMW twins going as far back as at least the 1934 R11 and R16 models.

While the frames were solidly built and required little attention, a defect was soon noted in the sidecar attachment that fitted through the right-hand frame tube near the saddle. The 12mm bolt that went through the hole in the frame broke on occasion, so when the R51/2 was replaced by the R51/3 model, a larger bolt was soon fitted. According to a service bulletin issued at the time, all frames after 530230 for the R51/3 and frames after 613317 on the R67/2 had the frame hole bored out to 13mm to accept the new, thicker bolt. Dealers were warned not to use the older, smaller bolt in the new frames, and to enlarge older frames by 1mm to accept the 13mm bolt. If you're planning to mount a sidecar, verify that the parts you're using are correct for the frame, or bore out the frame appropriately. The R68 prior to July 1953 had no sidecar fitting installed by the factory. It was not until frame number 650 924 that the R68 was also provided with sidecar mounts. The only other change to the frames in those years was the application of a small top-mounted engine clamp, beginning with the 1951 R51/3 and R67 series.

Swingarm Frames 1955–1961

After 1954, BMW changed the front forks to a leading link version built on the Earles pattern and modified the frames considerably. At the rear, the plungers were replaced by a swingarm and shock towers which housed hydraulic shocks and coil springs. These were adjustable to accommodate added loads and varying road surfaces. The frame itself mirrored the earlier double-loop tube design, with the exception of the rear swingarm modification. Consequently, earlier engines fit perfectly into later frames, and vice versa. The central spine was a bit thicker, as was the steering head, so gas tanks from the earlier models will not interchange. The mounting brackets below the central spine, which supported the tank, were also located at different points. The fork lock was now in the steering head, at the left side, and was hidden by a pivoting chrome cover. The key to the fork lock also unlocked the standard gas tank toolbox lid. Steering head bearings were still of the loose ball variety running in pressed-in cups.

1962–1969

There's little to differentiate the later frames from the earlier ones other than small, triangular frame gussets welded to the vertical tubes by the rear swingarm pivot points. These first appeared in February 1962 beginning with serial number 656276 on the R69S model. The only other improvements are a welded-on sidestand attachment lug at the frontmost engine mount bolt pad on the left-hand side. The sidestand lug appeared in 1955 beginning with frame number 552 230 on the R50. Consequently, all frames from 1955–1969 will interchange. Steering head bearings were still the loose ball variety.

Improvements by the Enthusiast

The best thing you can do for the handling of your BMW is to replace those loose ball bearings in the steering head with tapered rollers. These press right in replacing the existing races, are of modern manufacture, and cost little. They're available through a number of firms catering to the vintage BMW enthusiast or you can purchase them yourself over the counter less expensively at most bearing supply houses. Ask for MCI bearing 51W (the number on the cup) which accommodates tapered roller bearing 34W. Full cross-reference numbers are in the appendix.

You'll need a complete set (one bearing with its mating cup) for the top, and one for the bottom of the steering head. The difference in handling will astound you. If you don't opt for the better bearings, you'll have to constantly check your old ones for looseness, and keep them well lubricated. This is a tedious task, usually accomplished with lots of cursing as the bearing will invariably fall out just as you're almost finished and roll all over the dirty garage floor. Why BMW never used tapered rollers in the first place is a question, like the Riddle of the Sphinx, that may never be answered.

Another view of the rear suspension section of the 1950–1954 plunger framed twins. Note the location of the horn on the pre-1955 machines, as well as the size and shape of the rear fender striping. *Michael Gross*

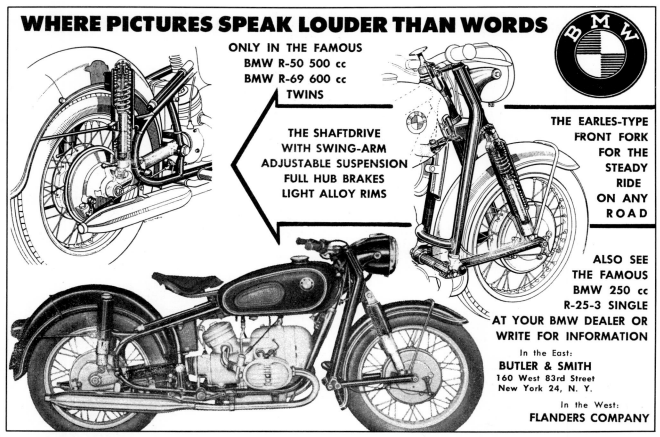

In 1955, BMW introduced the Earles fork twins in both the U.S. as well as overseas. Their big selling point was the ultra-smooth ride the automotive type shocks provided. Note that the R69 was the only 600cc Earles fork twin in 1955.

BMW delayed the introduction of the 600cc R60 until remaining stocks of the plunger frame R67/2 and R67/3 had been delivered. *Richard Kahn, Butler & Smith, Inc.*

BMW Forks
1950–1954

In 1950, when the R51/2 was introduced, it was fitted with the same oil-filled telescopics used on the prewar R51. They were robust, simple in design, reliable if kept filled, and strong enough to withstand the stresses of sidecar work. Disassembly and reassembly is straightforward, and unless they've suffered an accident, the tubes should be straight and true. Damaged tubes can be straightened, or new tubes made, without difficulty by specialist firms. A problem area was the lower bushings, which were of fibrous material now hard to come by. Upper seals are the same as those found on the post-1970 /5, /6, and /7 series. Ask for BMW part number 31 42 1 230 001.

A point that caused some owners a lot of trouble was the oil the 1950–1954 forks required. Most owners assumed the forks used hydraulic fluid, when in fact they used nothing more exotic than engine oil! The consequence of using the wrong fluid was damage to the original seals and oil leaking from every joint. Usually a straight 40-weight was correct summer and winter, unless the BMW was run under Arctic conditions. If you have access to the original owner's manual, oil recommendations and refill capacities are listed there; they are also listed in the various shop manuals for your model.

By September 1952, the early metal fork covers were replaced with rubber gaiters, to help eliminate wear from the dust and grit which crept under the old forks' metal covers. If your BMW is an R51/3, all numbers from 529380 on should have been fitted with rubber fork boots. For the R67/2, all frames from 631281 had the boots, and for the R68 from 650604 on. If your model has an earlier number, and now has rubber boots, don't despair. Once the original forks got damaged or rebuilt, most owners and dealers opted for the newer parts, which could be fitted to the original forks, per service bulletin 4/52. Since some of these parts may be required today if you're restoring your machine, see the reprinted service bulletin below. The same bulletin also told of improved seals, so I urge you to check your forks for that upgrade as well.

56

BAYERISCHE MOTOREN WERKE
AKTIENGESELLSCHAFT

Rundschreiben der Kundendienst-Abteilung

Circular-Letter of the Service Department
Motorcycle: Chassis Group No. 4/52

Munich, 25/9/52
KVK/Ba/Wi./eb

Dear Sirs,

SUBJECT: Front fork equipped with rubber gaiters
          R 51/3 from motorcycle No. 529 380
          R 67/2 from motorcycle No. 631 281
          R 68   from motorcycle No. 650 604

To protect inner fork elements from the penetrating dust, rubber
gaiters have been fitted now instead of the **lower** fork coverings in
sheet metal. This arrangement entails the following alterations:

		old parts	new parts
2	spring cover tubes	251 3 62 424 09	–
1	lower shroud, left	251 2 62 504 09	–
1	lower shroud, right	251 2 62 514 09	–
2	rubber sleeves	–	275 1 62 021 03
2	spring cover securing nuts	251 3 62 434 09	251 4 62 434 09
2	spring retainers, top, solo	251 2 62 483 09	251 4 62 486 09
2	spring retainers, top, side-car	251 2 62 473 09	251 4 62 476 09
1	fork yoke, bottom	251 2 62 544 09	251 4 62 544 09/19
2	joints tripartite	–	251 4 62 605 14
2	hexagon screws	M 6x30 DIN 931	M 6x22 DIN 931-8 G
4	sleeve securing clips	–	251 4 62 640 04

On the motorcycles R 68 No. 650 304 - 650 603 the fork sleeves have
already been fitted, but with a smaller oil seal instead of the tri-
partite packing 251 4 62 605 14. In order to have the fork tube top
cover fitted properly with the said packings which are still used, the
fork bottom yoke No. 251 4 62 460 11 should be shortened correspond-
ly on its tube holding lugs or a rubber washer of 2 mm thickness should
be added in compensation to the fork top shroud rubber seal No. 251 1
62 104 04.

SUBJECT: Sealing of front fork R 51/2,
          R 51/3, R 67, R 67/2 and R 68

It has become evident that the seal rings 251 3 62 620 04 with the dust
lip have a tendency to leak, as the dust lip did not work successfully with respect to the alternating movements on account of the fork
suspension. Moreover it was ascertained that the paper joint between
the main tube top bush and the oil seal was not centrically fitted at
assembly, producing thus leaks. In order to remedy these troubles we
have developed a new oil seal 251 3 62 007 14 which has shown good results. This seal is no longer fitted with a dust lip, but has a rubber
envelope on its front surface, so that the new oil seal must be
fitted without the paper joint.

   The new oil seals will be available within about two months,
through our spare parts department. In the meantime, please remove
the old oil seals in case of leakage, cut off cautiously the dust
lip by using a sharpened knife and refit the seals equipped with
proper paper joints, taking care that they should be placed centrically.

                              Yours truly,

                    BAYERISCHE MOTOREN WERKE
                       Aktiengesellschaft

If you've lost your rubber fork boots, or need to replace damaged ones, try your local British bike parts supplier. Fork gaiters from early-1960s BSAs or Triumphs are a "near enough" replacement, having only one less pleat than the BMW's (16) and somewhat thinner rubber. If you want to get the more readily available British replacements, get them from DomiRacer/Accessory Mart in Cincinnati, Ohio, by ordering their number 05-00694. They're close enough for government work, and certainly good enough to fool most judges, though German replacements are also becoming available. I suggest you keep a set on hand just in case you get really serious about winning some silverware at the shows. The hardest thing to keep in good shape, and something you will have to replace with the correct items, are those screw clamp (sleeve securing clips) called out in the service bulletin. They were again available at this writing, so stock up on at least four of them while you have the opportunity.

Earles Forks 1955–1968

By 1955, BMW felt it had to upgrade its whole line, not only to make it look more modern, but to help it compete with the handling of the British machines. What better way than to give the customer a set of front forks currently in vogue on the racetrack? The new leading link forks, invented by an Englishman and built by BMW under Earles license, looked very much like the championship Rennsport forks used so successfully by BMW on its sidecar racers. There certainly was no doubt that these forks were strong enough to handle the loads of a sidecar, and indeed, they came fitted with alternate mounting points for the front shocks, should sidecar use be desired.

The forks are robust and fitted with a forward-facing lower swingarm and two automotive type shocks and coil springs under steel and aluminum covers. Upper mounting points had two positions, for sidecar and solo work. If sidecar work was chosen, the lower mounting holes were used, which increased the trail of the swingarm. The longer rear springs were switched to the front, and special sidecar springs were used at the rear. If you're buying a solo Earles fork machine, check where the shocks are mounted. A machine set up for sidecar and ridden solo will not handle very well. It's best to find out before you try it out. Some owners have been known to ride their machines with the incorrect setup, fortunately without mishap.

In February 1965, the factory made available a stiffer "solo" spring, which replaced the existing spring then used on the Boge front shocks. BMW began installing them on the R50/2 with frame

The Earles fork frame was again a conical section double-loop tube design with a fitment for the adjustable rear shocks welded on. The front fork was adjustable for trail, which was useful when a sidecar was fitted. All that was required was to undo the two top shock bolts and move them to a second locating hole. *BMW Archives*

An excellent view of the innovative Earles forks, which were based on an Englishman's design that BMW had previously tested on their world champion Rennsport solo and sidecar machines. This photo of the Earles fork prototype also gives the restorer an excellent view of the fender and tank striping. A sharp-eyed BMW expert will have noticed by now that the flat steel brace is missing from this front fender. The brace was added to production models after the press kit photos were published in 1955. *BMW Archives*

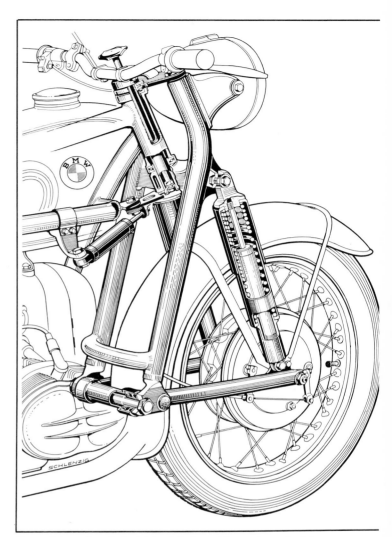

Some interesting industrial art is in evidence here in this Schlenzig phantom view of the R50S Earles forks. Schlenzig was the artist who did most of the cutaways for BMW in the 1950s and 1960s. In this drawing the hydraulic steering damper, a direct adaptation of the Rennsport item, is clearly visible. Only the R50S, the R69S, and the R69US models had the hydraulic damper. It was adjustable for high-speed riding by turning the knob ahead of the handlebars. By 1961 BMW had upgraded to tapered rollers for both front and rear swingarm bearings, but still used the archaic loose balls and races in the steering head, which demanded conscientious attention and adjustment. *BMW Archives*

number 637018, on the R60/2 with frame number 626401, and on the R69S with frame number 658929. All dealers were asked by BMW to use only the new style springs in cases where the motorcycle was brought in for repair. These springs will work on all the Earles fork models back to 1955 and should be used.

The lower cross brace on the front forks was normally just a conical tube, slightly curved, which crossed in front of the alloy electrical cover on the engine. After 1961, when these covers received a pronounced bulge, designed to clear the vibration damper on the "S" models, these cross braces were

altered. BMW felt that a slight risk existed of the cross brace striking the front engine cover in cases of severe frontal impact, so the back of the cross brace was flattened. Indeed, I've seen cases where some object was struck sufficiently hard to allow the fork to flex enough, causing the cross brace to hit the engine. Such cases are probably rare, however. The earlier forks can still be used on the later machines without causing a clearance problem.

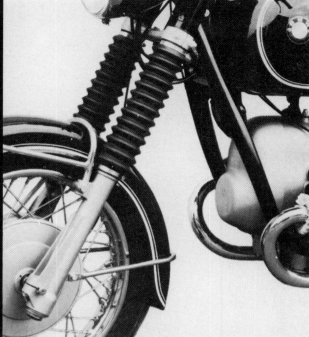

In 1968, BMW introduced its innovative US-fork models, which featured a robust steel and aluminum alloy hydraulic telescopic fork. Alongside the new models, which were touted as superior handling BMWs "for the byways," the prospective buyer could also consider the tried and true Earles fork highway machines. *Richard Kahn, Butler & Smith Inc.*

One problem that should be addressed by the owner of a pre-1965 Earles fork BMW is lubrication of the front swingarm bearing. Prior to frame number 636591 on the R50 series, number 626361 on the R60 series, and number 658624 on the R69S and R69 types, there was no grease fitting tapped into the swingarm cross tube. BMW discovered that water could be better kept out of the swingarm bearings by injecting grease from the inside of the swingarm cross tube, and subsequently fitted a small, convex cup type grease fitting to the models mentioned above. Owners and dealers were urged to retrofit this grease nipple, and service bulletin 1/64 (212) of June 18, 1964, spelled out in minute detail how this was to be done. To complete the job of water exclusion, bearing washers and seals were also to be replaced. For your information, and since dimensional data is involved, service bulletin 1/64 with its associated drawings is reproduced below.

The Earles forks will fit the US fork models of the late 1968 model through the end of the 1969 model run, and some owners prefer to retrofit their US fork models with the earlier design, primarily for reason of aesthetics. If you plan to haul a sidecar, the Earles fork is the only way to go, as the later US telescopics were just not suited for the job. Similarly, US forks can be made to work on the Earles fork models, for those wishing to do so. Again, I urge you to install tapered roller bearings in the steering head as described in the frame modifications section.

Rear Suspension
1950–1954

The rear suspension on the plunger twins is straightforward and a holdover from prewar practice. The coil springs that support the rear axle are located by a vertical rod, and the whole business is hidden under tin and aluminum covers. The shaft and its bushings should be greased liberally via the little fittings found just above the axle points.

There is no provision for additional dampening or adjustment for load, except by replacing the

With a backward glance at the past, BMW cautiously stepped into the 1970s, using this R60US to test the waters. This particular example, fitted with the large sport tank, was stablemate to the R50US and R69US. Note that the sidecar lugs, a feature on all BMWs since the 1920s, have been deleted from the frame members. Not sure of the strength of the new forks, and after weighing certain liability issues, BMW chose to discourage owners and dealers from mounting a sidecar on the new US-fork models. *BMW Archives*

Cust.Serv.-Techn.Dept. VKT er/lü/wi/fm	Motorcycles R50,R60,R69S,R27 Grp:Springs&Shock Absorbers	Munich, 18 June 1964 Nr. 1/64 (212) en.

Re: Lubrication of the Front Wheel-Swinging Arm Bearing

Dear Sirs,

By the introduction as standard equipment of a funnel-type grease fitting (nipple) for the lubrication of the front wheel swinging arm bearing commencing with frame Nr.

> 636 591 (R 50)
>
> 626 361 (R 60)
>
> 658 624 (R 69 S)
>
> 382 853 (R 27)

the maintenance of this bearing has been simplified considerably.

If the customer wishes, this funnel-type grease fitting may subsequently be installed (against charge) on the front wheel swinging arm for the lubrication of the bearing, on the models R 26, R 27, R 50, R 50 S, R 60, and R 69 S.

The following parts are necessary for this:

Description of Part	Part Nr.
1 Funnel-type grease fitting	99 60 270
2 Flat washers	10 20 136
2 Seal rings	20 00 331

Parts superseded:

2 Seal rings	20 00 330
2 Flat washers	20 00 322

For the installation, to which the following guidelines pertain we refer to the Repair Manual R 50, R 50 S, R 60, and R 69 S, from which the corresponding installing operations may be perceived.

1. Remove swinging arm from front fork and dismantle the bearing.

2. Drill a 7.0 mm ∅ hole into the cross-tube of the swinging arm
   and tap-in a M 8 x 1 thread. The center of the hole is located
   37.5 mm away from the left hand border of the swinging arm cross
   tube and set up by 8° against the axis of the swinging arm (also
   see sketch), as seen in the driving direction. Around the thread-
   hole, carefully file a surface not larger than necessary for the
   flat adaption of the fitting head; when doing this, care should
   be exercised to not produce any sharp edges on the borders of the
   surface.

3. Coat the thread of the funnel-type grease fitting with caulking
   compound (for instance Coril) and install the grease fitting.

   After thorough cleaning, reinstall the bearing into the swinging
   arm. When doing this, please note that the new washers 10 20 136
   with the larger supply hole for the grease and the seal rings
   20 00 331 with the metal case are now used.

4. Reinstall the swinging arm into the front fork and adjust the
   bearing.

   Subsequently, lubricate only by means of a manual grease-gun
   with a tapered mouth-piece, until the grease comes out on the
   sealing lip of the sealing ring on each side of the bearing.
   Don't wipe off grease, but spread it around the gap between
   fork-prong and swinging arm, as this constitutes an additional
   protection of the bearing against splash-water.

                    With friendly greetings,
                    BAYERISCHE MOTOREN WERKE
                    Aktiengesellschaft

           i.V.   i.A.
                Ortmann   Ansorg

springs with heavier ones, which was required when the use of a sidecar was planned.

Removal of the plungers and springs is spelled out in the workshop manual, but a few points need to be mentioned. On the 1950 R51/2 and some of the earlier 1951 twins, do not pry at the mushroom cap that covers the top of the plunger. It's purely decorative and made only of pot metal—it will break. Instead, after loosening the various pinch bolts, drive the plungers upward with a drift, something that's best accomplished with the bike lying on its side. Naturally, having a work stand will allow you to get at everything from underneath quite handily. On the models fitted with hex headed caps, carefully unscrew them before you remove the plungers.

1955–1969

The rear suspension of the swingarm framed models was a bit more complex than that found on the 1950–1954 plunger frame machines. Progressive wound springs were used, and road shocks were absorbed by automotive-type shocks. Both the springs and the shocks were hidden under the shock towers and their alloy lower covers. Adjustment for load was done by rotating a lever on either base of each shock.

The shocks required no maintenance and were replaced when leaks developed. Most shocks lasted for years, unless extraordinarily heavy loads were frequently carried. The rear springs had to be replaced with heavier ones when a sidecar was attached.

A common bit of damage one sees all too often on these older machines concerns the two adjusting levers. If they've been cut off by some cretin who owned the bike before you, it was probably done because they interfered with some sort of homemade saddlebag arrangement. All the previous owner had to do was exchange the adjusters from one side to the other, thereby placing the levers on the inside of the shock rather than on the outside. All bag interference would have been avoided, and a set of hard-to-find shock bottoms would have been saved. Incidentally, the bottom parts with the adjusting levers are made of cast iron, which was usually coated with a sort of silvery cadmium plate. Just wiping them periodically with a rag soaked in silver paint will make them look almost as good as the originals. Fanatics have been known to polish and give them a brushed nickel plating, but that's really gilding the lily and an unnecessary expense.

Rear Swingarm Improvements:
Earles Fork Twins

Prior to 1962, rear swingarm bearings could only be lubricated by the tedious method of removing the entire rear swingarm and its pivots posts every 7,000 miles. Not only was this costly and time consuming, but because of the effort involved, it was often passed over by the private owner.

BMW's solution was the fitment of drilled out pivot posts beginning in April 1962. All the owner or mechanic now had to do was remove the aluminum acorn nut, insert a grease gun with a tapered tip, and grease the bearings. This solution is so simple one is amazed that no one thought of it during the design stage prior to the introduction of the Earles fork machines.

Chapter 7

Wheels, Brakes, Axles, Tires

The 1950–1969 BMWs always came with what you'd call pretty wheels. Not your crude garden cart variety as found on other brands, but true quality items fabricated out of steel or aluminum, with brakes more adequate than those used by its contemporaries. Road tests, even in the British magazines, often raved about the BMW's fantastic stopping abilities, especially when compared to the anemic brakes the competition offered. The old saying went: "BMWs were meant to stop, not to go" and stop they did, especially when the production models moved up to front duplex brakes and full-width hubs.

While 1930s BMWs (from which the machines of the 1950s were the direct descendants) had skimpy brakes when compared to most postwar models, they did stop the machines adequately and were a snap to adjust and service. True to form, the 1950 R51/2 continued this tradition with single leading shoe brakes front and rear, actuated by a single cable in the front, and a rod and lever at the rear. Later, the pre-1955 machines went to duplex brakes in the front, then to full-width aluminum hubs with shrunk-in iron liners. By 1969 the limits of drum brakes had nearly been reached, yet BMW, of all the manufacturers, continued well into the mid-1970s with its famous drum and twin-leading front brake shoe system.

Wheels also followed prewar design. The R51/2 had the same black half-hub iron drums as the prewar R51 and R66, and black and silver painted steel rims. A few years later, small fins were added to the drums, and steel rims eventually gave way to alloy in 1954. At the end of the model run in 1969, drums were gargantuan (relatively speaking) and the rims were either alloy or plated steel.

Tires gradually grew from the narrow section 19in ones found on the pre-1955 models, to fat, high speed 18in ones in 1969. Putting all the various combinations together in the right order for your bike and the year it was produced can be perplexing and frustrating, especially if prior owners discarded the original pieces or modernized their machines with custom or performance parts.

Which Wheel Is for You?

The 1950 R51/2 only came with all-steel 19in safety center rims and drums. A silver center line was added to the rims, a practice also common to the late 1930s machines. All BMW rims, right through 1969, had safety notches across the centers that prevented the tire from rolling off the rim in case of a sudden loss of air at high speed. Spokes were black in the very early R51/2 versions, then a semi-gloss cadmium plate, soon to be replaced by polished chrome. The spokes were of unequal length and had cranked ends, again as on the prewar machines. Wheels and most frame parts will interchange with the prewar R51 and R66 series. The wheels were also interchangeable from front to rear. Splines were often neglected and should be greased regularly. The half-hub iron drums are easily recognizable because they have no finning. Similar wheels were seen on the early R51/3 and R67 models in 1951, probably because BMW was still

Typical steel wheel of the 1950–53 era. A half-hub iron drum housed narrow, single leading-shoe brakes. The rim center was painted a gloss silver, with no other colors separating the silver from the black. *Michael Gross*

The 1953–1954 duplex front brake, alloy drum, and aluminum rim, as seen fitted to a 1954 R68. The cast-aluminum drum had straight-pull spokes and a shrunk-in steel liner. *BMW Archives*

using up existing stocks.

By late 1951, the need for better brakes became evident, and BMW shrunk onto the drums a small iron collar with three short fins. Drums were still painted black, and the wheel rims were still the two-color black and silver. By mid- to late 1952, the hubs were enlarged, and by 1953 all the twins had full-width aluminum drums, and a choice of alloy or chrome plated rims. Spokes were still the cranked variety for the half-hub drums until 1952–1953, and straight pull for the full-width wheels thereafter. All rims remained at 19in until 1955, except for the R67/3, which had the optional wider section 18in rim fitted at the rear for sidecar use.

In 1955, all the new BMW twins received 18in wheels and full-width aluminum drums with iron liners. Rims were first alloy, then chrome over steel in 2.15Bx18in size for the front and rear on solo machines, and 2.75Cx18in for the rear for sidecar use. The spokes were of the straight pull variety and were chromed. BMW never mixed alloy and steel rims on the same machine, though a number of owners occasionally put a steel rim at the rear, especially when using the machine to haul a side-

car, which helped to handle the extra load.

Stopping the Beast

As mentioned previously, BMWs always had good brakes, but again, that's a relative term. As described, the tiny half-hub brakes soon gave way to finned ones, then to alloy full-width drums with twin leading shoes. If kept in proper adjustment, they worked well and even stayed dry in the rain. All BMW brake shoes were aluminum, with riveted asbestos linings, even as far back as the mid-1920s. The diameter of the early half-hub linings was a meager 15/16in, but by 1969 these had widened to 1-11/32in, with a marked increase in braking efficiency. The brake backing plates were

By 1955, all BMW twins and singles were fitted with 18in rims and duplex front brakes. Seen here on the BMW Earles fork prototype are the high-lipped aluminum rims used in the mid-1950s. Restorers should note that the brake levers were painted black at this time. Note also that on the prototype, the front fender still hadn't gained a flat steel center brace. *BMW Archives*

In 1968, BMW introduced the US-fork twins, which still used the same front brake, wheel, and drum. The backing plate was located and secured by the addition of a long aluminum brace, but the brakes were the same as on the Earles fork models. *BMW Archives*

For the privateer racer, a number of firms, such as Hoske, provided aftermarket racing brakes. Early examples used the single leading shoe backing plate, and simply added air holes and scoops. *Paul Seibert*

Tires and Tubes

BMW was always concerned about items of safety and reliability, and this was especially true when it came to tires. True, right after the war, anything that held air was being used, so tires were not a major concern. But once BMW began exporting their machines in ever increasing numbers, the factory made certain that the tires fitted to the machines were the best that were then available, from either the German firms of Metzeler or Continental. Other manufacturers were also represented, among them Veith, Fulda, and Englebert.

A glance at the owner's manual for your ma-

always quality aluminum castings, undrilled and unvented, and were fixed with a shrunk-in pin to the lower left fork leg of the pre-1955 models, and by a slot to the Earles fork swingarm on the 1955–1969 models. The US-fork models used a short alloy strut to keep the plate from rotating.

Occasionally, one sees a pre-1955 machine with Rennsport-style brakes, which were available from several accessory manufacturers such as Hoske, or even from BMW on special order, primarily for those intending to go racing. Some manufacturers simply resorted to drilling out the aluminum brake backing plate, allowing built-up heat to escape. Others had sophisticated fins and air scoops cast into the plates. Some even provided matching extra-width alloy hubs to help stop the beast even better. If you come across such a set, don't hesitate to buy it. The improvement in stopping will amaze you and the looks of the machine won't suffer in the bargain.

Another variation on the same theme, this time with extra wide hubs and shoes, still of the single leading shoe variety. *Paul Seibert*

This upgrade featured double scoops and wider drums, a practice seen most often on the pre-Earles fork Rennsport machines of the early 1950s. This particular setup is from the author's 1953 R68 ISDT Replica.

The front brake setup on the author's special 1952 R68 has an aluminum finned collar pressed over the half-hub iron drum, and duplex front shoes. The same collar was also used on the rear wheel.

The left side of the Rennsport wheels as fitted to an R68 ISDT Replica of 1953 vintage.

A stock 1952–53 steel half-drum wheel, with three shrunk-on iron fins. This wheel is correct for all R51/3, R67/2, and R68 models prior to the advent of alloy hubs.

chine will tell you what tires were recommended. To back up the manual, BMW periodically issued detailed service bulletins to its dealers telling them of alternatives that could be fitted or of changes in factory recommendations.

First, if your old machine still has its original tires, you're to be envied. It means that either the bike got little use in the last quarter century, or that a previous owner found a priceless stock of old tires. If you can find a perfect original pattern tire, and if you plan on showing the machine exclusively, then by all means mount it. But, if you plan to enjoy the BMW on the road as it was intended, spring for a more modern tread and better rubber compound.

There's now no excuse for using discount brands of Asian manufacture. Quality German tires in the correct pattern, in particular for the 1955–1969 machines, are once again available, and the cost is not prohibitive. Showing up at a concours with Asian tires will cost you points. After all, owners of British bikes wouldn't be caught dead with anything other than an Avon or Dunlop on their rims, so why should your BMW run on something made in the shadow of Mount Fuji?

Avoid, however, the modern high speed brands, especially the radial ply ones intended for tubeless applications on one-piece alloy rims. They will not look correct, will probably be oversize, and will not improve the handling. They could, in fact, be dangerous. BMW rims, especially the older variety, were intended only to carry narrow profile tall and skinny 19in and 18in tires.

The R51/2, R51/3, R67, R67/2, and R68 were all fitted with 3.50x19in tires and used natural rubber tubes. Brands were either Metzeler or Continental, as well as other German manufacturers. A particularly nice pattern was the 3.50x19in Continental LB. Eventually, export machines had tires fitted by the receiving dealers or owners that were common to their own particular country. For originality's sake though, try to mount a German tire whenever you can, and always use a new natural rubber inner tube when changing tires, along with a new rim strip. The latter costs less than a dollar, and a good tube is the cheapest life insurance you'll ever buy. In fact, in a service bulletin of July 1968, the factory again strongly stated that only natural rubber tubes should be used, and that butyl rubber tubes (at that time identified with a blue stripe) were to be avoided due to their tendency to deflate suddenly in the case of a puncture. Tire pressures for the 1955–1954 models were approximately 22lb for the front and 24lb for the rear. When in doubt, stick to 24lb in the front and 28lb in the rear, unless carrying heavy loads.

The R67/3, which was specifically intended as a sidecar machine, and was usually only available from the factory with the Spezial version of Steib's

TR500 attached, came with a wide section 18in rim at the rear, and consequently required a 3.50x18in rear tires. A 4.00x18in will also fit, but the tire might rub either the fender or the driveshaft.

By the late 1950s, BMW had settled on Metzeler as its tire supplier, but within a few years authorized the use of both Metzeler and Continental tires on its machines. It should be noted that all BMW twins built from 1955 until early 1968 had only 3.50x18in tires front and rear. This was done primarily for ease of wheel interchangeability and for handling considerations. If you've ever tried to stuff a 4.00x18in tire and rim into the narrow space available between Earles fork and brake plate when changing a front wheel, you'll know what I mean.

To further assure its customers that the company was looking out for their interests and safety, BMW stated in February 1962 that, after extensive testing, only two brands of Metzeler tires were authorized for use on their machines. These were the Metzeler 3.50x18in Rille 10 for the front, and the 3.50x18in Block C5 for the rear. By February 1967, a need for a wider rear tire had been recognized, but only for sidecar work. The factory bulletin of that date stated that for solo work, tire pressures were to be 24lb in the front, and exactly 25.6lb in the rear (to help maintain your sanity, we'll allow rounding to the next highest pound). If carrying a passenger, the rear tire was to be pumped up to 30lb. If riding solo but hauling a sidecar, the rear tire was now to be a 4.00x18in, pumped up to 27lb, with 27lb in the sidecar tire, which was still a 3.50x18in. Finally, if you carried both a passenger and hauled a sidecar (no mention was made of luggage, lunch, or pets), the rear tire had to go up to 38lb pressure. With instructions like these, its amazing anyone ever found the time to ride. No wonder all the old tire pumps on the 1955–1969 models are worn out.

Not content to rest, BMW in July 1968 approved the use of Continental's 3.50x18in Profile RB tire on the front, and 3.50x18in Continental Profile K65 on the rear, but only up to frame numbers 646685 for the R50/2, frame number 1816267 on the R60/2, and frame number 664650 on the R69S. After that, due to a change in rear end ratios to 27:8, the Metzeler 4.00x18in or 4.00Sx18in was to be used on the rear.

Finally, by March 1969, BMW announced that the newly introduced Metzeler 3.50x18in four-ply Rille 10 and "S" Rille 10 were the approved front tires. The factory claimed these tires markedly reduced the wheel shimmy that some owners had experienced. Rear wheels continued to be shod with the 4.00x18in or 4.00Sx18in Metzeler Block C5, presumably also now in 4-ply construction.

Heed the factory's advice. As nice as those fat 4.00in tires may look, stick with the 3.50x18in ver-

ℭontinental TIRES*

"Continental" Tires are approved by BMW for use on BMW motorcycles.

"CONTINENTAL" TYPE RB

A . . . . .3.50 x 18 . . . .**$21.15**

"CONTINENTAL" TYPE K65

B . . . . 3.50 x 18 . . . .**$21.15**
4.00 x 18 . . . .**$26.55**

"CONTINENTAL" TYPE K62

C . . . . .3.25 x 18 . . . .**$17.60**

"CONTINENTAL" TYPE LB

D . . . . .3.50 x 19 . . . .**$19.20**

"CONTINENTAL" TYPE GS-2

E . . . . .3.25/3.50 x 18 . . . . . .**$18.40**

"CONTINENTAL" TYPE GS-6

F . . . . .3.25/3.50 x 18 . . . . . .**$19.30**

❋ Federal Excise Tax included in all prices.

Dealers, Please Note: For all orders of 10 tires or more, freight will be prepaid.

An American accessory catalog of the late 1960s shows what the tread design on most BMW tires looked like at the time. Some of these patterns are now again available from Germany. *Richard Kahn, Butler & Smith, Inc.*

sions, at least for the front of pre-1968 models. Try to use the appropriate brand of Continental or Metzeler whenever possible, in either 3.50in or 4.00in size, depending on your BMW's year of manufacture.

Axles and Nuts

All the 1950–1969 BMW twins had plated axles front and rear that unscrewed from the fork leg or swingarm in the usual manner. Only certain prewar models had left-hand thread axles, but for the postwar twins just unscrew them in the normal manner by turning them to the left. Don't forget to loosen the nut as well on the safety pinch bolt on the left fork leg or swingarm. On the rear, it's the same procedure. The front axle on all machines is always the less robust of the two and cannot be interchanged. Axles from the 1950–1954 models will not fit the 1955–1969 models, and vice versa. To swap wheels from front to rear, a reducing sleeve on the 1955-1969 twins must first be removed from the front wheel and inserted in the rear, which will require the use of a special drift to push it out.

When rechroming the axles, make sure the plating shop masks off the threads with special tape, otherwise you'll have to chase the threads with a suitable metric die. The hole in each axle was meant for the little breaker bar that's in the tool kit, and is useful in loosening frozen axles. The British call this a "Tommy bar" and, contrary to popular belief, no such bar was ever fitted permanently into these axle holes on production machines. Only the racers and ISDT competition models had the bars pressed into them. There's also no need to turn the axle so the hole faces into the direction of travel. Any decrease in wind resistance is too small to be measured.

Things to Worry About

Spokes will loosen over time and if left unattended, will break. This holds true for any motorcycle and is not unique to BMW. Check them for tightness periodically by rapping them in succession with the end of a screwdriver or wooden dowel. Those that emit a dull, flat sound need to be retightened or may even be broken. It's cheaper in the long run to replace all of the spokes for any given wheel at one time than to replace a few. It's also better to buy new ones, in either chrome or stainless steel, than to attempt replating used ones. Hydrogen embrittlement from the plating process will weaken used spokes.

When replacing the spokes, remember that the 1955–1960 R50, R60, and R69 originally used spokes that were only 3.5mm in diameter. After 1961, all models were fitted with 4.0mm thick spokes. It's a wise idea to retrofit the larger sizes to the older machines, along with the appropriate nipples, of course. Don't forget to grind down any pro-

truding spoke ends before you install the rubber rim band. Any extra long ends will guarantee a puncture in a short time. Retighten any spokes fitted to aluminum rims after 1,200 miles. They have a tendency to loosen more quickly than those fitted to steel rims. Incidentally, the 1955–1961 machines had dull chrome spokes, but by 1961 the spokes in the 4.0mm size could be had in both dull chrome and mirror polished chrome. Stainless spokes will be of a slightly thicker gauge than the originals, but if you do both wheels at once, it's almost impossible to notice the difference.

Have the provider of the spokes also include a set of nipples in matching stainless. Nothing looks worse than having them half and half. If the provider will do it, have them relace and true the wheel. That way, if there's any problem with length or thickness, they can correct it on the spot. Again, don't send the shop dirty and greasy wheels; do them the courtesy of at least cleaning off everything. Naturally, remove the tires and tubes, but leave the bearings in; the shop will need them in order to put the wheel onto a machine to true and align the rim.

In December 1968 BMW sent out a factory warning to all its dealers that replacement hubs (listed as part number 36 31 2 030 017) could have an undersize inner diameter, which could cause drum distortion, especially when the wheels were rebuilt. The factory suggested that the drum be turned to a nominal size of 200mm plus 0.185mm to avoid such problems. There might still be some of these drums left over in old dealer's stocks, so check them before installation.

An Improved Brake Lining Solution

The original asbestos linings are no longer available, and even if you located some old stock linings, they're bound to be too hardened by age to be of much use. Even on the best cared for machine, the original linings would eventually glaze over, become brittle, and crack with hard use.

There is, however, a modern equivalent, which is superior to the old linings in every respect. The material is made of something called 232 AF, and it's available from Industrial Brake and Supply Company, 1606 Elsmore Street, Cincinnati, Ohio 45223. Order the 5/32in thickness. For the 1950–1969 twins, specify a lining width of 1-11/32in. For the 1950–1954 twins, specify 15/16in wide. Measure your own linings before ordering. The company will cut the material to the width you specify and sell it by the foot, rather than in individual sections. A good rule of thumb is to order 20 percent more than you need. Cost is reasonable.

When it's time to fit the lining, don't cut off the length you think you'll need, but leave it all in one piece. You'll have to drill the lining for the rivets beforehand. Use of small clamps or padded ViseGrips

71

will greatly expedite the process. Use a 1in drill bit, and drill the linings one hole at a time from the center out. Countersink the holes with an old 1/4in bit that has had the tip ground square to resemble an end mill. Chuck the countersinking bit into a T-handle from a tap set and counterbore the holes by hand. Cut away the excess material with a razor blade. Lay the lining onto one shoe, start riveting from the front, and work your way to the end. Rivet the linings using either the factory copper rivets (still available from your BMW dealer) or use 1/8in aluminum "pop" rivets, which are cheaper and easier to install. Cut off the excess material, after it is all riveted. You'll get a tighter fit that way.

Others prefer to glue the linings on with one of the new modern adhesives, but this will cause some problems later on when it comes time to change linings once again. Stick with the rivet method. It worked for BMW and they probably investigated adhesives long before anyone else even thought of it.

Tire Changing without Tears

Nothing is worse than changing a tire by the side of the road, unless it's having to do it with only the tools provided in the BMW tool kit. Unfortunately, when you need them most, your extra long British tire irons that you bought for just this purpose are probably at home. Try packing a pair of short and fat machined solid round aluminum tire levers, such as those available from J. C. Whitney at under $8 each. They will fit, with some repacking, into the toolbox, or can be carried in the bottom of your saddle bags. These, plus some liquid soap (dish washing detergent works best) will help zip that tire off the rim. Leaving the tire out in the hot sun for a while will also soften up the casing to

make your job easier.

Make sure that the tire pump clipped to your frame works and always carry an extra tube with you. A perfect place to put it is inside your headlight bucket, which has all sorts of wasted space. Protect the extra inner tube by inserting it into a small sleeve made of a section of old inner tube. If your sidecar gets a flat, and you do not have a spare wheel, you can attempt riding home with it deflated. Conversely, if your BMW gets a flat, and if you're lucky to have a Steib or other sidecar using a BMW wheel as a road wheel, swap wheels. Leave the flat tire on the unloaded sidecar axle. A trick like this once got me home, late at night, from Vermont to New Hampshire without difficulty. The tire had to be discarded, but it saved me hours of frustration and a few skinned knuckles.

While you may think changing a tire is child's play, a lot can go wrong. If done incorrectly, your mistakes could kill you. The BMW factory, in addressing complaints about defective tubes, felt that this was caused by improper tire changing techniques, and issued a detailed set of guidelines in May 1968. Most will seem obvious, but for those who have never changed a tire or replaced a tube, I've combined them with some other time-tested techniques that I urge you to follow.

First, never use a tube twice, no matter how good it looks. If you're lucky, you'll get a flat sometime later. If you're unlucky, this warning could be carved into your headstone. Used tubes have all sorts of weak spots earned through thousands of miles of bad roads or unseen particles of imbedded grit, even metal slivers caused by overzealous contact between tire iron and steel rim. The old tube can be cut up into rubber bands to use as emergency bungee cords or to tie luggage into tight little bundles.

If there's still air in the tire, remove the tire valve and let all the air out. Lever the tire casing away from one side of the rim and pull up the beading all the way around on one side.

If just replacing the tube, skip the next step.

If replacing the tire, lever it successively off the rim on the other side and reverse the procedure to install a new one. Most tires are usually marked with a colored dot indicating its heaviest part. Place the tire so that this paint dot is opposite the valve stem hole. This will help offset the weight of the stem and aid in balancing the tire and wheel when done.

Whether installing just a tube or replacing a complete tire, only push the tire half onto the rim before attending to the tube. Protect your painted rims (if dealing with a wheel from a 1950–1953 BMW) by taping the tire irons with plastic electrical tape, and by greasing the rims heavily with liquid soap. Chrome and alloy rims usually fare better, but a little extra caution will pay dividends.

The J. C. Whitney tire changing kit. While the iron tire spoon is more useful than the shorter examples found in the BMW tool kit, the round aluminum bar is the best thing in the set because it makes peeling the casing off the rim much easier and protects the wheel from damage.

The tube is inserted into the tire partially inflated with just enough air to allow it to hold some sort of shape (some find it easier to insert the tube into the tire before putting the tire back on the rim). Pull the valve stem out through its hole, and secure with the locking ring.

Push in the other side of the tire by working around the edge. Use of talcum powder will make the tube more slippery and prevent pinching. Always work in the tire irons at points opposite to the safety notches on the rim. Partially inflate the tube, bounce the tire a few times to seat the bead. Deflate the tire, and repeat the above bouncing and inflating a few times to assure that no part of the tube is pinched. If the valve caps are black plastic (most common), replace them eventually with metal Schrader or Michelin caps of the period.

Bearings and Seals

While you have the wheel off, check your bearings. Eventually, they will need repacking or replacement. Again, this is not something you want to be doing by the side of the road, at night, in a rainstorm (when things like this usually require attention). Ideally, you will have packed along a set of bearings, but if you haven't, any auto parts shop should carry them. Bearings have been standardized for nearly seventy-five years, and all numbers can be cross-referenced with modern equivalents. If the ones you just took out weren't handmade in a mud hut by native laborers, the man behind the parts counter should be able to find you some that will fit. Aftermarket bearings and seals for the R51/3 and R67/2 wheels are available from New Departure and carry number ND 3204 or CR 6206-22J. Bearings for the 1955–1969 are all tapered roller, front and rear, and should be replaced in pairs on each axle.

To get at the bearings, you must first remove the covers, which will require a special four-pin wrench. To attempt the removal without this factory tool will be well nigh impossible and will result in damage to the holes. Your BMW, or the one you're about to buy, will probably have such damaged holes. If it doesn't, it means one of two things. Either the seller took excellent care of the machine and used only the proper tools or he never greased the bearings.

The four-pin tool for the 1950–1969 twins is number 517. It can be purchased through your BMW dealer or made for you by Ed Korn. The tool costs little when compared to the cost of the parts you will damage by not using it. I keep one with the machine I'm riding and one in my workshop.

Grease the bearings with a general multipurpose grease with a drip temperature of 180deg C (356deg F).

There is also a special tool made that pops into the axle hole and is supposed to grease your bearings without requiring their removal from the wheel. Although I have one, I have never tried it, preferring instead to rely upon the time honored method of hand packing, which also gives me the opportunity to examine the bearing while it's out of the wheel. A good device, available cheaply anywhere, is a repacking tool, which is a set of two tapered plates and a central grease fitting. Simply clamp the bearing between the plates, introduce grease through the fitting, and you will force out all the imbedded crud and water that accumulated over the years.

Again, like tires and tubes, good wheel bearings are the cheapest sort of life insurance you'll ever buy. Repack or replace them at the first sign of trouble, and always check them before attempting any long trips.

Chapter 8

Sheet Metal, Fenders, Tanks

Nothing makes or breaks a restoration more than the amount of attention paid to the BMW's most visually exciting aspects, the fenders and gas tank. Lack of attention will spoil the motorcycle for you and make it less salable in the future.

First, the correct fenders and tank for the model *and* era must be fitted. True, it is possible to swap fenders and tanks between models to some extent, but nothing spoils a restoration more than to have the wrong items for the model fitted to an otherwise well-finished machine.

Avoid aftermarket reproductions, especially those in plastic or aluminum, unless your particular tastes run to riding a custom, exotic, or hand-built special. All BMW fenders were always fabricated in steel, as were both versions of the original BMW supplied accessory tanks. Not only are fiberglass tanks incorrect, but they are also dangerous because they are prone to develop leaks and cracks. They also have a nasty habit of losing all their fuel at once in an impact, with disastrous consequences.

A correctly striped 1952 R67/2, showing the twin fender lines set back from the edge of the front fender and just next to the edge on the rear. The lower brace swung down to prop up the front forks when changing wheels. The ultra-large tank is a Hoske, also most commonly striped in this fashion, with the lining following the outer contours. The narrow seat is also an option for these years, although it was less often seen than the sprung Pagusa saddle. *Michael Gross*

Stick to what the manufacturer originally fitted, or what was available as an accessory option from one of the major German tank manufacturers, such as Hoske or Heinrich. If your BMW does not have the correct tank, one will eventually turn up. If yours is of the wrong era for the bike it can always be traded for the one more suited to your particular machine, as discussed in this chapter.

Fenders

Starting with the fenders, the front fenders of the R51/3 and R67 series were identical in construction and were of the "elephant ear" variety, as they are popularly called in the U.S. They are easily recognized by the large bell-shaped valance at the bottom, and have deep valances on the sides, unlike the narrow profile of their prewar counterparts. The bell elephant ear fenders were fixed to the fork legs by a riveted-on flat steel brace, which also served as a center fork brace. These fenders were located at the bottom by a swing down, tubular prop-stand, which was attached to the bell portion of the fender by a large captive (non-removable) acorn nut. When it came time to change

Although the fender is correct for this 1953 R51/3, the striping is too close to the edge and is only a single line. The earlier R51/2 was striped in this fashion, but with a double line. Note the riveted-on flat steel brace and the single fixing bolt for the swing-down brace. *Bill Sawyer*

Factory striping on the Earles fork models followed the fender edges as well as the tank contours, as seen on this R50/2 with narrow bench seat, Europa bars, and Hella bar end signals. The tank is the standard 4gal item, with swing out toolbox lid under the left knee pad. The Earles-fork fenders were firmly attached to the lower swingarm, and not to the upper fork assembly, and moved up and down with the front wheel. In extreme cases, the fender could contact the base of the headlight rim, but usually only after a serious accident or by driving your BMW into a large deep hole at high speed.

wheels or repair a tire, this prop-stand cum brace made the task easier. Unfortunately, BMW did away with this feature with the R68 and all subsequent 1955–1969 Earles-fork models. The 1950–1954 singles did not enjoy the benefit of such a brace. If your brace is missing, it can be fabricated without too much difficulty if you find someone willing to loan you theirs as a pattern. The R68 had its own unique steel front fender, a narrow racing design, similar to some English examples, which had a tubular steel center brace, bolted on, which acted as fork brace, and two tubular steel top and bottom braces, which were also bolted on. The bottom one did not swing down to act as prop-stand.

Fenders fitted to the Earles and US-fork machines were not as sophisticated, complex, or handsome as on the 1950–1954 models. All Earles-fork twins had the same front fender, a simple pressing with a long riveted-on center brace of flat steel that attached only to the bottom of the lower front swingarm on both sides. There was a single, front, chrome plated, bolted-on upper brace. The bottom of the front fender was then firmly attached to the lower swingarm cross tube, and moved up and

down with the swingarm, thereby maintaining a constant distance from the tire. On the pre-1955 models, the front fender moved up and down with the lower fork legs, to which it was firmly attached. Fenders between the 1950–1954 and 1955–1969 models do not interchange, although unsuccessful attempts to do so can be seen now and then. The end result is an ugly combination, with the penalty being the destruction of the original fender through the alterations required to make it fit.

The front fender fitted to the US-fork models of the R50, R60, and R69S was similar in shape and size to its Earles-fork counterpart, but it came without any flat steel center brace and was held on instead by a complex chrome plated U-shaped brace that bolted to the alloy lower fork legs of the US forks and served as a stiffening member as well. The front of the fender did not have a chrome brace as on the Earles models, but instead had only a similar chrome brace on the bottom at the rear. US-fork fenders can be made to work with Earles-fork models. The only reproductions now coming out of Germany in steel for the 1955–1969 twins are similar to the US-fork design and have no flat steel

Another view of a 1954 R68 with the original striping still visible on the rear fender and Hoske tank. Compare the shape of this Hoske with the one on the earlier 1952 R67/2. Most Hoske tanks swallowed up the small Pagusa solo saddles. The R68 front fender was always a narrow one, with two

braces and a bolt on tubular steel center brace. The rear fender was similar to all other 1951–1954 fenders, except that on the R68 there usually were no sets of holes on top for a pillion rack or seat.

metal center strap.

Rear fenders are a simpler matter, but there are still some quirks that will fool the untutored. On the face of it, all of the 1950–1954 Twins appear to share the same rear fender: a deeply valanced, two-piece unit with a swing-up rear flap allowing access to the rear wheel. The rear braces are flat stock and bolt to the rear plunger towers. There is a small shallow cutout on the right side to clear the exposed driveshaft. This cutout should have a plate inside it, held on with two bolts. On a number of machines, however, this has either been lost or removed to clear tires larger than the stock 3.50x19in size. On the R67/3 (which had larger rear tires) it was usually left off by the factory. If it has been lost, one can easily be made up from sheet stock.

The rear fender main section bolts directly to the frame, with no other braces. When fitted, the pressed steel pillion rack bolted to four prepunched holes in the fender, and comes with its own supporting braces, which also bolt to the rear plunger towers. The R68 rear fender did not originally come with four holes on the top surface, since this model was never intended to have pillion rack or normal type of pillion seat fitted. The fine points of rear seating on 1950–1969 BMWs are discussed in Chapter 14. However, over the years, fenders tend to rust out or get damaged so don't be put off if your R68 has what appears to be a rear fender from an R51/3 or R67. Holes can easily be filled permanently with braze, or plugged with four small rubber caps, which were used on all machines during the 1950–1969 era.

The R51/2 (although cataloged as a 1950 model, it was actually sold from the last months of 1949 through early 1951) had a rear fender slightly different from the other pre-1955 twins. The R51/3, R67, and R68 (and all of the Earles and US-fork models) enjoyed a rear wiring harness concealed inside a tack-welded tunnel on the underside of the rear fender. The R51/2, on the other hand, continued with the prewar practice of clipping the rear wiring harness to the outside of the left side of the rear fender. While having the wiring hidden inside a tunnel underneath the rear fender is certainly more pleasing to the eye, such aesthetics came with a price. The 1951–1969 rear fenders now carried with them an ideal starting point for sand, salt, and rust to collect, all leading to the eventual destruction of the rear fender. This tunnel also contributed greatly to electrical problems as wires got pinched and insulation cracked. This destruction happened out of sight of the owner, who otherwise might have caught such problems before they got serious.

The rear fenders on all the Earles-fork and US-fork twins from 1955 through 1969 were identical, and all had the rear wiring harness tunnel mentioned earlier. The rear flap was hinged, but this time the hinged flap could be clamped tight in the down position by two captive aluminum acorn nuts. The rear side braces were tubular (not flat like on the pre-1955 twins or on the R26 and R27) and bolted to the upper rear swingarm shock towers. As on the prior models, all rear fenders were provided with four holes to accept the pressed steel pillion rack, which was similar to that on the pre-1955 twins, with the exception of having shorter side braces.

All fenders were painted in glossy lacquer, with no undercoating. Pinstriping was the same in execution, with one thin and one thick line, and was done freehand at the factory. The vast majority of fenders were black, as were the motorcycles. Some models, in particular those built after 1955, could be ordered in several shades of white, red, and the occasional blue or gray.

The location of the pinstriping differs markedly from 1950 through 1969. The R51/2 front fenders had stripes almost on the edge of the fender valance. The R51/3 and R67 series had the striped set back from the edge by 3-1/16in in the sides, and 3-1/16in on the bottom of the bell. The R68, in spite of all sales literature photos to the contrary, could have either a single 5/16in stripe on the front fender, 5/16in from the edge, or the usual double stripe. Rear fenders on all 1950–1954 twins were striped the same, with a single thin and thick stripe. The stripes, incidentally, were configured thick nearest to the edge, thin above it, with the thickness being 5/16in and 1/16in respectively. They were separated by 5/32in, and the wider stripe was set back 5/16in from the edge.

On the 1955–1969 Earles-fork and US-fork models, thankfully, all fenders (front or rear) were striped identically, with the thick line 1/4in from the edge of the fender, and the thin line 5/32in separated from it. The thick line was 1/8in thick, the thin one 1/16in. If the fenders were black, the striping was always white, although some models with red striping have been seen. (The red striping may have been a good custom restripe commissioned by a previous owner since it is doubtful that the factory had either the time or the inclination to do such special order work.) It should be mentioned that the above dimensional data was taken from original, unrestored BMWs in my collection. As both fenders and tanks were hand striped at the BMW factory, some minor variations in both thickness and location of stripes is to be expected.

Gas tanks

Nothing sets off the BMW more than the unique shape of its tank and the two blue and white enamel emblems it carries. A properly fitted and correctly striped tank can make all the difference in the world when it comes to showing a bike. Unfortunately, a bewildering and wonderful variety of gas tanks is available, all of which can spell

The standard small tanks as used on the 1951–1954 twins. On this example the worn striping is probably original and correct. The small rubber knee pads snapped over lips on the sides of the tank, and the toolbox lived in the top. *Bill Sawyer*

disaster to the unwary.

First, BMW offered the prospective buyer a choice of several tank sizes, to which could be added several exotic variations in sizes as large as 46 liters, from the firms of Hoske, Heinrich, and Meier. There were tanks with chrome side panels for the police force, all chrome models, and tanks with toolboxes inset in the tops or sides. Also available was a variety of lids: hinged at the rear or on the side, with and without keyed locks, and painted, chromed, or ones padded with rubber. To know which is right for your models requires extensive research

First, lets eliminate the problem of mismatching the standard tanks, as originally fitted by the factory. The 1950–1954 twins all appeared to have identical tanks, which to the casual viewer looked identical to the tanks that first appeared on the R5 in 1936. The shape is of the classic teardrop, with small, tapered, rubber knee pads clipped to the sides over a welded-on lipped mounting plate.

All standard tanks for the R51/2 through the R68 carried 17 liters (approximately 4.5gal U.S.), and with a few minor exceptions, appeared to be identical. The reserve capacity of 2 liters could vary from tank to tank, as it was dependent upon the length of the reserve pipe attached to the fuel tap.

The R51/2 tank had its top-mounted toolbox (actually, all top toolboxes were inset into the tanks) fitted with a sideways opening lid. All the others had the lid hinged at the rear. It should be noted that some of the early 1951 R51/3 models and the R67 had sideways opening lids as well.

All had two lines of striping, like the fenders in size and shape, following the contours of the tank. Please note that while the fenders had the thick stripe closest to the edge, the tanks always had the thick stripe as the inner stripe of the two. No lids were ever chromed when they left the factory. All lids had the square cut, four-sided key, the same key as used by the R26 and R27 and on the larger 6.5gal sport tanks, through 1969. All were fitted with a slightly convex-top aluminum cap made by BLAU, which had no center vent hole but was edge vented. Locking caps were available and are discussed in Chapter 18.

All standard tanks had a single fuel tap on the left side and balance tube fuel line fittings underneath joining both sides.

A similar tank as seen on the 1951–1954 models, with appropriate striping. However, although the lines follow the contours at the top, rear, and bottom, on the lower front surface they seem to cut in a bit too sharply, encroaching the emblem. Compare these lines with some of the factory photos seen in earlier chapters. The gas cap is the correct item for the period. *Bill Sawyer*

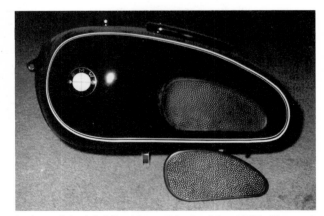

A nice original 6-1/2gal "sport" tank of the 1955–69 era. A reproduction kneepad is shown below the mounted original.

Standard tanks for the 1955–1969 Earles and US-fork models were of a more rounded and (to some) less pleasing shape than those used on the 1950–1954 models. From 1955 on, all the tanks carried 17 liters and had a locking toolbox hidden behind the left rubber knee pad. The key for the toolbox lock was identical to the one used for the fork lock. A word to the wise is needed at this time: If you come across a BMW with no key for the tool box, or if you lose your own key *do not* drill out the lock. Simply pry off the rubber knee pad to expose the metal lip. You will see that the lock is held with three flush aluminum rivets. Drill out the rivets and the lock will fall into the tool box, which can then be opened. Taking the lock to a locksmith, along with a few dollars will get you a new key made, and save you the expense of a new lock (which will now no longer match the fork lock) and which will leave you with little change from a $50 bill.

Striping was again the same configuration as on the 1950–1954 tanks, but now followed the more rounded contours of the 1955–1969 tank. Gas caps were the same as for 1950–1954, and, again, only a single tap and balance tube fittings were standard.

The factory offered an optional 6.5gal tank for the 1955–1969 models, referred to it in sales literature as the sport tank. It is instantly recognized by having a toolbox lid on the top; hinged at the rear; and flat, nubby finish knee pads, which again are clipped over a welded on lipped plate. Current versions of these tanks are still being manufactured but without the knee pad lip. The pads must now be glued on. Striping again is two lines and follows the contours of the tanks.

Just before the 1954 twins ceased being produced, a large tank similar to the 1955–1969 series sport tank became available. This was called the Meier tank, after Schorsch Meier, the former BMW racer and 1939 Tourist Trophy winner. Meier had established a BMW dealership in Munich and marketed a number of BMW accessories. Among the accessories were a large tank and a narrow bench seat that replaced the swing rubber saddle found on the 1950–1954 twins and all the 1955 Earles-fork models. While the Meier tank looks almost

With the larger sports tank, the striping looked smaller than on the standard tanks, especially as on this R69S. It's really an optical illusion in this photograph because the tank and fender lines are both basically the same width. It should be remembered that all the striping was done by hand, and not necessarily by the same person at the same time, so some variations should be expected. *Richard Kahn, Butler & Smith, Inc.*

A nice 1954 R68, with an equally nice optional Meier tank. Unfortunately, the front fender belongs on a 1951–54 BMW other than the R68, and is striped in the 1950 R51/2 pattern.

Another R68, this time a 1952 model, with yet another Meier tank. In the background, an Earles-fork machine with a Meier look-alike, BMW's own sports tank of 1955–69. Although virtually identical in looks and shape, the tanks will not interchange. *Dave Harden*

identical to the later post-1955 tank, the two do not interchange and cannot be swapped. Meier tanks can be recognized by a smaller, more tapered knee pad shape. Usually they have a lipped, rather than flat, toolbox lid, which was often chrome plated. Both the Meier and the sport tanks had one fuel tap and balance tube fitting between the tank halves.

For the long distance tourer or for the BMW rider wanting something different, the firms of Hoske and Heinrich offered a wide variety of tanks from the merely large to the gargantuan, in both steel and aluminum. Capacities ranged from about 7.5gal to as much as twelve! Both manufacturers provided a choice of tanks with or without toolboxes. Heinrich tanks, when fitted with the toolbox, had the gas cap hidden under the locking polished aluminum lid. The tanks are easily differentiated by their shape. Hoske tanks were generally slab sided with rounded fronts, and looked like a keyhole when viewed from the top. Most had glued on knee pads, with the earlier ones being teardrop-shaped pads clipped over bolt-on brackets. Tanks had either one or two fuel taps, with the larger ones usually having two. Hoske used a special design coarse threaded Everbest fuel tap, which screwed into the tank, rather than over the more common fine threaded fitting.

Tanks made by Hoske for the pre-1955 plunger twins were stamped underneath with a series of numbers, such as "R.51" or "RST 51" indicating they fitted the R51-67-68 series. Later, tanks were stamped "R.50" or "RST 50" or not stamped at all. They are not interchangeable, due to the opening at the front that allows the tank to clear the steering head. Most tanks, whether made by Hoske or Heinrich, had a cutout on the lower right side to clear the sidecar mounts. Due to their rounded front shape, most Hoske tanks required specially curved tank emblems, which were different for each side. Striping was again of the two-line variety, and generally followed the contours of the tank. Custom striping was also frequently available.

Heinrich tanks are still being produced today; their shape gives the appearance of a humpbacked whale. They can be either in aluminum or steel, and some were fitted with BMW car emblems

The larger the tank, the larger the cutout had to be to clear the front sidecar mount. This R69S carries one of the more radical examples of the Hoske tank.

rather than the more usual enamel ones held on with two screws. Most are so big that they practically touch the cylinders. Striping of Heinrich tanks was always radical, when compared to BMW or Hoske tanks, with large cutouts favoring the contours of the tank being the most common. Knee pads were an option and were glued on. The addition of either a Heinrich or Hoske tank to a machine can add nearly a $1,000 to the asking price. For sidecar use, a large tank is highly recommended, due to the increased fuel consumption you'll experience once you start hauling even a lightweight Steib.

Hoske also made a number of tanks for racing BMWs. Since the motorcycle frames were generally similar, at least on the pre-1955 twins, some of these tanks occasionally turn up on road machines. A steel racing version of a pre-1955 Hoske tank has small indentations at the rear for your knees, a top mounted toolbox (which was often filled in with a leather-covered chest pad), and a single fuel cap. Rubber knee pads were omitted.

Repairs and Restorations

Any repairs to either fenders or tanks should be done by panel beating, welding, and brazing. Use of putty or plastic is to be avoided, as it will eventually shrink, damaging the paint above it. Knowledgeable judges can easily spot plastic re-

The most interesting aspect of a Hoske tank is undoubtedly the rider's view, as seen here on a 1952 R67/2. This angle gives you a good idea where the striping line should go on most Hoske tanks. *Michael Gross Photo*

Another large Hoske, this time on a customized 1954 R67/3. Not all the Hoske tanks had a top-mounted toolbox, and those that did could have the lid in either chrome or paint finish. This tank has been fitted with BMW car emblems. *Jurgen Amtmann*

pairs without resorting to a magnet. Some success has been found with a product called AlumaLead, an epoxy filler containing metal powder, but this type of repair is best left to others. Filling in irregularities with such compounds prior to painting may be successful, but large dents should first be pounded or pulled out. Tank dents can be pulled out by the use of a screw and slide hammer. The holes drilled for the puller's attaching screws are later filled in by brazing. Some tanks, especially aluminum ones, can have their dents removed by filling the tank with water and using air pressure to pop out the dents. A competent radiator repair shop or facility catering to race cars should be able to fix most any tank. Tank repairs are best left to the experts since an amateur repair can have disastrous consequences should the repair fail and fuel spill onto a hot exhaust.

Tanks and fenders are best stripped by chemical dipping or by the exotic method of blasting them with carbon dioxide crystals. Use of abrasive grit will wear away the metal or harden it. BMW paint is persistent. Tell your chemical stripper to keep it in the tank longer, and make sure it's boiled or steam cleaned afterward to remove all the chemical residue. If you don't take these precautions, you will not get a good bond when paint is applied.

Chapter 9

The Engine

From 1923 through 1969, BMW motorcycles for sale to the general public were fitted with one of three basic engines consisting of a single-cylinder unit (displacements from 200 to 400cc) and two types of twins (a side-valve and overhead valve in displacements of 500, 600, or 750cc). There were also overhead cam racing engines, available in 500 and 600cc normally aspirated or supercharged form, but these differ so much from the production twins that they are best left as the subject of a separate book. Similarly, the singles, of which thirteen distinctly different models were produced during the years 1925–1967, are deserving of a book of their own.

Of the varying types of twin-cylinder engines that are left, their production can best be categorized as falling into three distinct eras. The first is the Early Split-Case Era, which covered all twins

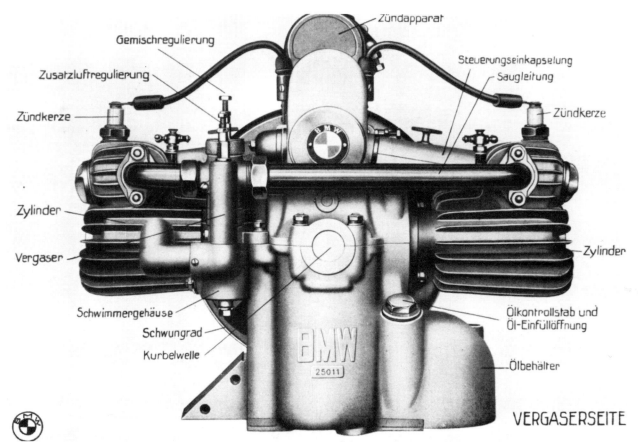

The original BMW M2B15 engine as fitted to the Victoria and other German machines. It was usually mounted fore and aft in the frame with either belt or chain drive being taken off the external flywheel. *Oscar Fricke*

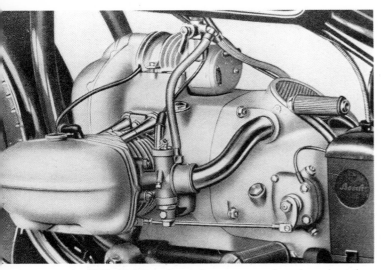

In 1936, BMW embraced a new one-piece tunnel casting. This is the 500cc R5 engine, which was in use virtually unchanged through the 1950 R51/2. *BMW Archives*

from the 8.5hp 500cc R32 of 1923 through the 33hp 750cc R17 of 1935–1937. The engine blocks were split lengthwise at the centerline and removal of crankshaft, rods, and cams was a simple matter. Most repairs could be accomplished without removal of the lower half of the engine block from the frame.

The second era brought us the First Series Tunnel Blocks, where the entire engine block was cast as one piece and the pressed-together crank, with rods attached, was inserted and removed through the front of the engine. The cases were no longer split, which made for a much tighter engine, soon to become a hallmark of all subsequent BMWs. The second era ran from the 500cc R5 of 1935 through the 750cc military R75 (production of which ceased in 1945), and should also encompass the 1950 R51/2.

The third and final era, which is the subject of this book, consists of the Improved Tunnel Blocks, which were used in basically the same configuration from the 1951 R67 and R51/3 through the last R69US of 1969. Again, since this book tries to deal with all the postwar BMWs available to the restorer, through the end of the Earles and US-fork era of 1969, we will also cover to some degree the prewar holdover, the 1950 R51/2.

Basic Points in Common

All 1950–1969 BMW twin-cylinder engines shared a crankshaft that was pressed together after the one-piece connecting rods were attached. All big end connecting rod bearings were of the caged roller type. All pistons were aluminum with iron rings. The cylinder heads were also of aluminum, with a hemispherical combustion chamber and inclined valves. Valve actuation on all the twins of

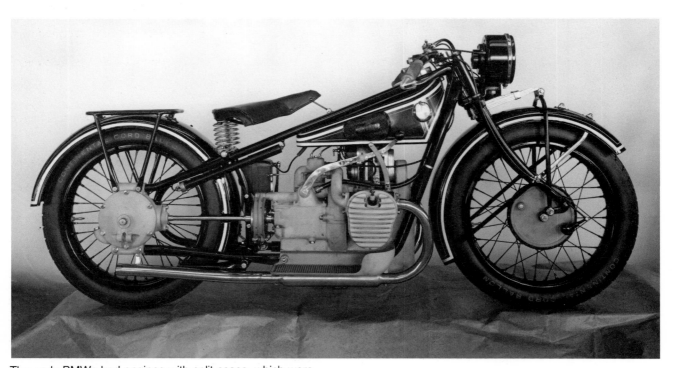

The early BMWs had engines with split cases, which were nevertheless quite oiltight. Note the split visible just aft of the cylinder head on this 1928 R52. *BMW Archives*

this era was by pushrods, which ran above the cylinder barrels in chrome plated tubes pressed into the cylinder barrel. All cylinders were iron, without separate sleeves.

All oil pumps were of the geared type, and lubrication was a rudimentary combination of pressure feed and splash, utilizing oil galleries in the block and slinger rings attached to the crankshaft. Oil capacity was measured with a screw-in dipstick, and a maximum of 2 liters (a shade over 2qt) was held in a pressed steel oil pan held on by a series of bolts. There was no provision for either an oil cooler or an oil filter.

At the front of the engine on the 1951–1969 BMW twins were the electrical components, with the magneto keyed to the camshaft taper and the generator armature keyed to the crankshaft. Again, the 1950 R51/2, being a prewar design, varied from this layout by having not one but two camshafts, driven not by a set of helical cut aluminum gears but by chains and sprockets. On the R51/2 the generator was mounted externally, on top of the engine, and ignition was by coil and distributor rather than magneto.

All engines from 1950 to 1969 had a massive steel flywheel attached to the back of the crankshaft, which was connected to the transmission cases via a single plate clutch. The dry clutch facing was asbestos. All engines were fitted with one carburetor per cylinder, each of which drew filtered air from a common air filter attached to the transmission case via a chrome air tube on each side.

Serial numbers were stamped onto the engine cases in a raised area over the right-hand cylinder, and the numbers were boxed in with a small BMW roundel at each end to prevent alteration. All engine numbers matched the frame numbers, a practice that had started with the R75 military twin of 1941–1945. The same number is repeated on the aluminum ID plate screwed into the steering head behind the headlight, and on the head lug of the frame on the Earles and US-fork models, and either on the head lug or on the top of the left rear plunger bracket on the 1950–1954 telescopic fork models.

Engine Number Breakdown

Before we proceed, let us review the engine numbers. Since the BMW you are looking at may have been altered with the addition of large tanks, special brakes, and wheels or a variety of saddles over the years, inspection of the engine number is usually the first and best clue as to the year and model of your prospective purchase.

All BMW engine and frame numbers were of six digits until late in the production run of the 1961–1969 R60/2 and R69S and US series. At that time, BMW had run out of numbers and had to prefix a new 800 000 range with a "1." These seven digit numbers were used only in the last years of the decade, around 1968–1969. The serial numbers are *not* to be used as a rough indication of engine displacement, since both the 500 000 and 600 000 series were used on the 500cc machines, and the 600 000 series, along with the 1 800 000 series, were also used on the 600cc displacement engines.

Unfortunately, BMW never published production figures by month or year and related them to the engines numbers, but some clues exist and have been summarized here. Remember, all numbers, years, and dates are at best approximate, since they have been gleaned from dealer service bulletins, factory modification notices, and other sources. For sake of readability, and since this is how BMW chose to reference the numbers, I have inserted a space between the hundreds and thousands position, though in actual practice there was no such gap on the numbers stamped in the blocks or on the frame and ID plates.

Plunger Frame BMW Engine Numbers: 1950–1954

1950 R51/2 began with 516 001 and ended with 521 005.

1951 R51/3 began with 522 001 and ended with 526 209.

1952 R51/3 began with 526 210 and ended with 536 000.

1953–1954 R51/3 began with 536 001 and ended with 540 950.

1951 R67 began with 610 001 and ended with 611 449.

1952 R67/2 began with 612 001 and ended with 614 946.

1953–1954 R67/2 began with 614 947 and ended with 616 226.

1954 R67/3 began with 616 227 and ended with 617 700.

1952–1954 R68 began with 650 001 and ended with 651 453.

Earles and US-Fork Frame BMW Engine Numbers: 1955–1969

1955–1961 R50 began with 550 001 and ended with 563 515.

1961–1969 R50/2 and 1968–1969 R50US began with 630 001 and ended with 649037.

The 1961 R50S began with 564 001 and ended with 565 634.

The 1956–1961 R60 began with 618 001 and ended with 621 530.

The 1961–1969 R60/2 and 1968–1969 R60US began with 622 001 and ended with 629 999, as well as with 1 800 001 through 1 819 307.

The 1955–1960 R69 began with 652 001 and ended with 654 955.

The 1961–1969 R69S and 1968–1969 R69US began with 655 004 and ended with 666 320.

Another view of a nicely restored 1936 R5, which in overall looks could be mistaken for a 1954 BMW. *Marie Lacko*

Dead or Alive?

Assuming you have determined that the opposed twin-cylinder engine you're looking at is indeed from a BMW, and not a Marusho, Zündapp, or Harley-Davidson XA, and that it is more or less mounted in the correct BMW frame, what you do next is of critical importance. Too hasty a decision at this stage could mean irreparable damage to the engine, or at the very least a less than advantageous purchase on your part. Remember, this book is not designed to replace the BMW factory shop manual, which should be consulted before the engine is torn down or serviced. However, this book intends to show you how to troubleshoot a balky engine or investigate a BMW about to be purchased to a degree that a rational decision to buy or not to buy can be made.

First Impressions

Your first impression of the engine will probably be what determines your decision. If you are unfamiliar with the particular BMW you're about to buy, a little bit of education and some forensic activity, subject to the seller's concurrence, will make that momentous decision much easier. If the engine can be started, more than half the battle has been won. If the engine will not start or if the bike has

been languishing in some damp barn for years, there are still a number of things that can be done to determine the engine's condition.

Starting a Dead Engine

Duane Ausherman is a Vintage BMW Club member, former long-time BMW dealer in Fort Bidwell, California, and a collector of vintage BMW motorcycles. Ausherman once set down some words of advice on how to start even the most neglected of engines; I've combined some of his comments with my own experience in the paragraphs below.

First, determine whether there is any mechanical interference. If the engine is seized or the crankshaft broken and the rods bent, things should be left alone (see the section below on how to free a seized or stuck engine or how to remove a crankshaft without resorting to a cutting torch). If things seem to be moving inside in more or less the right direction, you can proceed. If the engine turns freely but still refuses to start, either through neglect or misadjustment, a number of things must be investigated.

Without fuel, compression, and ignition, no internal combustion engine can ever be made to run. It also helps to have a little oil inside for cooling and lubrication, so your first check should be done by pulling out the dipstick, wiping it clean, and reinserting it. To get an accurate reading, put the BMW on its centerstand and read the oil level without screwing the dipstick in. If the engine is low on oil, add some.

If the oil is black, sticky, or contaminated with water, drain everything out and maybe even drop the pan. If the pan contains shiny metal objects larger than the average size of coffee grounds, look elsewhere, since what you're looking at in all likelihood are bits of bearings, rings, or pistons. If the oil is silvery, that's a sure sign of contamination with aluminum pieces of the engine or the remains of the bearing cages. If it's gray or rusty, it has been contaminated with water, which means that the bearings are probably at the least pitted with rust.

Rub the oil between your fingers and thumb; if it feels gritty, that's a sure sign of serious metallic contamination or of sand or dirt entering through an opening somewhere. Of course, if the BMW is priced so low that the cost of an engine rebuild and new bearings and maybe a new crankshaft has been taken into account, or if it's a particularly rare BMW, buy it without trying to start the damaged motor.

If the condition of the oil tells you everything is all right so far, proceed to the next step. Test the compression of the engine with either a compression gauge or by putting your thumb over the spark plug hole. If your thumb can't hold the pressure when the engine is kicked over, you have enough compression. A gauge should read at least 30 to 50psi, but you may need to warm up the engine and oil a bit to get it going. A better reading is 50 to 80psi; anything above 80 should make starting a snap. If you get no reading, it means broken rings, holed pistons, or burnt, stuck, or missing valves and probably a wasted trip on your part.

Next, check the fuel supply. Avoid using whatever gas is in the tank, unless the owner insists all is clean, the bike has been recently ridden, or everything is in good condition. Remember, we are talking about a neglected BMW here, not a pristine show winner. If the engine won't start after many kicks, check the fuel lines, carburetor floats, and jets. It may be best to avoid dealing with the carburetors at all. Try squirting fuel directly into the carb air intakes. Don't use an aerosol starting fluid such as Ether. The excessive power of such an explosion will probably damage the engine. Plain old gasoline in an old atomizer works best. Something like a hand pump bottle that once held window cleaner will give you a usable mist of fuel and air.

After squirting in the fuel, half choke the carb by covering a portion of the air intake with a gloved (not a bare) hand. The glove will not stick to the carb like bare skin; it will also protect you in case of a backfire. Better to have the glove get sucked in than your fingers. If the engine has no carburetors at all, squirt the fuel directly into the intake port in the head.

If fuel and compression are accounted for, you'll still need some way to ignite this mixture of air and gasoline inside the engine without blowing everything up or burning down the seller's garage. After you've made certain you're not about to fiddle with the spark plugs or magneto coil in a damp garage filled with gasoline fumes, test for a spark by pulling off a plug wire and holding it about 1/8in from a ground, such as the cylinder barrel or frame. If you insert an old spoke or nail into the plastic plug cap, it'll make seeing a spark much easier. If there's no plug cap, stick a pin into the end of the plug wire. If you want to avoid a jolt or tingle, protect yourself by holding the plug in the jaws of an insulated pair of pliers, instead of with your bare fingers.

As the engine is turned by kicking it over, the points will open and a spark will jump to ground. Test for strength by slowly moving the wire away from ground, to about 3/8in. If the spark won't make it or if the color is red or yellow, you've got problems in the ignition area. If the spark jumps 1/2in or more and is blue or purple, all will go well. Naturally, if the BMW is a non-magneto ignition R51/2, you'll need a strong 6V battery. A 1951–1969 magneto-fired BMW will start perfectly well without a battery. Repeat the sparking test with the plug wire attached, but lay the spark plug against the head or cylinder. It's a good idea to use new plugs if you had the foresight to bring them. They should be Bosch W240T1 if you plan to use them in the machine, but for testing purposes, even plugs from a lawnmower will do.

If you have no spark at all, you will have to improvise an ignition system, something that is not as difficult as it sounds. If the engine has no points, any set of points that work off the cam lobe on the camshaft will do, including points from a car. If the magneto is missing, set up a simple battery/coil system with any old battery, including 6V or 12V automobile types or a large, square lantern batteries. The coil should be the same as the battery, but if in doubt use a 12V battery. If the magneto is known to be defective, disconnect all wires to the points except the one from the original condenser. Use your own wire and alligator clips to make all connections. Negative goes from coil to condenser. Positive goes from the battery to positive on the coil.

Hook up the plug to the high voltage line and turn the engine by hand (or by foot) until the points open. The plug, laid next to ground, should spark. If it won't, replace the original condenser with a temporary one such as an automobile type. Once the plug fires, reinstall it, squirt some fuel into the air intake as discussed earlier, and partially choke the carb or intake with your gloved hand. Once the engine starts, keep squirting in fuel and adjust the size of the air intake for even running. Don't worry if you're only running on one cylinder. A twin-cylinder BMW can run this way, especially if you ease the strain a bit by removing the spark plug from the other cylinder.

Freeing Up the Seized Engine

Naturally, if the engine will not turn over at all you need to ascertain and eliminate the mechanical interference. If the owner tells you the bike has been sitting for a while but that it was running when parked, your problems may be minor. At the very least, the rings have adhered to the cylinders. Don't try to free them without taking some precautions first. Just jumping up and down on the kickstarter without a little forethought will guarantee either broken rings or a damaged kickstarter pawl or damaged transmission. First, remove the plugs on both cylinder heads, and fill the combustion chamber with a penetrating solution, such as commercially available penetrating oil, diesel fuel, kerosene, or automatic transmission fluid. Your task will be made much easier if the valve covers are removed first, and the rocker arms and pushrods are detached from the heads. Leave the head bolted in place, and the valves and springs and collars and keepers attached.

If the valves do not reseat once the rocker arms are removed, gently tap the valve stems with a small brass hammer until they snap back against the valve seats. If you have the time to spare, let everything percolate for a week. If you do not have the time, try inserting a threaded air chuck fitting into the spark plug holes and using compressed air to force all the fluids past the stuck rings. If that still does not free the engine, more drastic measures must be considered.

The first thing to do now is to remove the heads. Undo the head bolts and, using the air chuck, pop off the heads with air pressure alone. If this will not loosen the heads, gently rap them with a hammer using a block of wood or a chunk of rubber mat to protect the aluminum head. Whatever you do, do not pry between the head and barrel joint with a screwdriver or chisel unless you plan to

Compare this 1950 R51/2 engine to that of the 1937 R5. Except for the valve covers, the engines are virtually identical.

The finned assembly on top is the Bosch generator. *Bill Kuhlman*

replace the heads. Also, do not insert something like a crowbar or breaker bar into the exhaust port in an attempt to pop off the heads. Things can be hastened along by gently heating the head and then the barrels alternately with a small propane torch or heat lamp. The expansion and contraction will eventually free the heads. Remove all fuel sources and containers, such as the gas tank, before resorting to this measure and try to do it outside.

Once the heads are free, you can see what is really inside those cylinders. In most cases you'll discover a messy layer of carbon mixed with white oxide from the pistons. If the crankshaft stopped at any point other than top or bottom dead center, the next task will be much easier. If not, you'll have to rotate the crank using the kickstarter or by rocking the bike back and forth on its wheels while in gear. Whatever you do, don't try to rotate the crank by inserting a hex key into the generator armature fixing bolt, which is screwed into the crankshaft taper at the front of the engine. You'll only end up with a sheared off bolt, which will compound your restoration effort and increase your overall expenses. Also, don't even think about using a ViseGrips or a Stillson wrench on the end of the crankshaft taper, unless you plan to start over with a brand new crankshaft after you've thrown away the one you have just ruined.

With the heads now removed, gently tap on the tops of the pistons. If you haven't obliterated the markings on top of the piston, you'll know what size pistons were originally in the engine. Try to write down all the marks before you start beating on the top. Having soaked everything beforehand in a penetrating solution will make the eventual freeing of the pistons much easier. Again, use heat gently to free things up. Doing all this outside will keep the fumes and smoke in your house down to manageable levels. Keep tapping, gradually increasing the severity until the rings break free. Don't worry if you damage the rings or even dent, crack or hole the pistons. In all eventuality, you'll probably want to replace them anyway. They're cheap compared to replacing the crank.

Eventually, the pistons will start to move. You'll now see the rusty, blackened inner side of the cylinder barrel. Keep squirting in oil and turning the engine with the kickstarter. If you have enough strength, spin the engine with the transmission in gear by rotating the back wheel until you can see some sort of clean surface on the inside of the cylinders. If the place where the rings were stuck isn't too deeply pitted, you may be able to get by with just rehoning the cylinders and installing new pistons and rings in the same size as those removed. When reinstalling the pistons, use the same size and type, which have the same number of rings as those removed.

Removing the Cylinders

With the heads off and the pistons free, the cylinders can simply be unbolted and slid off the pistons. As you are removing the cylinders, jam some rags or small pieces of wood between the connecting rod and the engine block to prevent damage to the latter. Mark the cylinders on the outside so you'll know which side they came from. Save all the old gaskets in case you need to take them to a BMW dealer or flea market to find replacements. Happily, most gaskets for the 1951–1969 twins are still available, but you may have some difficulty with some of the gaskets for the R51/2 engine.

Engine Removal

The crankshaft can be removed with the engine still in the frame, but since you're embarking on a complete teardown, let's get the engine out of the frame and do all the work up on your workbench. If nothing else, your back will feel much better after you are done.

Unbolt the transmission case from the engine and remove it (see Chapter 10). After that, remove the front electrical cover, which is secured by one bolt on the R51/2 and two bolts on all others. (On the earlier machines after the R51/2, the hex bolts were replaced with much nicer looking slot-headed ones.) Carefully disconnect the wires leading to the generator assembly. Undo all fixing bolts on the generator, remove the brushes, and pull off the generator armature with the appropriate puller. Remove the generator body. Disconnect the rest of the wiring harness where it passes through the top of the block.

Disconnect the top engine support bracket, as fitted to all but the R51/2 engines. Support the engine under the oil pan with a box or block of wood. Undo the four nuts from the two long engine bolts, and tap out the bolts starting with the rearmost one. After the front bolt is removed, slip the spacers that fit between the left side of the block and the frame onto the bolts and put the bolts aside. Don't forget that when reinstalling the engine the spacers go back in on the left side, otherwise you will never get the engine to mate up with the transmission.

Although the engine can be removed with head and cylinders still attached, it's much easier if all this excess weight has already been taken off. If you have someone to help you, pulling the engine is easy; if you do it alone, taking off all the dead weight beforehand will help out immeasurably.

Start by moving the engine to the rear, then dropping the nose down. Raise the engine out of the frame with the clutch facing the bottom of the gas tank. Take care that the exposed magneto coil or the advance unit doesn't bang against the lower part of the frame. Reinstalling the engine is done in reverse order, but may be easier with the help of

An unusual cutaway view of an R51/2 motor on display at the Zweirad Museum in Neckarsulm, Germany. Note the twin chain driven camshafts and ignition coil hidden under the front cover. *Paul Lewis Photo*

another person. Leaving the cylinders attached provides a better handhold.

Removing the Crankshaft

While all the procedures for removing and later reinstalling the crank are spelled out in great detail in the official BMW shop manual, some points must be mentioned. First, the crankshaft can be removed while the engine is still in the frame, although it makes more sense to do it with the engine on a bench. It is not necessary, nor in fact possible, to remove the connecting rods in order to remove the crankshaft. Unfortunately, not too many know this, other than BMW mechanics or owners who have done a bit of reading.

I once purchased a totally disassembled but complete R50/2 (which was probably running when parked) that had suffered unimaginable indignities by some ham-fisted and ill-informed prior owner or amateur mechanic. The crankshaft turned out to be in excellent condition, but had unfortunately been removed by rather unorthodox means. Whoever did

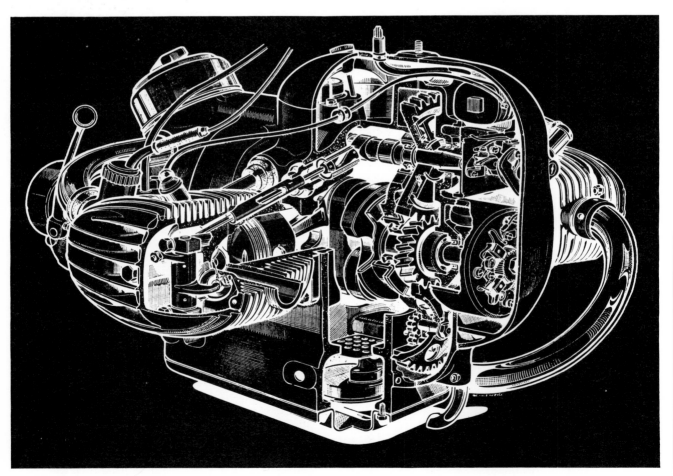

After the R51/2, BMW treated us to an engine design that was to remain virtually unchanged until 1969. This cutaway by the German artist Schlenzig is of the R51/3, which fol-lowed the R51/2 in 1951. The twin camshafts have been replaced by a single gear driven one, and the magneto and generator now live under the front cover. *BMW Archives*

The final development of the classic BMW engine was this R69S unit of the 1961–1969 era. It's easily recognized by its long, two-fin valve covers and finned exhaust clamps. The bulge in the front timing cover accommodates the crank-shaft vibration damper. In this example, the plug wires and plugs are covered with a radio interference suppresser, necessary for police use. *Wagner International Photos*

the job had obviously never opened a shop manual or asked advice from a mechanic or dealer. Rather than follow the simple procedures outlined below, he had just cut off the rods with a hacksaw a couple of inches below the wrist pin. Then, by just unbolting the timing chest, he had withdrawn the abused assembly by pulling it straight out the front. Naturally, everything was ruined, and a good crank now needed a total rebuild, as well as two brand-new rods.

The correct procedure requires the removal of the timing chest, the timing gears, and the front bearing carrier, all of which is spelled out in the factory shop manual. For the R51/2, you'll have to remove the camshaft sprockets and timing chain. Remove the oil slingers, the pistons, disconnect the flywheel from the crankshaft after removing the clutch, then push both connecting rods towards the

engine, rotating the crank as you do so. Once the rods are fully retracted, grab the front taper and tilt the front end of the crank downward toward the oil pan. With the crank standing on end, the whole thing can be pulled out the front. It's all very simple if you look at the pictures in the shop manuals.

What Next?

Again, as we said before, this book was not designed to replace the various reprints or originals of the factory shop manuals. However, there are a few things not mentioned in the manuals that might be of use, and which will make your restoration easier, save you money, and prolong the life of your BMW engine.

The Oil Pan

A simple repair, renovation, or retrofit concerns the oil pan, one of the most abused items on your BMW. There's no need to remove the engine to work on the oil pan. In fact, it's much easier to do everything related to it with the engine still in the frame and the BMW up on its centerstand. First, if you still have the original pressed steel pan, it's probably rusted, dented, and warped from over-tightening, unless you were fortunate enough to have found a well-cared for BMW or have taken the pains to properly care for your own. In most cases, the pan bolts will have been overtightened so many times that the entire edge of the pan is warped. At one time, new pans were cheap, but now there are few new ones available, and even used ones are likely in poor shape.

If the pan is warped, remove it and carefully lay it on a flat surface, such as the top of an anvil. With a small piece of steel rod, gently flatten out all the warped spots, which will be near each of the small bolt holes. Remember, metal once distorted is stretched and will never resume its original shape, so if things are not going well, toss the pan and install a better one. If, however, the pan can be saved and you want to avoid such overtightening damage in the future, replace all the lock washers over the twelve mounting holes with a small aluminum or steel strip, about 30mm long and 5mm thick. Now you can tighten the bolts to your heart's content, within the proper torque limits, of course, and never again worry about warping the pan. A much better solution is to replace the whole thing with one of several available finned aluminum pans. For a description of the pans, see Chapter 18.

Supporting Your Work

When working on an engine that's out of the frame, secure it to the workbench by bolting it to two pieces of angle iron that have in turn been secured to the top of the workbench with large clamps. Do not clamp the engine block in the jaws of a vise. Not only will you mar the casting, but also blocks have a disconcerting tendency to fall out of a vise with disastrous results. Better yet, purchase or borrow an engine stand or make your own using factory drawings as described in Chapter 4. A good engine cradle can also be made using an old BMW frame, which can usually be had for little money at flea markets. You can even use frames from post-1970 /5 and newer BMW twins. Cut off the lower frame tubes, preserving the engine mounting bolt areas. Have someone weld these frame sections to a piece of boiler plate, and you've got yourself a nice engine stand. If you have an old bare engine block, bolt the frame pieces to it first, making sure to include the spacers. That way all will be in alignment when the welding gets done.

The Piston Problem

BMW used a variety of pistons in their 1950–1969 twin-cylinder engines. Installing the wrong piston in the wrong engine will result in expensive noises and a distinct sucking sound as more money exits your wallet. More damage has been done by otherwise thoughtful owners and mechanics by installing pistons that looked right without first verifying that they were indeed of the correct configuration for your particular engine.

Pistons are identified only by inspection of the diameter stamped on the crown, the location and number of rings, and measurement of deck height. There are no BMW part numbers stamped on the pistons to tell you which model and which years they fit. It's good insurance to save your old pistons in clearly marked plastic bags so at least you'll have something to which you can compare your new ones. Even BMW dealers can make a mistake and send you the wrong ones. If you buy pistons directly from an overseas source, you will run the risk of not getting what you need or specified.

Most shop manuals describe the pistons you have to use in great detail, but for the novice, the following is a thumbnail description of what fits what.
• The 1950 R51/2 had a nominal 68mm bore diameter and four-ring pistons, with three compression and one oil ring above the wrist pin.
• The 1951–1954 R51/3 had a nominal 68mm bore diameter and used slightly domed five-ring pistons, with three compression rings and one oil ring above the wrist pin, and one oil scraper ring below the wrist pin near the skirt. Piston failures usually concerned the skirt, a weak point on these earlier machines.
• The 1951–1954 R67, R67/2, R67/3, and R68 had the same style pistons as the R51/3, but with a nominal bore diameter of 72mm.
• The 1955–1961 R50 and R60 had four-ring pistons similar to the ones used during 1951–1954. They will not interchange with the post-1961 models. Nominal diameter for the R50 was 68mm, and for the R60 it was 72mm.
• The 1955–1961 R69 had the same pistons as the earlier R68, with a nominal diameter of 72mm.
• The 1961 R50S had three-ring pistons, with two compression and one oil ring located above the wrist pin. Its nominal diameter was 68mm.
• The 1961–1969 R50/2, R60/2, and R69S had three-ring pistons, with all three rings above the wrist pin. Nominal diameter was 68mm, 72mm, and 72mm respectively.

Whenever pistons are installed, if they have an arrow stamped on top, the piston must be installed with the arrow facing forward in the direction of the motorcycle's travel.

Cylinder Head Notes

In April 1967, a valve clearance problem was caused by a change in the aluminum alloy mixture, which allowed migration of the bolt sleeves in the heads, reducing valve clearance. BMW remedied the problem on the R50/2 after engine number 644 184 and on the R60/2 after engine number 1 812 245 by installing bolt sleeves in the heads that had a larger bearing surface and by age-hardening the cylinder head castings. The problem was not apparent with the R69S, but the age hardening was also employed on this model.

As mentioned in Chapter 5, BMW encountered difficulties with poorly cast heads because of problems at the foundry under contract to BMW. The results were uneven expansion and contraction of the heads that resulted in the loosening and blowing out of the steel spark plug inserts. After September 1968, all engines were fitted with long-reach heads, which had no steel plug insert and were stamped with the letters "LK" on the outside for *Lange Kerze*. These improved heads can be used on all models back to the R51/3 of 1951. The original spark plugs marked W240T1 must be replaced with W240T2 long-reach plugs. Check your heads before installing any plugs. As a point of note, the original short reach plugs for the R50S and R69S were the Bosch W260T1 types.

Piston Notes

All BMW pistons were marked with colored dots which indicated their weight range and were useful in balancing a pair of replacement pistons. After June 1967, R50/2 pistons weighing between 342g and 347g were marked with a gray dot, those weighing between 346g and 351g were marked with a brown dot, and those weighing between 350 and 355g were marked with a green dot.

Valve Timing Errors

In April 1967, the BMW factory discovered an error in the valve timing notes in some of the owner's and workshop manuals. Valve timing for the R50, R60, and R69S noted on page seven of the owner's manual, as well for the R50S and R69S as indicated on page eleven of the workshop manual should be corrected to read: "Intake Opens 4 deg. before T.D.C, and closes 44 deg. after B.D.C. The exhaust should open at 44 deg. before B.D.C. and close at 4 deg. after T.D.C."

Rotating Valve Notes

Rotating valves were installed by the factory in all R50/2 engines after October 1966, commencing with engine number 641 473. On the R60/2, these valves were used beginning with engine numbers 629 956 through 630 000, and from 1 810 001 on. On the R69S, the new valves were used from engine number 661 545 on.

The R68 had 8mm valve stems for both intake and exhaust, while the other pre-1955 models had 7mm stems. The R50, R50/2, R60, and R60/2 also had 7mm valve stems, but the R50S had 7mm intake stems and 8mm stems on the exhaust valves. The R69 and R69S had 8mm stems on both valves. Needle bearing's were installed in the rocker arms on the R68 starting with engine number 650 304 and their use was continued on all the sports models thereafter.

Valve head diameters were as follows: Intake heads were 34mm on all the 1950–1954 models except the R68, which had 38mm diameter heads. Exhaust valves on all 1950–1954 models had 32mm diameter heads, while the R68 had 34mm diameter heads. Intake valves on the R50, R50/2, R60, R60/2, and R50S had 34mm diameter heads, and 32mm diameter exhaust valve heads. The R69 and R69S had 38mm intake valves and 34mm exhaust valves.

Pushrod and Base Gasket Notes

In July 1965, the BMW factory lengthened replacement pushrods for all R50, R50/2, R50S, and R51/3 models from 242mm to 243.5mm. The change was made to accommodate use of an optional thicker cylinder base gasket which decreased engine compression and allowed for the use of low-octane fuel.

Lubricating Oil Recommendations

Although the BMW factory changed its mind on oils numerous times, this was due to changes in seals and manufacturing tolerances and not due to mistakes or choosing oils by trial-and-error. True, often certain brands were favored over others at certain times, but by and large, BMW's latest recommendations are the one to follow. Following is a condensed version of the dozens of engine oil related service bulletins the BMW factory issued during 1951–1969:

- All R51/2, R51/3, R67, R67/2, R67/3, and R68: SAE 40 (summer), SAE 20 (winter).
- All R50, R50/2, R60, R60/2, and R69: SAE 30 (summer), SAE 10W30 (winter).
- All R50S and R69S: SAE 30 (summer), SAE 10W30 (winter).
- All R50US, R60US, and R69US: SAE 30 (summer), SAE 10W30 (winter).

For hard or fast riding, the 1969 edition of the owner's manual for the US-fork series recommended a single grade SAE 40 oil, which is probably a good idea for general all-around use if you can still find it today.

Naturally, during the earlier years, high detergent oils or synthetic mixtures were unheard of, but use of today's multi-viscosity oils will not harm your engine. Care should be taken that oil slingers have been cleaned of all sediment, and that the oil pan has been thoroughly cleaned prior to introducing high detergent oils for the first time. Failure to remove all the sediment, grit, and small metal flakes that have accumulated over the years will mean that they will suddenly all be freed to circulate and wreak havoc in your engine. If your engine has just undergone a teardown and a rebuild, none of these warnings will apply. If in doubt, stick with a straight-weight non-detergent oil if you can find one.

I have used the readily available Castrol 20W50 in most of my older BMWs (other than the prewar ones) with no trouble for nearly two decades. The prewar machines seem to prefer straight 40 for some reason; they sound loose and noisy with anything else. As I've had no experience with synthetics, I can't recommend or caution against them, but the best advice would be to stick with a good brand of quality oil and change it often, as well as cleaning out any sediment that's accumulated in the oil pan and slingers.

Bearing and Seals

Aftermarket and BMW bearings for both the 1951–1954 engines and for those fitted to the 1955–1969 Earles and US-fork models are still readily available. Some typical engine bearing and seals for the R51/3 and R67/2 are New Departure number ND 77507 for the main bearing and ND 77503 for the camshaft bearing. Chicago Rawhide also provides a rear engine main bearing seal for the R51/3 stocked under their number CR 20440. More choices can be found in the appendix.

A Rear Main Seal Fix

When rear main seals start to leak, oil will collect in the depression above the oil pan extension on the engine block underneath the transmission. It's a tedious process to replace the seal, but it's all spelled out in the various shop manuals so there is no need to repeat it here. What is not spelled out is that unless you have a perfect flywheel surface, you'll soon have to repeat the process. If there is even a slight groove on the surface that contacts the seal, leaks will continue. The problem can be solved with a new flywheel (an expensive proposition these days) or by using Chicago Rawhide's SpeediSleeve. This little item is a thin, hardened metal sleeve with a lip on one side. It comes with its own driver, and all that's usually required to install it is a heavy hammer and a good swing.

First, remove the flywheel and clean the surface that will contact the sleeve with carburetor cleaner. Lightly sand with 600-grit sandpaper. The next steps are a bit trickier. Since the surface of the flywheel that you'll be mating to is slightly under 52mm in diameter, you'll have to use red LocTite Stud and Bearing Mount mastic to retain the sleeve to the flywheel. Let the LocTite dry

Compare this front view of the R69S engine with the front of the 1950 R51/2. Although everything was much cleaner looking and much larger to the casual observer, a 1969 R69S engine could be dropped into a 1950 R51/2 frame without any interference or modification. The small triangular cover at the front housing allows for access to the oil pump gears and easy attachment of a VDO tachometer gearbox. *Wagner International Photos*

overnight before proceeding. This is an anaerobic compound used to retain bearings on worn shafts and is available from most bearing supply houses along with the SpeediSleeve.

Since all BMW twins from 1951 through 1969 used the same 52mm by 72mm by 10mm seal, Chicago Rawhide's number CR 99205 will fix them all. If you need a new rear main seal, the Chicago Rawhide number for the nitrile seal is CR 20440. A slightly more expensive but superior version, made of Viton, carries CR 20424.

Once you have installed the sleeve, cut off the excess length with a hacksaw, then use a good file to dress the raw edges. In all steps, exercise extreme care and patience or you'll have to start over with all brand-new stuff. If you would be more comfortable, take it to a local machine shop and have them turn off the excess. This would be a simple procedure for a machinist and should cost little more.

The same method of repair, using various types of SpeediSleeves, can be used on transmission output flanges or on the rear drive ring gear seal.

The Self-Destructing R69S

In July 1962, BMW learned of a number of complaints regarding the R69S. The complaints concerned such catastrophes as cylinders breaking off at the base, wrist pins floating loose and scoring the cylinder walls, and pins on the breather plates loosening. To prevent any future occurrences, dealers were asked to install new pistons having a shorter piston pin, which became standard equipment on the R69S starting with frame number 656 812. At the same time, reinforced cylinders, which had also become standard on the R69S, were to be used, in this case commencing with frame number 656 529. The defective breather plate was replaced with one having 6mm pins instead of the former 5mm ones. This modification commenced on the R69S with frame number 656 270.

The Vibration Damper Problem

All R69Ss and the R50Ss were fitted with a large metal disk at the front of the crankshaft taper, between the front engine cover and the generator armature. It was a disk composed of several plates held together around a flexible rubber center. Its purpose was to help smooth out some of the vibrations that were inherent in the operating band of these two engines. As the less stressed R50 and R60 series never experienced such vibration problems, they were never fitted with the vibration damper.

Unfortunately, the rubber center core demanded constant attention. If it was neglected, it soon disintegrated with disastrous consequences. If the steel plates didn't smash their way out through the front cover, they wobbled around enough on their loose center that damage to the delicate (and expensive) generator and voltage regulator was a certainty. Many frustrated owners simply took off the damper, which didn't do the engine any good, or switched to low-compression base gaskets, thereby decreasing the engine's power and diminishing the vibrations. Others tried various home brew solutions, such as garden hose gaskets, and nonstandard rubber rings.

In April 1966, BMW, probably beset by complaints from owners and dealers, stated that the vibration damper could only do its work if it was checked and adjusted every 4,000 miles. Testing was to be done by removing the front cover and rotating the damper by hand. If it rotated on the crankshaft end with a degree of difficulty, then it was still serviceable. If, however, it wobbled or spun relatively freely, then the inner rubber center was to be replaced and everything retorqued to 15lb-ft.

Chapter 10

Transmission and Clutch

All 1950–1969 BMW transmissions were of the automotive type in design, bolted to the engine at the flywheel end and connected to the engine by a dry plate clutch. All BMW transmissions of that era were four speed, shifted with the left foot, and all had an integral air cleaner and fittings for insertion of the chrome air tubes. All had a flexible internal coupling connected to either the main shaft or the output shaft, which helped absorb the shock of shifting. The shift pattern for all transmissions was one down for first, up one for neutral, then up again for second, third, and fourth gears.

Minor Differences

Again, the 1950 R51/2 had a transmission case slightly different from the other pre-1955 machines. While the 1951–1954 transmissions had a top-mounted air cleaner canister, the 1950 R51/2 contained the air cleaner element inside the case, a holdover from the prewar R51.

The early pre-1955 transmissions had no provisions for a driveshaft coupling cover, which was finally fitted to all twins after April 1952, starting with the R67/2, R68, and R51/3 after frame number 526 209.

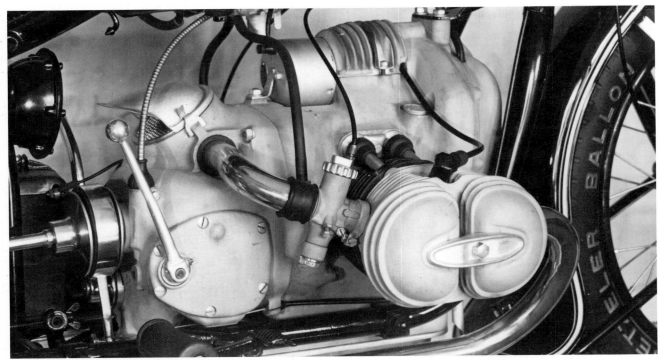

The transmission case on the 1950 R51/2 differed in several details from the 1951–1954 cases. Above the air tube socket were clips for the air cleaner scoop, the rubber output flange coupling had no shroud, and the cover on the right side (from which protruded the auxiliary hand-shift lever) had no socket for a neutral light wire. BMW experts will note that this R51/2 is the factory prototype, still fitted with a prewar fender and two-piece carburetors with separate floats. *BMW Archives*

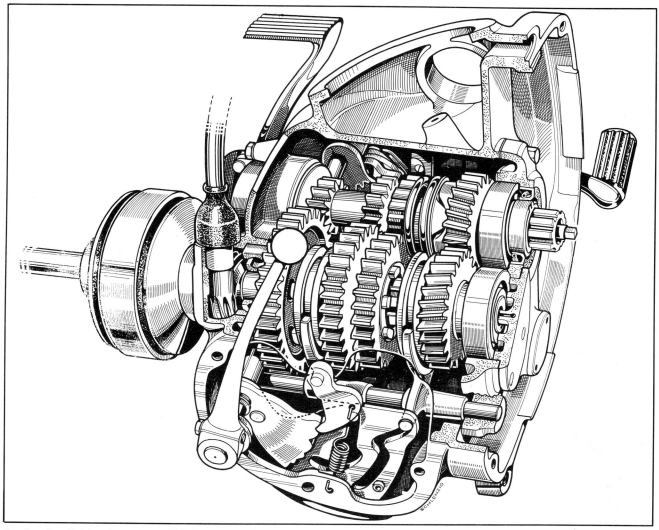

Another fine Schlenzig cutaway. This is the 1951 R67 transmission with a slightly redesigned case incorporating an air channel to the clutch housing. No half shroud was yet fitted over the driveshaft coupling. *BMW Archives*

Pre-1955 transmissions had an auxiliary hand-shift lever (attached to the right side), which was useful primarily as a neutral finder. After 1951, all transmissions had a neutral light switch incorporated in the mechanism and connected to a green indicator bulb in the headlight shell.

The 1950–1954 transmissions were coupled to the driveshaft with a hard rubber puck enclosed in either a painted or chrome plated ring. From 1955 to 1969, all transmissions were attached to the rear swingarm via a universal joint, hidden under a pleated rubber bellows.

1950–1954 Transmissions

All were four-speeds with no reverse; the gears shifted by means of internal dog clutches. The foot shifter was of the ratchet type, to which was connected an auxiliary hand shifting lever mounted vertically at the right side of the case. As the gears were shifted by the left foot, the lever moved in a short arc from the rearmost position, which indicated first gear, to the front (almost touching the right-hand air tube), when the mechanism was in fourth gear. Neutral was between first and second. The lever was intended primarily as an aid in the adjustment of the transmission while on the bench; the lever also allowed a rapid and easy finding of neutral, without having to use the left foot.

The transmission should be refilled every 6,000 miles with 800cc of SAE 40 oil. Hypoid gear oil was never used. The kickstarter was integral with the case, and its lever swiveled out and down from the left, at right angles to the frame. The kickstart lever was chrome plated steel and retracted by an internal spring. The speedometer cable was

This R67 clearly shows the spigot cast into the right-hand cover for the neutral light wire, as well as the early slotted-vent air cleaner. *Michael Gross*

driven off a gear set installed in the top of the transmission case. No provisions for a magnetic drain plug were incorporated.

Prior to April 1952, these transmission had no protective coupling flange shrouds bolted to the right side of the case. No instances have ever been documented of a rider's pants cuffs being sucked into the counterclockwise rotating coupling mechanism. Nevertheless, BMW began to fit protective shrouds as part of the rear transmission case to the R51/3, starting with frame number 526 210, and to all R67/2 and R68 models. However, since other owners apparently wanted to upgrade their machines (or possibly BMW foresaw some sort of a liability problem), a retrofit shroud was made available. It was listed as part number 250 4 31 690 09 and was designed to fit all examples of the R51/2, all of the R67, and all of the R51/3 until frame number 526 209. It bolted on using existing studs and bolts on these earlier cases, and should also fit pre-war transmission cases as well.

1955–1969 Earles and US-Fork Transmission

Like the 1950–1954 transmission, the Earles and US-fork model transmissions were of the four-speed, no reverse variety and also were shifted by foot. The previously used external hand-shift lever was eliminated. Internally and externally, the transmissions were totally different from their 1950–1954 predecessors, though they do bolt up perfectly to the engines in the earlier machines. The transmission was to be refilled every 16,000 miles with 800cc of either SAE 40 motor oil or Hypoid 90 oil, depending on year of manufacture. The kickstart lever was a polished aluminum casting

that swiveled out from the back of the case, in an arc to the left, across the centerline of the frame. The speedometer cable was driven by a gear set in the top of the transmission case. Transmissions were available in solo and sidecar ratios, and the cases were marked externally to indicated this. Drain plugs were at first non-magnetic; later they were magnetic.

1950–1954 Clutch

The 1950–1954 clutches were of the single dry plate design, actuated by a cable and levers. The clutch pressure plate utilized six coil springs to keep it engaged. It required no maintenance beyond adjustment to the cables and throwout levers. Periodic oiling of the small throwout bearings at the rear of the case was also required.

If the clutch fails, and if replacement parts are not available, it can be replaced with the clutch from an R69S, but in such cases the entire flywheel from the R69S must also be used.

1955–1969 Clutch

All clutches were of the single dry plate design. The mechanism was bolted to the flywheel and was actuated by means of a cable and release lever. It engaged via a single diaphragm type spring working on the pressure plate. No maintenance was required, other than periodic adjustment of the throwout lever and the cable ends, and

A 1953–1954 transmission with factory-installed coupling shroud and the latest air cleaner. The aluminum shroud was also available as an option for those wishing to upgrade their 1950–1951 machines. The shroud was bolted on externally, rather than cast as a part of the rear cover.

lubrication of the clutch rod bearings, which were easily accessed at the rear by removal of the throwout lever. Any noises associated with the clutch were usually attributed to dry throwout bearings.

Removal and Replacement

Removal of the transmission is straightforward on all models. Disconnect the cables, the battery ground wire, the neutral light wire (if fitted), the speedometer cable, and both air tubes to the carburetors. Remove the battery and straps. Remove the air cleaner canister. Disconnect the output flange connections to the driveshaft, either by removing the rubber puck on the 1950–1954 models, or by unbolting the four flange bolts on the 1955–1969 models. Loosen the kickstart bumper rubber and swing it away from the engine. Unbolt the case from the engine, pull it backwards slightly, tilt it to the left, and withdraw it sideways.

Lubrication

Oil is introduced on the left side by removing a hex headed plug located just under the left side air tube. Oil is drained by means of a drain plug at the bottom of the case. Fill oil to the bottom of the threads in the filler opening.

The Hypoid Oil Confusion

There is a common misconception that *all* BMWs used hypoid oil in the transmission and rear drive unit. In fact, all 1950–1954 transmissions used SAE 40 engine oil, summer and winter. From 1955 on, all the Earles-fork transmissions also used SAE 40 engine oil. In June 1967, however, the change was made to Hypoid 90 commencing with chassis number 646 358 on the R50/2, frame number 1 814 032 on the R60/2, and frame number 663 565 on the R69S. The use of Hypoid 90 in the swingarm tube was also instituted at that time with these numbers. Five new sealing rings were required in the transmission, which had the part number suffixes of 10 06 179, 10 06 135, 10 06 124, 30 38 513, and 10 20 109.

Additionally, the rubber boot between the transmission and swingarm had to be changed or risk being destroyed by the Hypoid oil. Accordingly, commencing with frame 646 486 on the R50/2, frame 1 814 032 on the R60/2, and frame 663 565 on the R69S, a new boot carrying part number suffix 30 38 225 had to be used. The earlier boot, part number suffix 30 38 224, could no longer be used when changing to Hypoid 90.

Drain Plugs and Other Problems

Oil leaks at the speedometer drive were eliminated in October 1965 by use of a redesigned helical gear. This commenced with frame number 640 039 on the R50/2, frame number 627 956 on the

1960 and earlier R50, R60, and R69 clutch plate.

R60/2, and frame number 660 144 on the R69S.

The original drain plugs were solid steel. Magnetic ones were fitted to the R50S and R69S and were optional on the others. It was discovered in April 1966 that overtightening the plug caused the sealing rings to deform, which in turn allowed the magnetic insert in the plug to contact the internal gear shifting mechanism. The solution was to drain the oil, pull the plug, grind 1mm off the magnetic insert, and reinstall everything.

In June 1964, BMW tried to remedy occasional clutch slippage complaints received from R60/2 and R69S owners by providing reinforced clutch springs. These were installed in the R69S commencing with frame number 658 624 and on the R60/2 at frame number 626 401. The spring, listed as part number 00 70 182, was differentiated from earlier ones by a red plus sign. At the same time, a reinforced clutch disk spring was available for the R50/2, starting with frame number 636 591, and in the discontinued R50S model. It carried part number 00 70 183 and was marked with a red minus sign.

Seals and Bearings

A number of aftermarket seals and bearings are now available for the earlier models, from sources listed in the appendix. You can find transmission seals for the R51/3 and R67/2 from Chicago Rawhide. For the kickshaft, order CR number 7910; for the hand shift, CR number 4715; for the foot shift CR number 5805. You can also retrofit CR number 14704 on the transmission output shaft, but in this case you must first turn down the seal surface of the output flange diameter by 1mm.

Transmission bearings for the R51/3 and R67/2 are now available from FAG as number 6205 (of which one is required) and as FAG number 6304, of which two are needed. Another bearing that will work is VKF number 20LN, of which one is required.

Making a Case for Silence

All 1950–1969 transmissions shift with a pronounced clunk, although the pre-1955 cases seem to prefer a rattle and clatter over the sharp clunk of the Earles and US-fork models. None of this is cause for alarm; it's an unfortunate part of the design. This is not to say that BMW intended the transmissions to be noisy shifters. The automotive design, the heavy flywheel, and relatively slow spinning engine all combine to make for noisy shifts. Don't attempt to muffle the clunk by using heavier oil. The best solution is to shift slowly and deliberately, and avoid harsh downshifts when slowing down the machine or when pulling up at a light.

Downshifting noises are probably why use of the 1950–1954 auxiliary hand-shift lever is so popular with owners of the 1950–1954 machines. It makes downshifting to neutral at a light a snap, and it can be done in almost absolute silence, with little wear and tear on the mechanism. It can also be used to impress spectators and young boys with your obvious skills at handling such an exotic machine. You can also tell the curious that it's really a reverse gear lever, or that you use it to engage overdrive when you approach 100mph.

"Disagreeable noises" (to use BMW's actual terminology) that developed from the kickstarter ratchet when the transmission oil was still cold and thick, were eliminated by changing the pitch of the kickstarter return spring to the left. This change went into effect November 1966 with frame number 643 865 on the R50/2, frame number 1 810 530 on the R60/2, and frame number 662 145 on the R69S.

Further noise reductions were attempted in June 1967 by reducing the end play of the transmission shafts to 0.00 + 0.1mm. This went into effect with frame number 643 990 on the R50/2, frame number 1 814 026 on the R60/2, and frame number 662 545 on the R69S. Make sure whatever shop manual you are using reflects this change.

Quicker and easier shifting was obtained in July 1968 by enlarging the radii of the cam plate and chamfering the faces of the shifting pegs on the spur gears of the output shaft. These modifications were introduced with frame number 646 686 on the R50/2, frame number 1 816 037 on the R60/2, and frame number 664 451 on the R69S. Happily, the new gears exchanged directly with the older style gears, but all other new shifter parts had to be replaced in unison with all other parts they mated with.

The things that went bump in the night ap-

parently never went away, so in March 1969 BMW again modified the kickstarter coil return spring by increasing its wire gauge by 0.2mm to 1.3mm. This was supposed to eliminate the annoying noises caused by the "clonking" (again, BMW's words) of the kickstarter dog plate while the transmission oil was still cold.

Still vainly trying to improve shifting, in particular the tendency to jump out of fourth gear, BMW in November 1969 also changed the diameter of the detent spring, part number 23 31 1 066 131, to a wire diameter of 2.25mm.

None of this seemed to work, however, because in January 1970 BMW hurriedly issued a service bulletin indicating that the above improved spring might not solve the problem. Possible causes to be investigated by the servicing mechanic were excessive play of the transmission output shaft, misaligned third and fourth gear shifting forks, or twisted sets due to faulty installation. Also seen as causes were badly worn shift dowels on the fourth speed gear, pounded out detents on the third and fourth gear sliding coupling, or a pounded out fourth speed gear bushing.

The list goes on and on. If you or your mechanic are unable to solve the shifting problems that BMW tried to resolve, ask to see service bulletin No. 275 (3/69) dated January 1970. It spells out the problem and its solution in clinical detail.

Sidecar Gears for the Transmission

Sometime around 1958, BMW realized that sidecar owners were in need of something better than using lower ratio rear end gears. The constant experimentation by BMW with various ring and pinion ratios seems to bear this out. Accordingly, many BMW trained mechanics were taught that certain gears from the R25/3, R26, and R27 single-cylinder transmissions could be installed into the standard 1955–1969 twin cylinder case. This in effect gave the sidecar owner a number of extra-low bottom ratios, yet did not alter his final gearing. Consequently it was no longer necessary to have the speedometer recalibrated. To do it properly, you will need to find an R25/3, R26, or R27 intermediate shaft (without fourth gear), and the first, second, and third speed gears from the output shaft. While these parts are no longer available, it's still possible to cannibalize a spare transmission from a BMW single, so keep an eye out at a flea market or swap meet.

The S Box and the Other One

All 1955–1969 transmissions were either stamped with an S on the case, near the filler plug and by the speedometer cable insertion point, or not stamped at all. The S stood for solo gearing, but the absence of an S did not necessarily mean that your transmission was originally set up with sidecar ratios. Remember, transmission do get rebuilt, especially after twenty or twenty-five years of hard use, so it's best to check the insides if you're unsure. Specially geared sidecar transmissions were intended only for use on the R50 and R60 series, and not on the R69S.

Like identifying the age and type of a fossil, solo transmissions can also be identified by counting the number of teeth. The drive gear had thirteen teeth; the fourth speed spur gear intermediate shaft had twenty-one; the intermediary shaft had twenty, sixteen, and twelve; the fourth speed spur gear output shaft had twenty; the third speed spur gear output shaft had twenty-four (and was marked with a green dot); the second speed spur gear output shaft had twenty-seven; and the first speed spur gear output shaft had thirty-one.

The non-S sidecar ratio transmission had the same number of teeth, except as follows: The intermediary shaft had nineteen, fifteen, and ten (not twenty, sixteen, and twelve). The third speed gear did not have a green dot. The second speed spur gear output shaft had twenty-eight (not twenty-seven) and the one for first had thirty-three (not thirty-one). Simple, isn't it? Too bad you'll have to tear into your transmission to find all this out.

Chapter 11

Rear Drive and Driveshaft

All BMWs since the first R32 of 1923 had an in-line arrangement of engine, transmission, driveshaft, and geared drive to the rear wheel. Some configurations were exotic, culminating in the locking and limited slip differential drive of the military R75 sidecar outfit of 1941–1945. That model was also fitted with a transmission that had four speeds forward and one reverse, plus high and low ranges, making for a total of eight speeds forward and two reverse! Unless examples of BMW's military offerings are part of one's collection, the average enthusiast will only be faced with a four-speed, foot shifted transmission, and either an exposed driveshaft or one enclosed in a swingarm, either of which is connected to a set of helical gears in the cast aluminum rear drive case. All three items are straightforward, but to the untutored can present a number of perplexing and serious maintenance problems.

The famous Cardan shaft, complete with universal joint and showing the chrome-plated dome and rubber mushroom, as fitted to all 1950–1954 BMW twins.

The Cardan Shaft: A Philosopher's Legacy

All shaft-driven motorcycles, be they BMW or some other brand, employ a power transmitting device said to have been invented by the Italian philosopher Girolamo Cardano (1501-1576). The term "Cardan Shaft" is from the French term *transmission a cardan*. At the end of the nineteenth century, the phrase described a connection between engine, transmission, and the road wheels by a turning shaft, instead of the more common belt or chains. Prior to the introduction of the R32 in 1923, only one other European motorcycle, the Belgian FN, was transmitting the power of the engine to the rear wheel via a shaft.

There had been attempts to develop shaft-driven bicycles, and by 1923 virtually all automobiles utilized a driveshaft, but by and large, most motorcycles and heavy trucks still employed a chain drive from the transmission to the rear axle. Prior to 1923 and the BMW's debut, most motorcycles were either belt driven, chain driven or, like the 1894 Hildrebrand and Wolfmüller, propelled by levers, cranks, and planetary gears like a locomotive. Even the world's first motorcycle, Gottlieb Daimler's 1885 wooden-framed experiment, had a rear wheel turned by belts, pulleys, gears, and cogs.

The Driveshaft: 1950–1954

All of the pre-Earles-fork BMW twins had a beautiful chrome plated exposed driveshaft located on the right side of the frame. It was connected to the transmission output flange by a thick, hard rubber puck. This served as both a flexible connection, since no universal joint was fitted to the driveshaft at the transmission end, as well as a shock absorber to help take up shocks and surges as the transmission was shifted.

At the end of the driveshaft, where it met with the rear suspension, was an automotive type universal joint, housed under a chrome plated steel or dull-finished aluminum cover. The cover had to be unscrewed and pushed towards the transmission in order to service the universal joint, which required conscientious lubrication via a grease fitting. Failure to exercise a modicum of caution here, or neglecting the U-joint's lubrication, could lead to disaster. BMW fitted a white mushroom-headed rubber cap over the driveshaft to cover the open end of the U-joint dome. The cap also served as a dust excluder. All of this was assembled as a pressed together unit at the factory; replacement of the various parts is difficult. When the motorcycle is moving in a forward direction, the driveshaft rotates counterclockwise as viewed from the transmission output flange facing the rear wheel.

The Driveshaft: 1955–1969

After 1954, BMW revised their frame, transmission, and rear drive designs and housed the driveshaft inside the right-hand swingarm member. Since the rear suspension was now capable of far greater travel than before, a universal joint was fitted to the front of the driveshaft at the transmission flange, and a sliding spline was used at the rear drive end where it connected with the pinion gear. Hand lubrication of the U-joint was no longer required and the whole thing was enclosed under a flexible accordion pleated rubber boot between the transmission and swingarm. Unfortunately, the rubber boot gave rise to a number of problems, not the least of which was the effort it took to replace the boot when it developed cracks. Provision was made to fill the swingarm with a measured quantity of oil, a point too often neglected. When the motorcycle is moving forward, the driveshaft rotates in a clockwise direction when viewed from the transmission output flange in the direction of the rear wheel.

By 1953, as seen on this R51/3, the rubber coupling on the driveshaft was covered by a half shroud, cast as part of the rear transmission cover. *Bill Sawyer*

The rear drive case moved up and down on two plunger shafts. Under the tin cover on the 1950 R51/2 were coil springs. The whole assembly had to be conscientiously greased via two external fittings on either side. *BMW Archives*

The Rear Drive: 1950–1954

All 1950–1954 BMW twins had sliding plunger rear suspension. The rear drive casing had cast integral with it on the right-hand side the rear plunger fittings. The other fitting was attached to the frame on the left-hand side. The transmission of power from the driveshaft was via helical-cut gears, utilizing a mated set of ring and pinion gears. The gears were lapped in at the factory and should be replaced in pairs. A number of ratios were available for both sidecar and solo use, and both the ring gear and pinion gear must be replaced as a set.

The ring gear is bolted to the hub carrier and can be removed from the hub carrier without difficulty for replacement or service. The carrier itself is supported on needle bearings and has splines machined to the end that mate with the rear wheel. Neglect of the splines will spell disaster and will require expensive and hard-to-find replacements. The pinion gear meshes with the ring gear on the surface closest to the center of the machine; that is, the cut gears mesh on the brake shoe side of the gear set.

The Rear Drive: 1955–1969

In 1955, BMW introduced a swingarm rear suspension member to which the rear drive case was solidly attached. The swingarm and the driveshaft it housed (and the attached rear drive case) pivoted on a pair of swingarm bearings. The gear sets were available in both solo and sidecar ratios and were interchangeable between all the 1955–1954 machines; they should only be replaced in pairs. Over the years, the venting of the rear case was changed, and several internal improvements were incorporated. Externally, however, all the cases look the same. Internally, the hub and splines share the same concept as their 1950–1954 predecessors. Again, the splines that mesh with the rear wheel must be kept clean and lubricated with grease. Unlike the gear set on the plunger machines, the pinion gear meshes with the ring gear on the outer side of the machine, with the teeth facing away from the brake shoe side.

Driveshaft Maintenance: 1950–1954 Models

Although it requires little adjustment and little maintenance, the BMW's driveshaft cannot be neglected. Like all machined objects, fits and tolerances must be maintained, and lubrication must be periodically checked and replenished. Moisture must be kept out and connections to the various other moving assemblies must be kept tight.

The main sources of failure of the 1950–1954 shafts concern the rubber puck and the universal joint. In fact, short of a catastrophic crash, that's all that will ever fail, if you discount peeling chrome and surface rust. In spite of its slender appearance, no driveshaft on the 1950–1954 BMW twins has ever been known to break. Most get damaged in the disassembly process, when injudicious use of a heavy press can distort them. Of all the things to be disassembled when working on a BMW, the 1950–1954 driveshaft is the most difficult.

The rubber puck typically fails from age or if the steel ring that's supposed to strengthen it is misaligned or removed. Some restorers have been known to forget the ring entirely, which leads to rapid and sudden failure. Happily, pucks are in good supply and are now remanufactured. They should be hard black rubber, with four evenly spaced holes and a centering hole. Use of the yellow plastic ones with the notches in the side is not correct, as these fit only the R26 and R27 singles. Replacement of the puck requires the removal of the rear drive so that it can be inserted between the transmission output flange and the shaft input flange. Use of a rubber lubricant, such as liquid soap, will help this process considerably.

With the introduction of the Earles-fork models in 1955, the rear drive was located by swingarms on both sides, rather than plunger shafts, and the Cardan shaft now lived inside the hollow right-hand swingarm. Note that the spring tension on the rear shock towers was now adjustable via short hand levers. *BMW Archives*

this rear drive and suspension... unstintingly designed

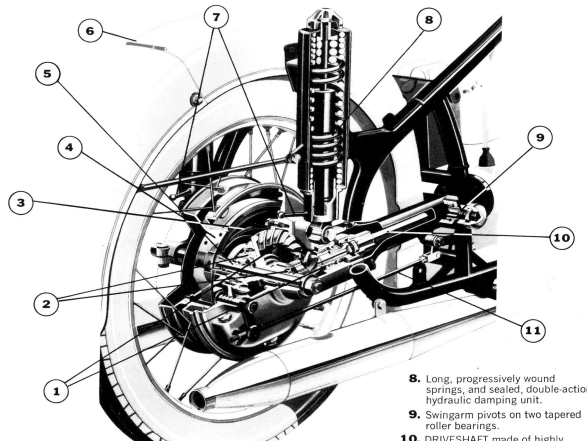

1. Precision-ground, matched, ring and pinion drive gears.

2. Ring and pinion gears supported by needle and ball bearings at each end.

3. Rear drive housing is fully enclosed and vented. Helical gears run silently in oil bath.

4. Full-width aluminum hub with cast iron brake drum. Brake linings conform to Quality Control Test Procedure SAE J661a.

5. Axle can be easily removed, allowing wheel to slip out of spline. Entire drive assembly remains undisturbed when wheel is removed.

6. Hinged rear fender section swings up to allow easy roll-out of rear wheel.

7. Levers for quick and easy adjustment of suspension to accommodate additional load.

8. Long, progressively wound springs, and sealed, double-action, hydraulic damping unit.

9. Swingarm pivots on two tapered roller bearings.

10. DRIVESHAFT made of highly resilient special steel, a product of years of BMW materials research. Needle bearing universal at front of driveshaft; splined, compensating cup-connection at rear.

11. Rod-operated rear brake, designed to compensate variations in brake force due to up-and-down movement of rear wheel. **The unstintingly designed BMW rear drive assures you of reliable, smooth operation requiring minimum maintenance.**

An excellent ad from the mid-1960s describes the intricacies of the BMW's rear suspension and rear drive. Fine points like this put the BMW miles ahead of the competition. *Richard Kahn, Butler & Smith, Inc.*

The universal joint is another matter altogether. It's hidden under the rear driveshaft dome. This is the place where most new owners and untutored restorers make their first major and costly mistake. The joint is left-hand thread and is clearly marked so with a bold letter "L" stamped near the cone end where the hook wrench fits. Unfortunately, the letter may be underneath the cone. If you've acquired a BMW with a damaged or chewed up cone, the L could stand for "lummox," since it was a ham-fisted previous owner who probably used a pipe wrench to strip off the dome after all normal attempts at undoing it failed. At the least, the dome has been destroyed. At worst, the damage extends to the rear drive, which has had its threads stripped off as well. All that's left is to replace both.

Undoing the cone is easily done with the wrench that's in the tool kit, the same hooked wrench that's used for the exhaust rings. Remember, loosen it by turning it to the right, and tighten it by turning it to the left, opposite to all normal inclination. It does not need to be overtightened. Use an anti-seize compound on the threads such as NevaSeize. Grease the universal joint via the grease nipple, using any commercially available lithium-based grease. You will need the original BMW grease gun with the concave tip, since all BMW grease nipples were made to the DIN standard and were not of the Zerk-type found on American cars. A pointed-tip nozzle can be used if you do not have an original BMW grease gun. Lubricate the universal joint every 1,000 miles and while you're at it, do the grease fittings on the rear plunger shafts as well.

Driveshaft Maintenance: 1955–1969 Models

Unlike the 1950–1954 models, there is no need to lubricate the U-joint by hand. All lubrication of the driveshaft at both the U-joint and spline ends is done by the oil that's contained inside the hollow swingarm tube. Care must be taken that the pleated rubber boot is oil-tight. Once cracks develop, the oil will leak out—a condition that is easy to spot since the rear wheel and rear frame will soon be covered by a fine oil mist. Replacing the rubber boot requires the patience of Job. The bolts holding the driveshaft U-joint flange to the transmission output flange must be disconnected. The best way to replace the rubber boot is to cut the old one off with a knife. After the four flange bolts have been removed, spread the flanges apart with a wooden wedge. Insertion of a new rubber boot without damaging it is a tricky and tedious task, but it can be done, and is best accomplished if small children are kept well out of earshot.

A Matter of Gearing

The standard gear ratio for the R51/2, R51/3,

and R68 when used as solo machines was 4.57:1, which was accomplished by a pinion-to-ring-gear ratio of nine and thirty-five teeth respectively. The numbers 9/35 (or sometimes 35/9) should be stamped in the rear drive case on top, near the cone mounting treads. Unfortunately, just having the number there doesn't necessarily mean the gears are still the same as originally installed. It's best to unbutton the case and count teeth.

For sidecar work, the gear sets were 7/32. When changing ratios, owners were supposed to obliterate the old numbers and stamp in the new ones.

For solo work with the R67 and R67/2, the ratio was 3.56:1 and the gear sets were 9/32. Sidecar ratios were 4.38:1 and the gear sets were 8/35. This sidecar ratio also applies to the R67/3, which was only sold as a sidecar machine.

The rear end ratios were changed numerous times with the advent of the 1955–1969 twins, and only the knowledgeable enthusiast can possibly remember all the ratios. Solo gears for the R50, R60, and R69 were first 11/35; that is, eleven finely cut teeth on the pinion to thirty-five on the ring gear. After 1961, the gears were changed to 25/8, which was also used on the R69S. The 1961 R50S used its own special solo ratios of 25/7. For sidecar work, all the machines used sets marked 26/6, except for the early R60, which had a ratio of 27/7. Bowing to popular demand in January 1963, BMW reintroduced the former 27/7 ratio, commencing with frame number 623 980 on the R60/2. The former 26/6 ratio, however, was still available on special order. Not content to rest, in July 1968, a rear end ratio of 27/8 was made available, commencing with frame number 646 686 on the R50/2, frame number 1 816 268 on the R60/2, and frame number 664 651 on the R69S. At this time, use of the new 4.00x18in rear tire was also instituted.

Shims, Seals, and Things

Comprehensive instructions for replacing shims, spacers, and seals are explained in the factory workshop manual, which can be purchased in reprint format from several sources listed in the appendix. A few things not spelled out in the manuals deserve mention at this time.

A good replacement rear pinion bearing for the R51/3 and all other plunger twins is the U.S.-made item from the Penn Ball Bearing Company, Philadelphia, Pennsylvania, (phone 215-423-3105). Ask for size 49.3mm x 34mm x 9.5mm.

Lubrication

All 1950–1954 rear drives used SAE 90 gear oil, of which 130cc were to be introduced via the top filler plug mounted to the rear of the case. Oil should be changed every 6,000 miles. When filling or topping up, measure it as full when it reaches the bottom of the threads in the filler plug opening. On no account is a Hypoid type oil to be used, as the seals and gears will be damaged.

Rear end and driveshaft lubrication for the 1955–1969 machines were an entirely different matter. If the previous owners of your older BMW didn't pay attention, they probably at one time or another used the wrong oil, at the wrong time, in the wrong place, and in the wrong proportions. At the very least, they dissolved or blew out their seals. At worst, they ruined the U-joint bearings, the gear set itself, or the rear hub carrier bearings.

First, let's get the Hypoid oil controversy out of the way. Unless the BMW you have bought was originally fitted with seals, gaskets, and rubber parts resistant to Hypoid oil and unless the BMW was described as using Hypoid oil (see the pertinent manuals for the year it was built), Hypoid oil should not be added. At one time, the only oil a BMW ever used in any of its cases was a good grade of motor oil. Unfortunately, as the machinery improved, and as the BMW's performance increased, better oils were introduced. To blindly put in the latest type of oil because the new BMWs require it is asking for trouble.

All oil used in the rear swingarms in the 1955–1960 machines was SAE 40, in the quantity of 200cc (about 7oz), introduced into the swingarm via the filler plug on top near the rear drive case. There is no way to measure how much oil is left when doing your periodic checking. You have to drain out the oil entirely into a graduated beaker, measure it, add any if needed to the maximum of 200cc, then pour it all back in. The R69 and R50S never used Hypoid oil, but the other models of the R50/2, R60/2, and R69S, as well as the US-fork versions of them, could use Hypoid 90 oil. Regardless of which type is used, the fill quantity was the same and the service interval was 16,000 miles or at least once a year. Again, if you plan to use Hypoid 90 in the other models, you must use the proper seals.

The same caveats as stated above apply to the oils used in the rear drive. All oil used in the rear drives of the 1955–1960 machines was initially SAE 40, in the quantity of 150cc (about 5oz), added to the case via the rear mounted drain plug. Fill only to the bottom of the thread in the opening. Again, the R69 and R50S never used Hypoid 90, but all the others eventually did. If in doubt, check your manual. You can tell if the oil is Hypoid by its pungent odor. The service interval for the rear drive was also 16,000 miles or at least once a year.

The Oil Problem

According to factory notes, service bulletins, and manuals, Hypoid oil began to be used on the various machines, at various times, and in various locations. It's all extremely confusing and you can't

rely on everyone having paid strict attention to all the notes. For your information, here are the frame numbers affected. Write them down. The information may save you a costly mistake.

• Swing Arm Oil went from SAE 40 to Hypoid 90 on the R50/2 commencing with frame 646 358, on the R60/2 commencing with frame 1 814 032, and on the R69S commencing with frame 663 565.

• Rear Drive Gear Oil went from SAE 40 to Hypoid 90 in July 1966, on the R50/2 starting with frame 641 986, on the R60/2 starting with frame 1 810 001, and on the R69S starting with frame 661 445. If Hypoid oil was to be used on earlier machines, BMW required the replacement of six separate sealing rings in the rear drive unit.

Naturally, if you're putting together a BMW from a number of disassociated pieces, you'll never know what's what, and you're better off replacing all the seals with Hypoid types. This is easy to do if you have to rebuild the rear drive and other components as part of the restoration effort. If you are not about to tear into everything, stick with the oil that was in the various cases when you got the machine. If nothing leaks out, it's probably all right to continue using that oil.

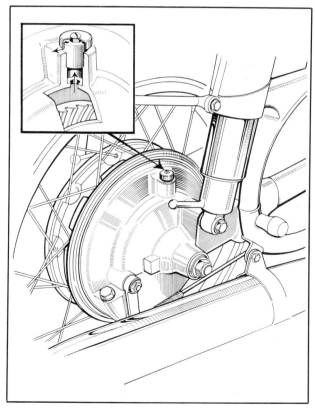

By 1961, oil seepage during excessively hot weather was cured by the addition of a vent plug cast into the rear drive case. Unfortunately, it could not be retrofitted to the earlier 1955–1960 rear cases. *BMW Archives*

Problems, Problems, Problems

BMW had more to worry about than oils used in the wrong places. Occasionally, assembly problems and manufacturing defects were discovered. Thankfully, they were few in number and most were corrected by the dealers before the machines ever reached the street.

However, in case your old BMW was never checked, here are a few notices worth repeating. Don't be alarmed. If your BMW hasn't self-destructed in the twenty-five or thirty years since these faults were discovered, they were either already taken care of or they never were present in your particular machine.

Having received complaints of the rear drives sweating oil in the more tropical climates, BMW in January 1963 fitted a vent plug to the top of all rear drive cases, commencing with frame number 657 099 on the R69S. It was also fitted at that time to all other models, but unfortunately could not be installed into earlier housings due to differences in the casting.

In January 1965, after a number of needle bearing failures on the driveshaft universal joints due to the shifting of the needle bearing bushing, BMW added two extra securing notches to the two already punched into the carrier. This was begun with the R50/2 at frame number 637 491, with the R60/2 at frame number 624 001, and with the R69S at frame number 658 929.

In June 1967, some of the new R50/2, R60/2, and R69S models that had been delivered after January 1, 1967, were discovered to have loose driveshaft mounting bolts—the four bolts holding the driveshaft to the transmission flange. Dealers were asked to check and retighten them.

The Driveshaft Bolt Problem

Now would be a good time to pull that rubber boot and inspect these four bolts. First, drain the oil from the swingarm tube. Undo the retaining clips and push the boot all the way to the rear. Check that the bolts are on tight. If they're the old style Allen head bolts used prior to 1967 without the ribbed sides, remove and discard them; replace them with the new 12 point bolts. Use a 10mm box wrench to check the new bolts. If the bolts are loose, don't just retighten them. Remove all four and replace the spring washers. In all cases, the spring washers should be replaced each time the bolts need to be retightened. Use of a thread compound such as LocTite would help here, too, but it will require total cleaning of the threads beforehand.

When retightening, keep the driveshaft from rotating by having the transmission in gear and holding down the footbrake pedal. If you don't check these bolts religiously, a loose one could fall out, come in contact with the U-joint, and lock everything up. The result would be a bent shaft that could cause a serious accident. At the least, you'll destroy the aluminum flange on the transmission end plate to which the rubber boot is attached, which will mean a transmission rebuild.

Chapter 12

Carburetors and Fuel System

Except for the single carburetor touring and military versions of the 750cc R12, all BMW twins since 1935 have enjoyed the benefit of twin carburetors controlled by a throttle twist grip from the handlebars. All carburetors fitted to the 1950–1969 BMW twins were one-piece,cast-alloy, semi-down draft versions, having a single throttle slide and integral float bowl.

At one time, BMW manufactured their own carburetors, and later used purpose built units from SUM, Graetzin, or Fisher-Amal. By mid-1950, however, they had settled on the German firm BING of Nuremberg as their sole supplier.

Carburetors in General

All postwar carburetors were made with a float chamber cast as part of the carburetor body, which was made of zinc alloy metal similar to Zamak. The body is difficult to repair if damaged, but it can be done. All floats weighed 7g and were made of soldered brass with a central steel float needle, which fitted into a seat in the top of the float bowl

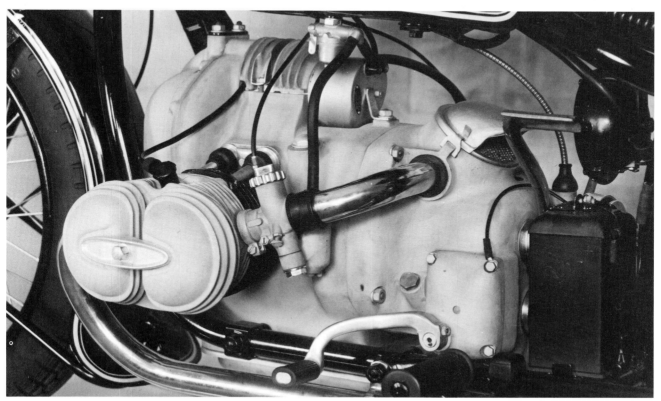

Carburetors on the 1950 R51/2 were one-piece BING items, although on this prototype and on early production models the carburetors were like this two-piece unit with separate float chamber. Note that the fuel tap is also of the prewar variety. *BMW Archives*

lid. Pushing down on the priming button enriched the mixture by flooding the carburetor and allowed starting under most circumstances without having to resort to use of the air cleaner choke lever. Again, only the first versions of the R51/2 were the exception. Instead of the one-piece BINGs, it had inclined carburetors with separate float bowls like those on the prewar R51.

Air entered the carburetors via long chrome-plated tubes inserted into the transmission case, which in turn contained either the air cleaner (as in the R51/2) or acted as a base for one mounted on top, as on the 1951–1969 models. The air was filtered either by passing through a metal mesh/oil soaked element (again, as on the R51/2 and early R51/3 and R67) or through a pleated paper filter after 1952.

Fuel was gravity fed from the fuel tank, with each carburetor having its own fuel line. Fuel lines were black braided rubber covered with a molded-in knit cloth casing. Most fuel lines were painted silver. Although the fuel lines can usually be purchased in either black or silver, it's common and appropriate to paint them.

The Fuel Taps

The fuel tanks usually had only a single tap, which screwed onto a fine thread boss on the left side of the tank's bottom. The two halves of the tank on either side of the frame spine were balanced by another fuel line, which was pressed over two small angle pipe fittings brazed to the tank bottom. BMW never used any sort of clips to attach the fuel lines, or any filters other than the ones built into the fuel tap body. The taps, if used singly, had a double outlet at the bottom to accommodate a fuel line for each carburetor. If two taps were used, as on some of the larger accessory tanks, one-half of each double outlet served as the balance pipe union between tank halves.

Fuel taps in use by BMW during the 1950–1969 era were made by Everbest in Germany, although a few other brands were sometimes seen. Most German motorcycles in the postwar era used similar taps from competing firms, so don't be surprised if your BMW might now be fitted with some-

In detail, the two-piece Everbest fuel tap, as used on all BMW twins from 1950 through late 1953. The sediment trap could be unscrewed for cleaning, and contained a fine wire mesh filter to screen out particles. Unlike the later versions, it could also be taken apart for repairs or renewal of the cork seals. *Rich Sheckler*

Another view of the pre-1955 Everbest tap. The unequal length tubes were the normal and reserve fuel inlets. In practice, they were also covered with a small wire mesh screen to keep large paint flakes at bay. *Rich Sheckler*

thing other than its original Everbest. All taps contained a small, wire mesh filter, and the pre-1954 taps had a removable aluminum sediment bowl that housed the filter. It can be cleaned easily with a soft bristle brush and compressed air. Everbest taps after 1953 were of one-piece construction, and a smaller filter screen was in the bottom outlet fitting, which was cleaned in the same manner.

Pre-1954 taps were rebuildable, and could be totally disassembled with a small screwdriver and wrench. Gaskets were cork and if not available, could easily be made. The taps in use from 1954 on were of the one-piece style and could not be rebuilt, although several solutions to that problem (covered later on) have been tried and proven. These so-called modern one-piece Everbest taps were used in 1954 starting with frame number 536 001 on the R51/3, frame 614 947 on the R67/2, as well as on the R68. While Everbest taps correct for the 1954–1969 machines are no longer manufactured, modern versions made by the firm of Karcoma will work just as well (though they are not correct visually). Reproductions of the 1950–1953 Everbest taps are now being made in Germany, and some success has been had with using similar original taps made for Zündapp and NSU motorcycles, and even early Volkswagen fuel taps.

All taps, rather than having the push-pull selection common to other machines, had an On-Off-Reserve position selected by rotating a small lever over a 180-degree arc. Once the taps became plugged or frozen through years of neglect, these levers were usually broken off, effectively ruining the tap.

The Gas Works

All BING carburetors came in left- and right-hand versions and are not interchangeable on the machine. Most do interchange with other 1950–1969 BMWs; decreased performance and poor starting are the consequences of fitting the wrong carburetor to the wrong machine. They are easy to get mixed up, since they all look generally alike. It's best to have the numbers for your model written down somewhere, in case you come across a set at a flea market or while rummaging through some old dealer's stock. If you find a set, or even a single one, buy it. Replacements are still available, but they will cost you dearly.

All BING carburetors were stamped with identifying numbers in the carburetor body, which faced outwards when the carburetor is mounted on the correct side of the engine. The last set of numbers after the slash mark indicate the side the carburetor should be mounted on. An even number, such as 1/22/42, says it's made for the right-hand side; an odd number, such as 1/22/41, says it's for the left. The middle number between the slashes indicates the size of the intake port, in millimeters.

The larger displacement engines or the sports machines such as the R68, R69, R50S, or R69S naturally were fitted with the largest (and highest numerically) carburetors.

The operation of the carburetors is straightforward. The only problems usually encountered are caused by fuel contamination, fuel restrictions caused by clogged filter screens, or flooding due to a sunk float. Jets can get clogged or plugged permanently after prolonged storage and varnish buildup. Occasionally, needles are misadjusted or the wrong needle for the altitude is used. BMWs that run well in Boston will run poorly in Boulder unless the needles are changed. The most common complaint is fuel leaking from the float tops, and this is usually due to either dried out float top gaskets, leaking fuel taps, or worn float needles or seats. All items are easily replaced or corrected.

The Air Cleaner

BMW did its best to confuse those who are now trying to restore their forty-year-old machines by changing air cleaner designs on an almost yearly basis. There is no precise way to tell you if your BMW has the correct air cleaner, since the use of certain styles seems to overlap. It's probably due to the fact that some owner's manuals were printed using old illustrations, or that BMW themselves used up existing stocks of obsolete air cleaners on some machines while specifying the new style for the new machines. Newer air cleaner housings will fit older machines, and vice versa. Some owners even prefer the look and utility of earlier air cleaners to some of the newer, chrome plated, and non-choke versions. When in doubt, refer to the manual that came with your machine or check factory photos and press releases.

However, certain specific points that are unique to several of the models must be mentioned. The 1950 R51/2 had an air cleaner made of wire mesh that set into the transmission case and not above it like on all 1951–1969 models. It was covered by what had been termed a "chimney vane air cleaner," looking all the world like an air scoop facing backwards. Its real functions were to keep rain from getting in and to dress up an unimaginative prewar design. The scoop was chrome plated, and secured to the transmission body with two clips. No other air cleaner from any other 1951–1969 BMW will interchange or even attach to the transmission of an R51/2. The air filter element must be removed and washed out periodically with gasoline or kerosene, and lightly re-oiled with engine oil. The air tubes are unique to each side, do not interchange, and will not fit any other BMW twin.

For the 1951 R51/3 and R67, the air filter was still oil soaked wire mesh, but was now made by Knecht and housed in a can on top of the transmission, which was also fitted with air intake slots. It

Carburettor

The carburettors cannot achieve their tasks unless ignition timing and valve clearance have been adjusted to their prescribed values. Moreover, only use BMW service proven types and sizes of sparking plugs and jets which must be in excellent condition.

Model		R 51/3	R 51/3 (1952)	R 67	R 67/2
Type of air filter		Knecht	Eberspächer	Knecht	Eberspächer
l. h. carburettor	Bing	1/22/41	1/22/61	1/24/15	1/24/25
r. h. carburettor	Bing	1/22/42	1/22/62	1/24/16	1/24/26
carb. passage		22 mm		24 mm	
main jet solo		100	105	100 *)	110
main jet side car		100	105	105	110
idling jet		40		40	
needle jet		12/08		12/08	
jet needle		standard		No. 2	
needle adjustment		1		3	
mixing chamber cap		5		5	
weight of float		7 grams		7 grams	

*) For solo sports riding of R 67 a main jet 105 can be used. With the driver crouched low this will allow to attain a higher maximum speed while fuel consumption increase at peak speed is moderate.

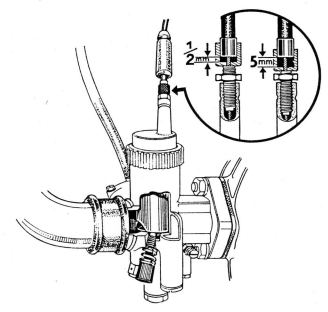

Carburettor Adjustment:

Before adjusting carburettors clean them with petrol.

Wash also common air filter with petrol or kerosene and re-oil metal screen after cleaning. To prevent disturbing irregular air suction make certain that suitable gaskets are inserted between the attaching flanges and also care to tighten clamp nuts evenly.

Make it a rule to regulate idling only with the engine brought up to normal operating temperature. Adjustment is to be done as outlined below:

1. Tighten up Bowden cable adjusting screw upon pipe connections of carburettor cover plates (free travel of piston slides approx. 5 mm = .20 ").

2. Pull down throttle stop screws until throttle slides rest no longer on screws, but upon mixing chamber bottom.

3. Turn stop screws clockwise until screws just touch the throttle slides. With the suction pipes detached this position can be clearly seen. Now rotate stop screws two more turns so that the throttle slides will be lifted thereby.

4. Turn pilot air screws clockwise fully in, tighten slightly and rotate them anticlockwise 1¹/₂ – 2 turns.

5. Crank the engine and let it run.

6. Regulate idling with throttle stop screws so that both cylinders operate uniformly.

7. In case there are still some slight discrepancies in engine operation, clear them one after the other separately for each cylinder (remove spark plug cable from opposite cylinder) by cautiously turning the pilot air screw until uniform idling on both cylinders is obtained. Turn the pilot air screw clockwise for richer mixture, and out, for leaner mixture.

8. Adjust for a Bowden cable travel of approx. 0.5 mm = .02 " in idling position by means of the cable adjusting screws.

After correct adjustment the engine will run smooth and uniformly at low speed. A slow opening of the throttle slide should continually increase the speed. Even with a large handful of grip the engine has to respond in regular flexibility.

Too high fuel consumption, when found, is mostly due to worn jet needles or needle jets.

Replacement of both above named parts will bring remedy in almost all of these cases.

Comprehensive tuning and adjusting instructions for the 1951-1954 carburetors, taken for the official factory shop manual. The principles apply to all BING carburetors through 1969. *BMW Archives*

was usually painted black. You'll seldom have to use the choke lever to restrict the air flow. Just tickling the carburetors with the float plunger knob is enough to enrich the mixture.

By 1952, both the R51/3 and R67/2 had Eberspaecher brand filters, which didn't require oiling and fit into a two-piece canister with a more flattened top and a single air slot at the rear. The choke lever remained the same. Colors of the can could be black or silver. For 1953–1954 and through the early years after 1955, a similar design with a flat, slightly angled top was retained on all models, all painted a silver color. In 1958, covers had a rounded top and by 1962 much larger canisters were in vogue, especially on the sports models, which were devoid of any choke lever.

Non-choke air cleaner elements used during the 1955–1969 era carried BMW part number 13 72 1 250 388. A good replacement is Purolator PM-1049, which almost fits; the excess 1/4in in height can easily be trimmed off. It's available in most auto parts shops. Another good replacement for the BMW item is WIX number 42147, made for the 1962–1974 MGA and MGB.

Air Intake Tubes

All the 1950–1969 twins had two separate chrome-plated air intake tubes that plugged into the transmission case just below the air cleaner housing. At the transmission end, they were sealed with a large rubber grommet; at the carburetor end, they were pressed into a short curved rubber coupling secured with two clips. The clips on the early machines were one-piece spring steel affairs; on later machines they were narrow aircraft-type clamps tightened with screws. For the S models, the air tubes had rubber inserts at the carburetor ends that pressed over the carburetor air intake flange and used no clips.

Although all the tubes appear to be similar, they are not alike. Left and rights do not interchange, nor will those from a 500cc machine fit a 600cc version. S pipes will not work at all on the R50 and R60 series, and vice versa. If they require more than the usual grunting and groaning to attach, they're probably the wrong ones for your machine. If you're restoring a number of BMWs simultaneously, if you have a sizable collection of motorcycles, or if you have a large accumulation of air tubes, mark the inside of the tubes with a scratch awl or vibrating marker, indicating not only the side the tube fits, but the year and model of BMW it came from. It will save you hours of frustration later on.

Carburetor Numbers and Notes on Air Filters

The R51/2, fitted with the Eberspaecher filter, had carburetor bodies stamped with 1/22/30 for the right side and 1/22/29 on the left-hand side. The R51/3, when using the Knecht filter, had BING carburetor numbers of 1/22/42 and 1/22/41 respectively. When the R51/3 was fitted with an Eberspaecher filter, the carburetor numbers were 1/22/62 and 1/22/61. The R67 only came with a Knecht filter, and had BING carburetors numbered 1/24/16 and 1/24/15. The R67/2 and R67/3 only came with the Eberspaecher filter and used BING carburetors 1/24/26 and 1/24/25. The R68, again using the Eberspaecher filter, had BING carburetors numbered 1/26/10 and 1/26/9. All machines used regular gas except the R68, which required premium.

After 1955, all BMW twins had 24 and 26mm BING carburetors, and a paper Micronic air filter. The R50 and R50/2 used numbers 1/24/46 and 1/24/45 for the right and left units. The R50/2 after August 1967 (commencing with engine number 645 590) and the R50US used numbers 1/24/150 and 1/24/149. The R60 used BINGs numbered 1/24/96 and 1/24/95. The R60/2 had carburetors numbered 1/24/126 and 1/24/125. The R60/2 after August 1967 (commencing with engine number 1 814 032) and the R60US were fitted with numbers 1/24/152 and 1/24/151. The R50S used 1/26/72 and 1/26/71. The R69, unique among all the post-1955 twins, used the same BING 1/26/10 and 1/26/9 carburetors as the R68 that preceded it. Finally, the R69S was fitted with carburetors stamped 1/26/70 and 1/26/69. After August 1967, the R69S (commencing with engine number 663 245) and the R69US had bodies marked 1/26/92 and 1/26/91.

Hints of Trouble

It was discovered in June 1952 that occasional fuel restrictions could occur when the rider switched from normal to reserve while riding the motorcycle at speed. These restrictions, even though momentary in nature, could lean out the mixture enough to cause the pistons to seize. To prevent such a rare occurrence, BMW had BING increase the feed diameter of the jet needle in the float and install new float covers having three feed holes instead of two, such as were already fitted to the R68 models. In June 1967, BMW responded to complaints of hard starting and uneven idling of the R50/2, R60/2, and R69S models fitted with lever float carburetors and micro-star paper filters, and came up with improved float guides, shorter float ticklers, and a modification to the main jets.

Better Breathing

In August 1967, all air filters were standardized, and a paper Micro-Star filter was employed. At the same time, beginning with engine number 645 590 (R50/2), 1 814 032 (R60/2), and 663 245 (R69S), carburetor main jets were recalibrated. Float tops now had offset fuel intake hose fittings, and the ticklers had black plastic caps instead of

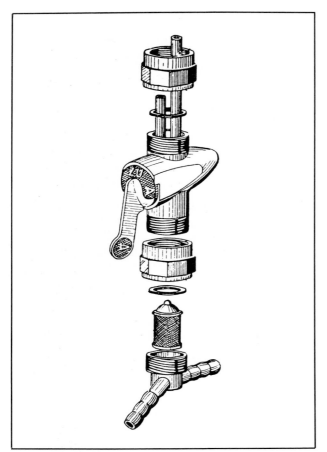

By mid-1954, all BMWs were using the one-piece Everbest fuel tap, which no longer had a lower sediment bowl. The small internal filter usually clogged after a year or two of use and many owners elected to fit in-line filters right into the fuel lines between the tap and the carburetors.

the former metal ones. Sliding choke levers on the R50/2 and R60/2 air cleaner canisters were also phased out with these numbers in August 1967. This is all useful information for those seeking to achieve an absolutely correct restoration, or for concours judges intent on penalizing unknowing owners to the fullest.

Fuel Tap Troubles

Some BMWs experienced poor power output after March 1967 due to restrictions in an improved Everbest fuel tap then being fitted. The problem concerned a "poorly machined cork plug" (as BMW so aptly described it) which restricted fuel flow. Dealers were asked to test the taps for flow in both the normal and reserve positions. All good taps should have passed fuel at the rate of 15 liters per hour, or 250cc per minute.

In April 1968, some owners complained that even with the fuel taps in the open position, fuel was either restricted or didn't flow at all. BMW dis-

covered the trouble was due to the excessive length of the longer (main) fuel pipe attached to the fuel tap, which could sometimes interfere with the bottom of the toolbox as it protruded inside the tank. A suggested remedy was to shorten the main fuel pipe by 4 or 5mm.

Fuel Tap Rebuilding

Although the 1950–1953 taps can be disassembled and reconditioned, the later 1955–1969 Everbest taps were cast as one piece and cannot easily be rebuilt. Since some of these taps were also in use on the 1954 plunger frame models, the following solutions should serve all restorers of 1954–1969 machines.

First, note that there is a Vintage BMW club member willing to undertake a rebuild of the above mentioned taps. Particulars are noted in the appendix. Another Vintage BMW club member who at one time offered me a solution was Harold Sharon, veteran car and motorcycle restorer. Sharon came up with the following fixes to leaking taps:

Carefully cut away the two small crimped edges that hold in the outer washer. After the handle is clamped in a padded vise, gently tap the valve body away from the handle pintle with a drift pin. Remove the cork sleeve, the cause of all the trouble, which will probably be cracked or shrunk up, but don't discard it. Clean the inside of the valve body. Next, coat the inside of the body and the outside of the old cork sleeve with No. 2 Permatex gasket compound, using a matchstick. Reassemble the cork sleeve, lightly grease the pintle, and install temporarily. You don't want the rotating pintle and

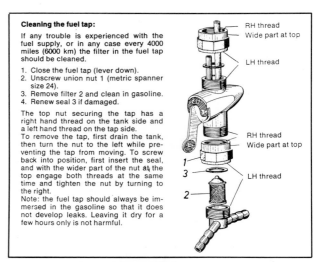

Cleaning the fuel tap:

If any trouble is experienced with the fuel supply, or in any case every 4000 miles (6000 km) the filter in the fuel tap should be cleaned.

1. Close the fuel tap (lever down).
2. Unscrew union nut 1 (metric spanner size 24).
3. Remove filter 2 and clean in gasoline.
4. Renew seal 3 if damaged.

The top nut securing the tap has a right hand thread on the tank side and a left hand thread on the tap side. To remove the tap, first drain the tank, then turn the nut to the left while preventing the tap from moving. To screw back into position, first insert the seal, and with the wider part of the nut at the top engage both threads at the same time and tighten the nut by turning to the right.
Note: the fuel tap should always be immersed in the gasoline so that it does not develop leaks. Leaving it dry for a few hours only is not harmful.

RH thread
Wide part at top
LH thread
RH thread
Wide part at top
LH thread
1
3
2

Note the various right- and left-hand threads necessary to get the tap and outlets to line up properly under the tank while still allowing a tight compression seal on the upper and lower gaskets. BMW provided some comprehensive instructions on how to attach a fuel tap in their owner's manuals.

handle to stick to the cork. Gently push the pintle back into the cork and body; leave it alone overnight.

The next day remove just the pintle, taking care not to disturb the cork that should be stuck to the inside of the tap body. Using a lathe, carefully turn an O-ring groove close to the handle end of the pintle after having purchased the proper O-ring. The groove depth should allow for 15 percent compression of the O-ring after installation. It's not really necessary to use an O-ring, but if you have a small lathe, you can easily modify your tap to accept one. Finally, permanently assemble the pintle, washer, and O-ring. Install them back into the cork-lined fuel tap body by lightly staking it in place as was originally done by Everbest. Remember, the metal washer will hold everything together, if it's properly staked.

If all else fails, or if you can't find anyone to rebuild your Everbest petcock, use the post-1972 Karcoma rebuildable petcock, which works just as well, but which unfortunately does not look like the original ones at all. Carry an extra Karcoma in your tool kit for that day when the old Everbest gives up the ghost and you're 500 miles from home and there's no BMW dealer in sight.

Balancing Your Carburetors

While the workshop and owners' manuals go to great lengths to tell you how to adjust and tune your carburetors for optimum economy and performance, there's an excellent tool on the market that will make it child's play. Remember, this tool still requires that you know how your carburetor works, and what all the little screws and things do. You need to have a manual handy, but having this tool in your workshop will make your BMW, regardless of model, run like it has never run before, and it will make you think you've suddenly become the world's best BMW mechanic.

The post-1970 BMWs all had a small vacuum hose fitting on their carburetors, to which a gauge was to be attached. Unfortunately, none of the 1950–1969 models ever had this device, so the Synchrometer carburetor synchronizer will have to be used. It's not an exotic item, and although it's imported from Germany, it's been listed in the J.C. Whitney catalog for nearly ten years, at a price between $20 and $25. Remember, if you can balance the air flow going into the carburetor, and if the needles and jets are set so that both carburetors are working more or less the same, the bike will run much better. This tool will help you do this and will tell you via a dial gauge as well. The English instructions with the Synchrometer are comprehensive, but here are some hints to assist you:

A small advertisement for the German-made carburetor synchronizer mentioned in this chapter. It's virtually foolproof and provides an excellent and accurate means of balancing both carburetors. It is available from J.C. Whitney via mail order.

Remove the chrome air tubes from both carburetors. Put the BMW on the centerstand and let it warm up at idle. Alternately pressing the gauge against the carb air intakes will give you readings from both sides. First balance the idle speed air flow by adjusting the idle stop screw and the mixture air screw until the needle on the gauge reads within 1 line on the scale between the two carburetor measurements. To adjust high speed air flow, run the engine up to about 2000rpm, and read the gauge as before. This time, do your adjustments at the cable ends where they enter the carburetor. Again, follow the fine detailed instructions in both the sheet that comes with the Synchrometer, as well as with your machine's relevant manuals. You'll be amazed how you ever got along without such a device. If you really want to impress your friends with your skill, buy a Synchrometer for each carburetor. It would speed things up, but two aren't really necessary or required.

When you order the unit, specify that it's for the 1955–1969 BMW motorcycle, models R50 and R60, and ask that they ship the item with Adapter 23/25. Even if you don't get the right adapter, any old rubber sleeve will do, including ones cut from old radiator hoses.

Chapter 13

Electrics, Lighting, and Horn

All 1950–1969 BMW twins had a 6-volt, negative ground system. The speedometer, all the major electrical switches, indicators, and junction boards were contained in the headlight shell. In addition, all models had a head and taillamp, horn, and provisions for attaching an inspection lamp or sidecar circuit plug. Ancillary switches for headlamp high and low beam and horn were clipped to the handlebars. With the exception of the 1950 R51/2, all 1951–1969 twins had magneto ignition and a generator running at engine speed, mounted to the front of the crankshaft and protected from the elements by a cast-aluminum cover.

Again, since the 1950 R51/2 was basically a prewar holdover, it had a 6-volt coil ignition system and distributor, rather than a magneto. The generator was mounted externally on the top of the engine case and was driven by a single row chain, which also was connected to the twin camshafts of the R51/2.

While the entire lighting set was dependent upon a rather anemic 6-volt, 7 ampere hour battery, road speeds were not what they are today, so no one seemed to complain. However, for the police, military, and other government users of the BMW, and for those enthusiasts or competitors in long trials or endurance events, a special order 12-volt system was made available in the mid-1960s. This system could be installed at the factory prior to delivery or retrofitted at a later date.

The R51/2 Electrical System

The 1950 R51/2 used a Bosch RD45/6 generator and coil ignition, all of which was a general upgrade of the prewar system employed as far back as on the R5 of 1936. The spark was sent to the plugs via a simple distributor housed under a cast cover at the front of the engine. Protection of the electrics had been a BMW hallmark since the mid-1930s. Those models that still had portions of their electrical system mounted outside in the open employed some bulletproof products made by the firm of Robert Bosch-Stuttgart.

The main circuit board, which also contained a simple grounding switch, was in the headlight shell protected from the elements. BMW's famous and ubiquitous spike controlled it. The spike was a removable key used in various forms since the 1920s and finally phased out in favor of a slotted Yale-type key in the mid-1970s. Unlike later models, the circuit board was fitted with a fuse, something BMW did away with in 1954.

The wiring harness was cloth and plastic wrapped wire, well protected by rubber sleeves here and there and rubber grommets as it passed in and out of the various components, such as the engine block and headlight bucket.

The rear end of the harness ran clipped to the outside of the rear fender, and headed towards the taillamp shell, entering it from the outside. All a very proper prewar configuration, and somewhat incongruous with all of the BMW's other niceties. A properly restored R51/2 must have the rear fender wire clipped to the outside, however, and a correct rear lamp and fender rack, not the later 1951–1954 versions.

The battery sat exposed on a bracket bolted to the frame, in an area below the seat next to the rider's ankles and the spinning driveshaft. It was secured with a metal two-piece clamp, which in later models gave way to a more practical but not as nice-looking rubber strap.

The R51/3, R67, and R68 Electrics

In 1951, with the introduction of the "new" R67 and R51/3 series, BMW upgraded all of its twin-cylinder models to Noris magneto ignition, and began using a generator supplied by either Noris or Bosch. What set the new engines apart from their predecessors was a redesigned block casting, incorporating a fully enclosed set of electrical components housed under a front cover seemingly cast as a part of the block. Only a thin line where the machined surface of the cover mated with the timing chest gave it away, as did two small recessed attaching bolts. The cover was vented internally, and cooled by forced air passing through passages in the block, all of it pumped by the flailing about of internal components and the rotation of a ventilating disk attached to the front of the camshaft. All very sophisticated, and all designed to provide cooling air to the electrical components without compromising weather protection.

The circuit board still lived inside the headlight shell which, except for the addition of a round green neutral light just below the speedometer, was identical to the R51/2 shell that preceded it. The ignition key was the same plastic-headed metal spike and the fuse plug was retained as well, along with the single red charging warning light to the left of the key socket. In mid-1954, the headlamp bucket was altered and resembled the 1955–1969 Earles and US-fork version in all but minor details.

The wiring harness was altered to accommodate the new electrical components, but all the changes were invisible to the outside world. However, at the rear of the machine the formerly exposed electric wiring harness had now disappeared and was routed in a neat, but problematic, tunnel underneath the rear fender's sheet metal, at the centerline of the fender. It entered the taillamp body from the back, finally giving the BMW a more finished appearance.

The 6-volt battery was still the same black cased item, still clipped outside on a little bracket and held on with a two-piece metal strap, which finally gave way to a rubber elastic in late 1954. The rating of the battery did not yet go up to 8 ampere hours, retaining the meager 7 ampere rating of the R51/2.

The 1955–1969 Earles and US-Fork Electrics

When BMW introduced the Earles-fork models in 1955, virtually every aspect of the motorcycle was changed except the electrical system. In any event, any detail improvements were hidden away underneath the engine front cover. By 1955, the headlamp bucket was a refined version of the one that had first appeared on the R68 and R67/2 and R67/3 of 1954. It had a chrome base surrounding the key socket and a spring-loaded, sliding black plastic cover. Finally gone were the separate red and green round indicator lights, which were now part of small triangular unit below the opening for the speedometer.

The wiring was still neatly enclosed underneath the rear fender and by 1960, with the upgrade of the R69 into the R69S, the last prewar vestige of a manual magneto/spark retard control was finally eliminated. Batteries were marginally increased in size and rating, as was the taillamp, which now resembled a cylindrical coffee can and to many looked too large for the rear fender. At least it now had a larger reflector and a less fragile plastic lens, which had replaced the smaller glass lenses used earlier. All the big taillights now had a stop-

lamp filament, something all but the last of the pre-1955 machines lacked. Thankfully, from an aesthetic standpoint at least, additional reflectors were not used until required by the authorities in 1969, and no add-on stalk-mounted turn signals were ever fitted.

The Generator and Voltage Regulator: 1951–1954

The early generators were Noris L45/60L units. After engine number 524 029 on the R51/3, and 611 179 on the R67, they were replaced with the L45/60L/CV, which was of a slightly different design. This was also used on the R68. Both were rated at 45W at 1800rpm, producing a maximum of 60W at 2200rpm. This was achieved at approximately 28–30mph when in top gear on the R51/3 and R67 series when fitted with solo rear end ratios. Both had a separate single pole voltage regulator and a wire wrapped ceramic resistor or rheostat. All had an external voltage regulator that had an adjusting nut for regulating the voltage, something the later two pole regulators lacked.

The system was generally maintenance free, requiring no lubrication and only occasional dusting every 6,000 miles to remove carbon residue from the armature, and wiping clean of the armature itself with a gasoline soaked rag or contact cleaner. The brushes had to be replaced periodically when worn. Dust particles or carbon chips were to be cleaned from between the regulator points with a small piece of cardboard.

The Generator and Voltage Regulator: 1955–1969

The basic generator used on the 1951–1954 machines was continued with the 1955–1969 series, with minor upgrades along the way. On these machines it was a Bosch LJ/CGE 960/6/1/1700 R5 model. The R69 had the earlier R68 L60/6/1500L version. The newer generator did however produce considerably more juice, namely 60W at 1700rpm and a rated 90W at 2100rpm. This came in at a lower speed than before as well, somewhere between 22 and 25mph in top gear, depending on the model.

The earlier Bosch Type F regulator was now replaced with a Bosch Z-type (Bosch RS/ZA), which had two armatures, one of which was a cut-out relay. Unlike the earlier regulators, the new version was not adjustable.

Magneto Ignition: 1951–1954

These models had the Noris MZ ad/R magneto, with an auto advance unit, driven at one-half crankshaft speed from the front of the camshaft. Due to changes in camshaft tapers, the magneto rotors are not interchangeable with later models. The auto advance on all including the R68 worked over a 30-degree range. The R68, however, had a manual retard feature, via a cable and lever, which allowed for an additional 10 degrees of retardation. Its primary purpose was to allow easier starting, especially when low grade fuels were used. It was also known to be an excellent anti-theft device, for if left fully advanced the resultant backfire would frighten off the unknowing thief or alert a nearby owner.

A feature often misunderstood by owners new to the BMW was the safety spark gap, which allowed high voltage spark to jump from the coil to ground on the breaker plate whenever a spark plug wire was disconnected during tuning operations, or when a plug ceased to fire due to damage or fouling. If the gaps were not kept at a separation of 10 to 11mm, the magneto would not fire or would fire erratically.

Magneto Ignition: 1955–1969

Although much changed with the advent of the Earles and US-fork models, the magneto setup remained the same. True, camshaft tapers were altered, precluding the swapping of rotors with earlier models, but that was the extent of it. The R69 still enjoyed 10 degrees of manual retardation via a manual retard/advance control on the handlebar, but that was basically the only difference between the various 1955–1969 models. Maintenance and lubrication was the same for all throughout the 1951–1969 era, and consisted of periodic greasing of the points mechanism where it contacted the cam lobe, and cleaning, adjusting, and periodic replacement of the points. As on the 1951–1954 models, the safety spark gap had to be maintained, or failure of the magneto would result.

Timing Considerations

Timing was adjusted by the laborious method of rotating the points mounting plate, something that has finally been improved upon and is fully described in the sections below.

To time the machine, follow the instructions in the various owner's manuals and in the BMW workshop manual. A timing light is useful but not absolutely necessary. Remember that the timing marks stamped into the flywheel are sometimes in the wrong place, and this is spelled out in the following "Problems, Problems, Problems" section.

BMW BATTERY SPECIFICATIONS

BMW MODEL	BATTERY				WHITNEY/ATLANTIC STOCK NUMBER
	TYPE	LENGTH	DEPTH	HEIGHT	
Most prewar (i.e.-R12, R17, R51, R66) plus R24, R25 series, R51-67-68 series.	6V-12Ah	3.5/8	3.1/4	6.1/2	G-1
R26 R27	6V-12Ah	4.13/16	2.3/8	5.3/8	B39-6 / G-3A 6N11A-1B / G-3A
R50-60-69S series.	6V-18Ah	3.5/8	4.3/4	6.5/8	B49-6 / E-1

Note: These sizes may not be correct for your particular model, as battery carrier or box may have been altered by prior owners. Japanese sizes may also vary.

Alternative battery dimensions for the BMW singles and twins. Note that most applications will work on BMWs all the way back to the mid-1930s. The stock numbers listed are the old J.C. Whitney and Atlantic Battery numbers from the mid-1970s, which you should still be able to cross-reference today. The important thing is the dimensions. If the case is clear plastic, it can be painted black to pass for an original.

Even if they're in the right position on the flywheel, it's best to check this with a degree wheel. Re-mark the flywheel if necessary. In any event, dress up the marks that are there with white nail polish, to help make then more visible. Keep an extra set of points in a plastic 35mm film can, which tucks handily into all that empty space in your headlamp or tail-lamp body. Also, keep at least one extra set of generator brushes there, but wrap them separately to prevent them from damaging each other.

Battery Alternatives

All early BMW batteries, even those going back to the late 1920s and early 1930s, were of the black case variety with a separate lid that fit loosely over the three filler caps. The outside of the case was of a hard tarry substance, like petrified rubber or old telephone cases, but was not a true black rubber case like some American and English varieties. If neglected, they leaked and froze in winter and generally ruined the finish of the bike. Fortunately, the BMW could be made to run without a good battery, but the voltage regulator and generator depended upon a working battery for ballast, so it's wise to keep a functioning one in your machine. The earlier brands were Sonnenschein, Varta, and Bosch, to name a few; most are no longer available.

Thankfully, black case batteries are again being made, but at a price. In a pinch, clear case Japanese ones will work and look almost identical, if you rough up the case and paint it black beforehand. Others have taken to using old Russian batteries that were take outs from Cossack, Ural, and Dnieper machines. Other restorers have been known to hollow out damaged batteries and insert small 6-volt units made for mopeds and such. Others use 6-volt toy car batteries, such as the ones marketed by Sears Roebuck for their ride-on cars. A good Sears alternative is their DieHard 6-volt battery, number 49-86567. It is of the sealed gel-cell type and has dimensions of 5-1/2in high, 4-1/4in wide, and 2-5/8in deep.

1950–1954 Batteries

All were of the black case variety, in 6-volt size, rated at 7 ampere hours. Dimensions were 6-3/8in high, 3-1/8in wide, and 3-1/2in deep. All measurements include the lid in place. The negative pole was grounded to a bolt head on the transmission case. Most common brands were Varta, Sonnenschein, and Bosch, and the maker's logo or decal was usually in a circle molded into the side of the case. All had hard black plastic or phenolic lids that generally broke when dropped. All batteries were secured with two separate metal straps. These were usually eaten away by battery acid and were eventually replaced with rubber bands that were not as pretty, but that at least bore the BMW logo.

A good alternative for the tall-case batteries is the "Made in the USSR" version, which measures 6in high (including the cover), 2-7/8in wide, and 3-3/4in deep. Like most Russian products, it's rough, crude, built like a tank, and will probably last a long time if cared for properly. It also looks good and fits well in prewar BMWs, from which it was probably copied.

Larger 1955–1969 Batteries

After 1955, batteries were somewhat enlarged in size and the rating went up to 8 ampere hours. Overall dimensions were now 6-3/8in high, 4-3/4in wide, and 3-3/8in deep. All dimensions included the lid. A common brand was the Varta 3 FL 3. Straps were now rubber bands for all the models.

A good, readily available alternative, if you frequent British bike restoration shops, is the SAFA 3L3. This one has a slightly ribbed black case, a nice black lid, and measures 6-3/4in high (including the lid), 4-5/8in wide, and 3-3/8in deep.

Alternative 12-Volt Systems

If you wanted to convert your factory 6-volt system to 12-volt (to match the system BMW fitted to police machines), an unbelievable number of parts had to be replaced. Most owners usually found it was not worth the bother or expense. If you want to embark upon this venture, the complete list of parts you'll need is in the appendices.

Early Horns: 1950–1954

On the 1950–1954 machines, the horn was a Bosch HO/FDF/6/1 unit mounted on a laminated spring bracket directly under the seat spring mounting boss. It faced forward like all proper horns should, not off to the side as the British were so fond of doing. It was a fine thing to see and hear, and looked much more prewar than the Bosch and Klaxon units that followed after 1955. These early horns had a small round or oval tag at the front, bearing the maker's name and model numbers, and it was usually lost after awhile. No restoration is complete without one. Scour old time junkyards that may still have some early examples of German cars of the 1950s rotting away. Mercedes and Volkswagen cars, not to mention the less common Opels and Borgwards, usually had identical horns, though some may have been rated at 12-volts. At the very least, they might have that little aluminum tag yours is missing.

1955–1969 Bosch and Klaxon Horns

After 1955, BMW variously used Bosch and Klaxon horns, all in the 6-volt flavor and all painted a somber black, devoid of any bright metal tags. Connections were still screw terminal and the mountings were still laminated spring brackets. Mounting location, however was now at the front of the machine, under the steering head and facing forward. The Bosch HO5 horns were non-adjustable and once they failed, were usually discarded. The Klaxon ETF/4 D models, however, had an adjusting bolt at the back.

Now that no old horns are available, conscientious restorers are starting to figure out how to make them work again. Some put new internals into the older cases, but the sound isn't quite the same. If you have a passion for trivial pursuits or for winning bar bets, ask your fellow BMW owners, the ones who don't know all that much about old BMWs, if all the parts on a 1955–1969 German built BMW were made in Germany. Most will say yes, some will disagree, but few will be able to point out that the one item not marked Made in Germany (or, as it used to say Made in Western Germany) was the Klaxon horn. The horn was clearly stamped Made in France. There's a lesson to be learned from all of this, but I'm not sure what.

If the camshaft driven tachometer was fitted to any of the 1951 and later models, the horn had to be relocated to the right side of the engine in order for the drive cable to pass in front of the steering head (outlined in Chapter 18).

Other Horns and Sirens

With the use of a 12-volt system, one naturally had to use a larger 12-volt horn, typically both physically larger and louder. Most Bosch auto horns of the period will work fine here, especially Mercedes car horns of the 1958–1966 era, which were massive items indeed. For police use, an electric siren was fitted in several variations either with a wailing or warbling high-low sound, such as preferred by the European police.

The Circuit Board

All the wiring and the 1950–1953 fuse and such come together at the pressed plastic/cardboard concoction called a circuit board, which was safely hidden inside the headlight shell. It was secured in such a safe place that it was usually the first (and in many cases the only) thing damaged in even the most minor of accidents. It was damaged as the headlight sheet metal to which it was pinned was warped or as the ignition key was ripped out of its socket. If the board survived these traumas, the owners usually broke them trying to get at the wiring or when trying to pry the board off the four bent steel tabs that held it.

It was pure hell to get at, although there was nothing else in the headlight to obscure it. Lying on one's back usually helped get at the upside-down terminals, but the little plastic-handled screwdriver included in the tool kit was seldom up to the task of loosening old screws or tightening new ones. Small wonder that the circuit board, along with the battery and those papier-mâché mufflers, was right

near the top of the list of things otherwise enthusiastic owners disliked the most about their beloved BMWs.

If you break a board, it can still be repaired, for it's not the true printed circuit board to which we are accustomed today. At least the BMW board contained no sensitive diodes, no transistors, and no microchips that something so simple as an errant magnetized screwdriver head can put into permanent disarray. It was nothing more than a primitive non-conducting terminal board to which the wires were connected.

The Ignition Key

It seems that from time immemorial, BMWs had those funny black plastic keys with a streamlined head on one end and a nail on the other. We've all seen them, we've all wondered where to put them other than to carry them in our hand like some sacred amulet or rune stone, and whenever a group of pre-1970 BMWs arrive together after a ride, the snapping of key slides and the snicking of keys is the first thing one usually hears after the motors are silent.

Something that few motorcycle owners (other than BMW owners) know is that these keys are not unique. They will start any pre-1975 BMW, back all the way to the R5 and R12 of 1936. The key is really not a key, but merely a removable kill switch. Unlike a kill switch, this one works in reverse in that it disconnects the wiring harness from ground when inserted, and reconnects the circuit to ground when removed. The fact that the spike is made of steel has nothing to do with it; in a pinch, if you've lost your key, you could start your bike and ride it home using a stick, a bent twig, or even two kitchen matches. All you have to do is stuff the objects into the key socket and push against the tension spring of the switch.

The 1950–1969 keys were of two varieties, with slightly different plastic heads and two lengths of steel shaft. The shorter headed keys, with the shorter spikes, will only work in the 1950–1953 headlight buckets, but they will also work well in all the prewar machines back to the R5 and R12 of 1936. After mid-1954, when BMW went to a covered and chrome plated ignition key slide, the shorter keys will no longer work, and the ones with the longer heads and longer shafts must be used. These will also work on all the machines back to 1936, but will not look correct. Happily, both types of keys are once again being made, but instead of selling at a cost of under a dollar, they now command much, much higher prices. Emergency keys were similar, but flat, with no bulging plastic top, and fit nicely into a wallet.

The spike on the end of the key served several purposes. It had a flat tab at the top which contacted a rotating switch that was part of the circuit board. Turning the key to the right, when fully inserted, turned on the headlight. Turning it to the left turned off the headlight but allowed the small parking bulb in the headlamp reflector to remain on, as well as the taillamp. While this may make little sense to us in the U.S., it was a requirement in Europe and England to leave these lights on whenever parking a bike unattended. In the leftmost position, the key could also be removed without turning off the parking lamps.

Bulbs, Fuses, and Warning Lights

With the exception of certain small taillamp bulbs, all bulbs on the 1950–1969 BMWs were of the bayonet type, which plugged into a socket and then were rotated to lock. All bulbs are readily available today, and the most common European makes are from Bosch or Osram. The Bilux brand was actually a label used by Osram to indicate twin filaments. Most bulbs were of such a low rating as to be almost ludicrous, but at least they managed to put out more candlelight, and at a more reliable rate, than the product of Jos. Lucas and Sons.

Bulb applications and ratings are usually spelled out in the manuals, but in case you're on a bulb hunt, here are the common types usually encountered.

Headlamp bulbs were of the twin filament type, and rated at 6-volt 35/35 watts, for the 1951–1954 twins. The rating went to a more useful 6-volt 35/45 with the 1955–1969 twins.

Parking lamps were 6-volt 1.5W on all 1950–1954 models, except the R51/2, where it was listed as 6-volt 2W.

The taillamp was a single filament 6-volt 5W, without a stop lamp, on the R51/2 and others until 1953. Fitting a twin filament bulb served no purpose, for there was not a stop lamp circuit or stop lamp switch fitted to any BMW prior to 1953. Naturally, you wouldn't leave home now without one, and you're required to have one in all states to get an inspection sticker. The common solution was to add a socket to the taillamp. If that was not possible, the owner could rip out the original and solder or rivet in a proper two terminal socket and use a regular auto bulb. It's really quite easy to do, and you can purchase a cheap trailer light and make it work well, as long as everything is hidden away under the taillights cover.

In 1953-1954, a second circuit was added and a torpedo type stoplight bulb rated as 6-volt 10W was used.

Dual filament taillight bulbs were 6-volt 5/18W rated on the 1955–1969 BMWs, and all are readily available today.

License lights were usually of the torpedo type having a contact at each end. Today we would call then dome lights, but of course they're not quite the same. They were rated at 6-volt 5W on the 1950-

1954 series, and doubled as a running light when fitted as such. From 1955–1969, they were of the round, bayonet type, and rated at 6-volt 5W.

Other bulbs usually found on the BMW were for the red and green indicator lights in the headlight. These were 6-volt 1.5W on the 1951–1954 machines, the same as the parking lamp. On the 1955–1969 machines, they were upgraded to 6-volt 2W.

The speedometer bulbs were 6-volt 0.6W or a larger 6-volt 1.2W. Either will fit, and the larger rated one is recommended.

Hella blinker bulbs for the bar end signals were 6-volt BL 81 types.

The fuse, as used on the 1950-1953 BMWs, was inserted via the fuse plug on the outside of the headlamp shell, and was of the 8A ceramic variety. It was only a part of the headlamp, taillamp, and parking lamp circuit and did not protect the rest of the harness. It did not disable the ignition when removed as many suspected.

Please note that use of any bulb will be a waste of money if the battery is not in good condition. Bulbs will quickly soot up with carbon, rendering them useless, if the battery is not keeping the generator and voltage regulator happy. Too few amps and too many voltage fluctuations will quickly ruin a bulb's delicate filament.

The Wiring Harness

Wiring is wiring, they say, but in the BMW's case this was a bit more so. The harness was complex, neatly wrapped together, and usually sold in two parts, a main and a tail section. The cost of a new harness, even at today's prices, is so reasonable that it's a foolish endeavor to attempt to create your own.

Spark Plugs, Caps, and Wires

Bosch was the major supplier of plugs to BMW for over half a century, although other brands, such as BERU, were often listed in the manuals. Finding the old style Bosch plugs with the unribbed insulators is difficult these days, and only the most knowledgeable of concours judges would know to look for the difference. Besides, like tires, modern plugs are almost a necessity for safe and reliable riding. If you can find the old straight sided plugs, cherish them and put them in your pre-1955 machine when you're at the show, but use the more modern ones at other times.

Plug recommendations were spelled out in the various manuals. For most, the Bosch W240T1, W260T1, or BERU 240/14 or 260/14 will work fine. If using the LK heads, you must use the long reach Bosch plugs, which were marked BoschW240T2 or W260T2.

All plugs were gapped at 0.024in, or 0.6mm. Again, keep a spare set in a hiding place in the headlamp or taillamp for emergencies.

Plug caps are another matter. Many a restoration has been flawed by the use of incorrect caps for the era. Unfortunately, the style of cap that BMW used in the early 1950s was of a design that often trapped moisture rather than excluded it; most owners threw then away in disgust. Some caps were of a brownish plastic, with an aluminum collar, which was intended to act as a suppresser and keep static from appearing on the radios of others in the vicinity. Once these caps started to age, the metal covers could contact the cylinder head. Mix in a little dirt, oil, and moisture, and your cap would ground out the plugs. If you can find an original set, use them when showing the bike. At other times, use a rubber type, such as the Spark-Ez brand, available at most auto parts and lawnmower supply stores.

If you must have something that looks like it came on the bike in the 1950s or 1960s, get a black plastic Bosch item, with the name embossed in the top. These can be found inexpensively at your friendly SAAB or Volvo dealer. The inlet hole for the wire may be a bit too small, but minor trimming of the wire's insulation will make the cable fit right in.

Finally, the high tension wires that come out of the engine block should be checked and replaced periodically. They are prone to cracks and are subjected to considerable heat in their run inside the engine casing. When replacing them, don't get a modern resistor core equivalent. Ask for the seldom used Packard 440 cable, which employs a non-resistor wire. Not only will this allow all of the spark

The two headlight styles used during 1951-54. On the right, the 1954 item, with covered key slide and using the longer ignition spike. The 1955-69 headlamps and keys looked identical, but the 1954 headlamp had a shallow depression under the rear. Note that the speedometer inserted in the 1954 headlight shell is of the post-1961 variety, with resettable trip odometer.

to pass from the magneto coil to the plugs, it will also last much longer than the resistor core type. Unfortunately, it'll also send static to the radio of the car next to you at the light, but by the time they figure it out you'll be long gone. Besides, you'll never hear it, since your BMW isn't festooned with CB sets, CD players, intercoms, and mega-watt stereos like some other two wheeled behemoths you're bound to encounter.

The Headlight Shell

From 1951 to 1969, BMW used four basic styles of headlamp shells, all made by Hella. Only the true student of vintage BMWs knows the difference, but knowing the difference can spell success or defeat at a concours. In 1950, the R51/2 had a simple bucket with a large round hole for the speedometer, a red generator warning light at the left of the uncovered key socket, and a reddish-brown plastic fuse plug to the right of it. There was no green neutral lamp. The rim was chrome plated, usually stamped Bosch and *Importe d'Allemagne* on the top edge, and the lens was slightly convex, with Bosch script in cursive Germanic letters at the bottom. There was usually a frosted half circle at the bottom. Most of the Bosch lenses had the characteristic series of nested U shapes in the center as

The most commonly encountered pre-1955 headlight shell, complete in this case with the correct Veigel black-and-white-face speedometer. Note the fuse plug on the right. The round light opposite the plug is the red ignition warning light. The light below the speedometer is the green neutral light. *Bill Sawyer*

The mystery revealed. As you can see, there's really little inside the headlight shell other than the small terminal board at the top and the body of the speedometer. Even with the reflector and lens in place, there's still room inside the headlight assembly to store extra bulbs or spare control cables, ignition wires, and a foot or two of fuel line.

well. Other appropriate lenses for the 1950–1954 era were ones made by Hella, with a significant cat's eye pattern vertical in the center. Yellow tinted lenses were made for the export market, primarily France and its colonies.

After 1951 to mid-1953, BMW used a similar shell that now had a round green light below the speedometer opening, which was the neutral indicator. All else remained the same.

In late 1953, to the end of the 1954 model run, all headlamp shells took on the appearance of the 1955–1969 Earles-fork models that followed, having a covered key slide and two triangular red and green lights below the speedometer. The headlamp bucket was unique, however, in that it had a shallow depression at the bottom, underneath, and near the pointed end, ostensibly to clear the fork lock bracket that was part of the steering head forging. After 1955, this shallow dish was eliminated.

From 1955 to 1968, more or less, all the headlamps looked like the 1953-1954 versions, minus that dished out bottom. Rims were now devoid of letters or markings, and the lenses had the Bosch name in block letters at the bottom. Gone was the frosted semicircle near the bottom, and the nested U pattern.

By 1968, the final version of this headlamp style was seen, with a round indicator bulb appearing to the right of the key slide, totally asymmetrical on a motorcycle that always was known for its beautiful symmetry. This add-on indicator, usually red or sometimes blue, was the relocated generator light, while the former triangular red lens at the bottom became the high-beam indicator, something required by the authorities in the U.S. and in other forward-thinking countries. On some machines, owners or dealers rewired them so that the old lens again indicated the generator's status, which made more sense. For a while, all replacement buckets only came with this add-on light, so many pre-1968 machines you see today may have been fitted with this after the fact, when a hapless owner found out that that's all there was available. Now they're highly sought after, especially by owners restoring the US-fork machines, which only had this sort of headlamp shell fitted from the outset.

The 6-Volt Headlamp and an Alternative

Rather than go to the expense of converting from 6-volt to 12-volt just to get a little more light onto the road ahead, you can choose from two other alternatives. The first is to not ride the BMW at night, a choice that might not appeal to everyone. The more practical one is to convert just the bulb, lens, and reflector to a 6-volt halogen unit being marketed by a member of the Vintage BMW Club in the U.S. Installation is a snap, and assuming the generator, voltage regulator, and battery are in tip-top shape, the improvement will be an eye opener. Unfortunately, the lens is of the more modern flat surfaced variety, with an asymmetrical pattern, but if you're serious about riding these older machines, such a conversion is a must. Current sources for the various components are listed in the appendix.

Speedometers

All BMWs from the 1936 R5 and R12 had the speedometer mounted in the headlight shell. Although in the prewar era speedometers were usually supplied by Veigel, after 1950 both Veigel and VDO were BMW's major suppliers. In the early 1950s, only speedometers reading in kilometers were available, but after 1953 ones calibrated in miles per hour started appearing on the American market.

All speedometers in the 1950–1969 era were internally lit, all had a chrome-plated bezel permanently crimped on and holding the lens in place, and all were fitted with an odometer. In the years after 1961, a separate trip odometer reading to 999 miles or kilometers was available, which was reset via a small chrome knurled knob that went straight through the glass lens. It eventually served as an entrance point for moisture, but most of the BMW

A proper view of a very proper R67/2, showing the correct single lens EBER taillamp. Unavailable for years, these lamps are now being reproduced and are available in the U.S. through various Vintage BMW Club members. *Michael Gross*

speedometers were prone to fog up as a matter of course anyway.

Early VDO and Veigel speedometers had black faces, which later became a two-color black and white. After 1955, all faces were a two-color black and cream. When new, all the faces had the instrument's ratio painted on in small numbers, but as BMWs were frequently regeared for sidecar use, these usually were painted over when the instrument was recalibrated. Specially geared instruments were also available from BMW directly.

The 1950–1954 speedometers had curved glass lenses, which can still be found now and then. If you have no luck, try a watchmaker or clock repair shop, or some of the instrument repairers advertising in *Hemmings Motor News*. After 1955, all lenses were flat glass.

It's impossible to repair the speedometer without destroying the crimped-on bezel. In any case, such repairs are best left to the experts who can also restore or provide a new face, which has probably faded badly on your own machine. Virtually any BMW speedometer can be repaired by the American VDO repair facility, or by such firms as Palo Alto Speedometer, which has been in the business of fixing German instruments for nearly half a century. The appendix lists the names of these firms and other sources.

Taillamps

From 1950 to 1954, all BMWs had small taillights made by Eber, but the ubiquitous Hella "coffee can" was available as an option as early as 1953. To compound the confusion, early examples of the 1955 R50 and R69 also came with small taillamps, which had, however, larger lenses held on with a chrome ring and three external screws.

For a while, the source of small lamps had evaporated, since no one in Germany was allowed to use such a small rearward facing lens for obvious safety reasons. Happily, reproductions are now again authorized for machines classified as veterans or antiques. These reproductions are true to the originals, although in some instances the lenses may be plastic rather than glass.

An unusual lamp of the small configuration appeared in late 1953. The lamp had a triangular, orange glass lens on top, above the regular round red one. This was an interim stop lamp lens, and when it went on, the sight of a bright orange light to indicate that the bike was about to stop caused all sorts of confusion, particularly in the U.S., where everyone was used to seeing only red lenses at the rear. The orange lens is not a turn signal indicator as is most commonly believed.

Sidecar taillamps on the various Steib models were identical to the small taillamps on the BMW, but had no window cutout for the license plate bulb. In a pinch, a sidecar lamp can be modified to work as a taillight for a pre-1955 BMW.

After 1955, all BMW twins were fitted with the large, round Hella coffee can, which is still being made by the original manufacturer. It used a round plastic lens that had a central reflector. Early reflectors were only 44mm in diameter, while the later ones were 53mm.

Problems, Problems, Problems

In January 1967, in response to complaints of wire securing screws working loose in the circuit board on the headlight shell, BMW secured them with a dab of green lacquer. Any subsequent work on the wiring required the use of such lacquer after the screws were tightened.

Everyone seemed to have a tendency to overfill the black case 6-volt batteries, due mainly to a lack of knowledge of the battery's design. It seems the battery contained what BMW called a splash protection box, basically a barrier between the tops of the plates and the top of the case above it. The barrier's perforated lower surface was about a third

Two EBERs and an impostor. On the left, the late-1953–1954 twin lens EBER, with the triangular top lens made of orange glass, which served as the stop lamp lens. It must have confused many following drivers. The more practical single lens EBER in the middle originally had only a running light circuit, but clever owners can fit a twin filament bulb socket without too much difficulty. On the right, the Spanish made GAMO impostor, which is in reality a Bultaco item. Although not authentic, and fitted with a screw-in plastic lens, it's close enough in looks to work in a pinch on a pre-1955 BMW.

of an inch from the top of the plates. If the battery was filled properly, no fluid should be visible when looking inside the filler holes. Unfortunately, the only way to accurately measure the amount of acid in the case was to tilt the battery, which meant undoing the strap, or inserting a small wooden stick through the plate's perforations. Not at all a good design.

Naturally, everyone usually put too much fluid in the battery, thinking it needed to be visible just below the edge of the filler hole, something taught to us at an early age when we first learned to work on dad's car. This attention to detail probably accounted for untold numbers of BMW having their paint and mufflers ruined by acid leaking out of chronically overfilled batteries.

In June 1964, centrifugal advance units with a modified timing setting were fitted to all models, commencing with engine number 636 000 on the R50/2, number 625 951 on the R60/2, and number 658 624 on the R69S. The intent was to eliminate pinging and pre-ignition when accelerating the engine to speeds of approximately 4000rpm. The new part number was 80 04 113.

Flywheel marks on the R50S and R69S were changed in June 1964. The former 12 degrees and 42 degrees for advanced and retard respectively before T.D.C. were no longer applicable, since the retarded ignition timing (initial) was now 9 degrees before T.D.C. This change commenced with frame number 658 164 on the R69S, and brought the R69S flywheel in line with the same ones already in use on the R50/2 and R60/2 models.

As indicated earlier, BMW told us in April 1967 that valve timing data as printed on page seven of some R50, R60, and R69S owner's manuals, and on page eleven of the repair manual should be corrected to read, "Intake opens 4 degrees before T.D.C., and intake closes 44 degrees after B.D.C. The exhaust opens at 44 degrees before T.D.C. and the exhaust closes 4 degrees after T.D.C."

Improving the Electrics

A modern solution to the vexing problem of adjusting points and replacing the Bosch condenser was recently provided by Dr. Robert Harms, a Vintage BMW Club member from Florida. His company, Pentacomm, has started to market a machined aluminum point plate that utilizes readily available American made components, including the condenser and automotive points. The points, which are made to fit a late-model Chevrolet, are

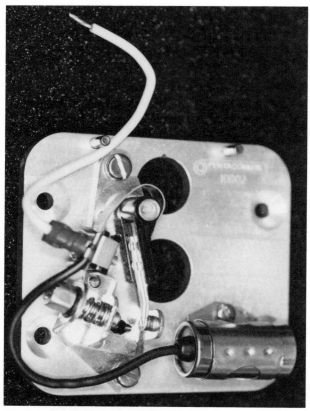

The Pentacomm aluminum point plate, which is made to fit all 1951–1969 BMW twins. It's a vast improvement over the difficult to adjust original it replaces, and the easy availability of automotive points and condenser it uses is an additional bonus. *Robert Harms*

not only in almost inexhaustible supply, but are also inexpensive. As an added bonus, the points can now be adjusted with the engine running. The old method of loosening the point backing plate and jiggling everything until it made a difference is gone. Furthermore, the American condenser comes with a wire already in place, whereas the older Bosch unit required a certain amount of skill with a soldering iron, an item you usually didn't have with you when repairing your electrics on the side of the road.

The points plate replacement comes with a beautiful and simple set of instructions, but some improvements to the installation process were recently provide by Craig Vechorik, frequent contributor to and technical editor of the *Vintage BMW Bulletin*. While the manufacturer's instructions indicate that the magneto body can remain in place when installing the new points plate assembly, Craig found it easier when he removed the entire magneto, rather than just the original pressed brass points plate. Others may prefer to follow the instructions to the letter, but if you decide to do it Craig's way, first rotate the engine by hand, using the kicklever, until the "S" mark is aligned with the stationary mark in the crankcase timing window. Check the alignment of the magneto rotor with the notches on the breaker plate, loosen and then rotate the body of the magneto until the two notches align, and scribe a line on the side of the magneto body and timing gear cover for future reference.

Next, remove the grounding lead from the magneto's upper right corner, and the two spark plug wires. Remove the advance unit from the shaft, and the two 6mm nuts that secure it to the timing cover. Lay the whole unit down on a bench, and remove the four screws, the points lead, the plate, and the spacers.

Follow the rest of the preprinted directions. Craig used soldered connections rather than the extra crimped wire and connector supplied, but that's a matter of personal preference. After all is reinstalled on the engine, put the magneto body back, using the marks you made earlier for reference. Get a long-shank 1/8in Allen wrench, start the engine, and, using a strobe light, adjust the points on the new points plate. It's a vernier type adjustment, similar to adjusting the sights on a target rifle. Keep your fingers and the wrench clear of that spinning auto advance unit. If you want to order a points plate conversion that will fit all BMW twins from 1951 through 1969, see the appendix for more information. You'll also find the Vintage BMW Club's technical editor listed there, in case you want to share some of your experiences.

The Problem with Brushes

The carbon brushes were the most common cause of all electrical problems. If left unattended, they were prone to hang up, causing the red light to go on. If allowed to wear down too far, they would begin to float, since the springs holding them against the armature could no longer exert enough pressure. The solution was to take them out, and either replace them or dress them with a nail file or fine sandpaper. If the red warning light still remained on, or got brighter when engine revs were increased, it meant that the generator was polarized incorrectly, probably due to momentary attachment of the battery with the wires reversed. This was a common error in the R26 and R27 singles, but relatively rare among the twins. To repolarize the electrical system, follow the directions in the BMW workshop manual. If all else fails, any good competent mechanic should be able to do it. Exercise a little caution at this point and you'll save yourself some time and money in the long run.

Key Tricks

The ignition spike had several detents built in that helped keep the key from popping out of the socket. If you look at the key closely, you'll see it almost fits into the square key socket built into the toolbox lock of the accessory 1950–1954 Meier tank, the accessory 1955–1969 6.5gal sport tank, as well as into the toolbox lids of all 1950–1954 twins. To open these locks, you need the square headed special BMW key. Most everyone loses that key sooner or later and has to use a screwdriver blade to unscrew the lock. However, the ignition key, due to its ungainly shape, is seldom lost, and if you carefully grind four flats into the portion of the shaft just below the first detent, the ignition key can be made to do double duty as a toolbox key. I first tried this trick about twenty years ago and neither the key nor the ignition socket have failed me yet.

Chapter 14

Controls, Seats, and Sidestands

The controls on a BMW are as important as any of the other assemblies on the motorcycle, yet they are the ones most often neglected. To make the restorer's task more complex, however, most of the controls from 1950–1954 can be substituted with those from the 1955–1969 series, resulting in an incorrect restoration. Unfortunately, once damaged, the cast pot-metal control assemblies are virtually impossible to repair, and an incorrect, though expedient, substitution using the later items is often the only alternative.

It should be mentioned that the restorer of the 1950–1969 BMW is at least spared the agony of hunting up many of the bewildering examples of air, throttle, and magneto levers that were to be found on the prewar machines. Gone, with only three exceptions, are the manual thumb levers that

one had to operate in order to advance or retard the ignition timing. Gone, happily, is the mechanical dip switch and lever assembly that the prewar rider had to contend with. Gone, and not missed by any but the prewar enthusiasts, are the beautifully designed and executed, but cumbersome, hand-shift levers built into the right side kneepad. Sadly, the graceful reversed levers of the prewar BMWs are gone as well, but any mechanic or owner who has jammed one of these in the back of his neck while working on the front wheel or forks won't grieve long over their absence.

Throttle and Clutch: 1950–1954

Basically, two styles of control castings for the throttle and clutch lever assemblies and three styles of lever blades were used. Horn buttons and headlamp dip switches are pretty much the same throughout the 1950–1969 period. These, however, require the skill and patience of a watchmaker to repair and are difficult to find in new condition. Fortunately for the enthusiast and the restorer, turn signals were not part of the design of a pre-1969 BMW, and from an aesthetic standpoint, their omission cleaned up an already clean design. Small orange lens aftermarket signals, which fitted into the grip ends of the handlebars, were available from Hella, and these will be covered in Chapter 18.

The 1950 R51/2 is again the exception to all this, but it must be remembered that in 1950 BMW was basically assembling and selling a prewar design. In some of the early press release photographs, the R51/2 is even shown with the prewar reversed levers, but few if any were ever sold to the public in that configuration. All examples of the R51/2, however, did have mechanical headlight dip switch levers, a round horn button held on with a knurled cap, and a manual ignition timing lever mounted to the top of the clutch control casting on the left end of the handlebar. All are purely prewar holdovers, and because of that are still relatively easy to find. Expect to pay dearly, nonetheless. Fairly good reproductions are now coming in from

An excellent view of the controls you would expect to find in 1950. Although this shot is of a 1937 R20, the steering damper, headlamp shell, and the mechanical dip switch on the throttle, as well as the manual ignition control on the left, were exactly as those used on the 1950 R51/2.

Germany; once painted, they are indistinguishable from the originals. In a pinch, 1951–1954 controls and switches will do, but their use will cost you points at some of the better judged competitions.

The R51/2 control castings, in spite of their holdover prewar switches and levers, are similar to the ones used on the 1951–1954 R51/3, R67, R67/2, R67/3, and R68. The only differences are in the location of some tapped holes, which can easily be filled and painted over, if you plan to use them on the latter models. Don't overtighten the set screws or other fasteners when mounting it. The casting could fracture and can only be repaired by expensive methods. Epoxy glue won't do the trick here. Only a firm specializing in restoring pot-metal castings will be able to help, and then everything will have to go to a machinist to be trued and trimmed before it will again fit on the handlebars. The use of a little caution here will save you time and money in the end. It's little wonder that many owners chose to use the easily available and relatively inexpensive 1955–1969 controls, saving the originals for when they put the bike out to show.

The 1950–1954 throttles were of the twist grip design, using separate cables for each carburetor. The cable ends were held captive in a small rectangular traveler, which worked its way up and down a spiral slot cut into the twist grip that rotated inside the control casting. A handy grease fitting is right there on the casting to help lubricate everything, and this is one of the few external grease fittings on a 1950–1954 BMW that must never be neglected. Failure to keep the throttle packed with grease will result in rapid wear of the mechanism. Use plenty of the best, black lithium-based grease, and use a gun with the special concave headed nozzle. In a pinch, a needle point nozzle will work. Better to wear black leather gloves that won't show the grease when riding, than to suffer a broken throttle miles from home. It's also a wise idea to carry an extra throttle traveler in the tool roll.

Controls and Levers: 1950–1954

The control levers for the clutch and front brake cables look identical on all the 1950–1954 machines, but are not interchangeable from right to left. The slotted hole must be on the bottom on each one when fitted. All blades are without ball ends and have no finger notches. Post-1954 levers may look similar, but will not work, due to the shape of the pivot end. Other German manufacturers of the period used similar assemblies, so checking around at NSU, Adler, and Horex stands at your next flea market might turn up the BMW items you're missing. The blades were highly polished, one of the few polished aluminum items on a BMW. Occasionally, you'll encounter blades where the ends have been trimmed off, either the result of accident damage or by an owner who got tired of being poked in the neck by the sharp end. Repairs can be made, if no new blades can be found, by having someone weld back on the tips from later blades. These repair parts need not be of German manufacture; any suitably shaped aluminum blade will do.

Getting a Grip

Rubber grips should only be of the pattern provided by Magura, Germany's largest throttle manufacturer. Left and right grips are identical externally, with closed ends. In May 1963 grips with open ends, stocked under BMW part number 207 21 77, were also made available to accommodate turn signals or bar end mirrors. The open ends could be closed with a small black plastic snap-over cap, which carried the part number 207 21 79. The number of the closed-end grips was 207 21 60. They were only used in black on the BMW, although other colors, such as gray, white, or beige, were available for other brands. The throttle grip naturally has a larger inside diameter.

If the rubber is beyond redemption, used and worn grips can be removed by slicing them off with a razor knife. If the rubber is still good, pry up the inner lip of the grip with a screwdriver and inject a lubricant, such as WD-40 or Armorall. The fitting of new grips should only be done using soap and water, not a lubricant. Otherwise you'll end up with rotating rubber grips at both ends. All grips from 1950 to 1969 were identical, are still being made, and are inexpensive. There's no excuse for having worn grips on any BMW you plan to show. One drawback of the Magura grips is that they were thin, with no cushioning effect provided. Since BMWs don't vibrate like other bikes, this was a minor shortcoming.

Bars and Posts

Handlebars on all 1950–1969 BMWs were also manufactured by Magura, and they came in varying lengths, shapes, and angle of rise. Finding the absolutely correct and proper Magura bar for your 1950–1969 BMW can be a frustrating ordeal. Everyone is suddenly the expert, telling you that the bar you spent years hunting for is not the correct one after all. Aesthetically, the best are the low rise Europa style bars, which are now suddenly in fashion. Years ago, everyone had to have high-rise American style bars, such as those manufactured by Earl Flanders specifically for the American BMW enthusiast. All bars, whether factory originals or aftermarket accessories, were chrome plated and 7/8in in diameter, while the prewar ones were made to the 1in pattern. Prewar controls consequently will not fit the postwar machines, even though they may look similar.

All handlebars on the 1950–1954 BMWs were of the one-piece, flat European design. Width from end to end on the solo machines was 600mm, or ap-

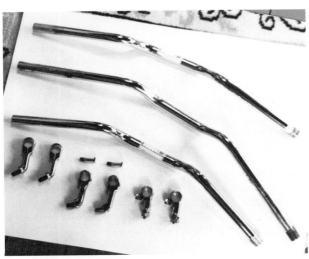

Three styles of Magura "Europa" bars, with the longer of the three being a sidecar item. The bar clamps on the left are those used on the 1950–54 machines, the middle set are those for the 1955–68 Earles fork twins, while the shorter, more vertical ones on the right are the posts for the R68.

proximately 24in, while sidecar machines used 30in width bars. A common slight-rise 24in Magura pattern is stocked under the Magura number L359.2-00 ch. A slightly longer version is the 26in Magura bearing the number L359-00 ch. All 1950–1954 bars were identical. Only the R68 had a slightly lower, racier shape than the others. Only the rabid R68 expert would be able to tell the difference. In all likelihood, he couldn't find any of the R68 bars either and is using the more common R51/R67 style.

From 1955 on, the Earles-fork and US-fork BMWs used two styles of bars, the Europa style, which was seldom fitted to American-export machines, and the 28in US-bars, which had a large cross brace across the top. To the uninitiated or non-BMW enthusiast, these look like enduro or motocross bars. They're now hard to find, difficult to straighten, and expensive to have re-chromed. Most owners of 1955–1969 models prefer to replace them with the low, Europa bars, which also give the BMW a more racy appearance. If the original Magura items for the period can't be found, a good looking and nearly correct substitute is the use of 24in BMW R90S bars, which look almost identical. Avoid using later BMW bars that have a knurled section. This may have been fine for the post-/5 or -/6 series, where the handlebar risers hid the knurling, but on the 1950–1969 machines it will show and look unsightly. Handlebars with a small hole drilled in the bottom surface at the center were intended to be used with the Hella bar end signals. The use of bars with this hole is no detriment to a correct restoration as the hole cannot easily be seen.

Bars were attached to the fork tops with a pair of split, one-piece risers, made of chrome plated malleable iron. Both left and right risers were identical but they came in several variations. Use of earlier risers on later machines, and vice versa, is possible but makes for an incorrect restoration. With the exception of the R68, all 1950–1954 machines used the same risers, which were angled affairs having a long slot down the center. They were pinched tight with plain hex headed bolts and nuts. The R68 had short vertical risers clamped shut with a single bolt.

The risers should always face toward the gas tank. Use of large tanks made by Hoske and others may require the reversal of the risers in order to clear the tank top. Test the position of the handlebars after mounting the tank. If they approach the top of the tank when swinging the bars from left lock to right lock, raise the risers with washers, reverse them, or fit R68 posts, which should do the trick. Unfortunately the R68 posts are the hardest to find these days.

All the Earles fork machines from 1955-1968 used angled risers similar to the 1950–1954 styles, but with spit collars at the bar end. They're difficult to pry apart. Use caution or they will be damaged. Naturally, if your BMW is fitted with the one piece Europa bars, they can just be slid off the ends. If you've got the American style bars, you'll have to do some serious prying to get the risers off the bars. If you have the risers re-chromed, have them chromed in the open position; you'll minimize the risk of fracturing the plating by only having to clamp them shut once, rather than prying them open and then shut again.

US-fork models of 1968–1969 had two-piece aluminum risers, which simplified matters. These will not fit the Earles fork models and their use should not be attempted. Risers from 1970 /5 models look like the 1968–1969 US-fork models.

Throttles: 1955–1969

The throttles on the 1955–1969 machines were of an improved design, using a geared rack and pinion concept and a short-linked chain inside the throttle casting. It all sounds very complex, but it was a vast improvement over the earlier 1950–1954 version. Some adjustment is now possible, but it requires partial disassembly of the throttle and is difficult to do successfully. One drawback is that the throttle is slow to respond. A common solution is to use the 1970-on /5 throttle cam and chain assembly, which is more progressive and quicker in action. If considering such a retrofit, you must also use the /5 version of the throttle cover. There are no provisions for lubrication, but a good solution is to carefully remove the center hold down screw and, without disturbing the lid, inject grease into the mechanism until is oozes out of the joints.

This process requires either a third hand or a friend.

Cables were again of the twin type, one for each carburetor. Use of the little rubber boot over the cables at the point where they enter the throttle is a nice idea, but it should be remembered that this little item was never available prior to 1970, and only first appeared on the /5 models! A knowledgeable judge will probably use it against you, so be careful. It could spell the difference between winning and coming in second.

More Controls and Levers: 1955–1969

Early on, the control levers were similar to the 1950–1954 style, without finger notches or ball ends. By January 1967 all levers had notches and balls, but the earlier styles were still available. Both interchange, but earlier machines should be fitted with the plain levers. The new levers, which also had nylon bushings in the pivot holes, were fitted to all R50/2 and R50US models starting with frame number 641 437; to R60/2 and R60US models from frame number 629 956 to 630 000; and to subsequent versions of this series starting with frame number 1 810 001. On the R69S and R69US, use of the new levers began with frame number 661 045. At the same time, switches were redesigned to incorporate the use of Hella bar end signals. Since there were three versions available concurrently in 1967, each with its own variations of the wiring diagram, those finer details are discussed below in the section on switches.

Again, like the R68, the sports R69 had an extra lever of its own. Like the R68, the R69 of 1955–1960 had a manual spark control fitted to the left control casting, with the cable entering the timing chest as on the R68. All quite natural, since the engines and electrics were identical. However, the R69 lever base is slightly different from the R68's, and they won't interchange.

No pre-1970 BMW had a front brake switch, something you will need to remember when it comes time to get your annual inspection sticker. Most states will not require you to retrofit one if the bike originally didn't come with one. If you do have to have one, use of the post-1970 /5 series throttle casting will solve the dilemma since it comes with a front brake lever actuated switch. The assembly looks almost identical, and judges should be informed if your state requires such an item. It's probably a good idea to use one anyway. Safety consideration should not penalize you in a concours. Note however that signal switches for horn and headlamp dipping are not identical to the pre-1969 items.

Note also that 1950–1954 and 1955–1969 machines had several styles of steering dampers, which differed both in form and function. Although these are basically handlebar controls, they are dis-

Another view of the 1950-54 "wing nut" steering damper and its friction plates, next to the flat style used on the 1955–68 Earles fork machines.

cussed in Chapter 2 dealing with recognition points.

Electrical Switches

Handlebar mounted electrical controls on the 1950–1969 machines are minimal, since the major ones are located in the headlight shell. On the left control casting, a small chrome Hella unit was usually clipped. The unit had switches for headlamp high and low beam and a toggle for the horn. Some had a third lever for headlamp flashing, but these are seldom seen in the U.S. If turn signals are fitted, they require a separate switch assembly, usually clamped over the handlebar on the right. The most common complaint about the horn/dip switch assembly is the rapid rate at which the short four wire cable that leads to the circuit board in the headlamp shell deteriorates. Once the rubber covering starts to crack, the insulation on the individual wires is soon to follow. It's best to keep an extra, new cable in your toolbox, or rolled up inside the headlamp shell, which has vast amounts of empty space for storing all sorts of spares. A wiring failure on the road, late at night, could mean no lights or a shorted out electrical system. It's best to plan ahead and be ready when disaster strikes.

The New 1967 Switches

As indicated previously in the section on levers, in January 1967 all BMW twins (and the R27) became available with redesigned throttle and clutch control castings, which accommodated the new switches for the optional Hella bar end signals. The starting and ending frame numbers for their use are the same as spelled out in the switch section above.

Two major versions of the switches were available, as well as the original version for BMWs to be sold in the domestic German market. The former two applied to BMWs sold in the export market without signals, and for all handlebars regardless of market with signals.

Of the signal switch types, there were also three variations, one called the "new" execution, the second the "original" execution, and the last the "intermediate" execution. It's all quite confusing. To best describe the variations, and in particular to help you rewire your machine, all three wiring diagrams are reproduced below. It should be noted that the new execution switches feature black plastic rotating toggles, similar to those that would be seen on the 1970 /5 series. Naturally, modified bases fitting onto the new control castings were required to attach these switches.

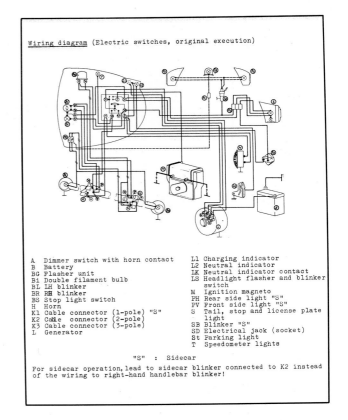

Wiring diagram (Electric switches, original execution)

A	Dimmer switch with horn contact	L1	Charging indicator
B	Battery	L2	Neutral indicator
BG	Flasher unit	IK	Neutral indicator contact
Bi	Double filament bulb	LS	Headlight flasher and blinker switch
BL	LH blinker	M	Ignition magneto
BR	RH blinker	PH	Rear side light "S"
BS	Stop light switch	PV	Front side light "S"
H	Horn	S	Tail, stop and license plate light
K1	Cable connector (1-pole) "S"		
K2	Cable connector (2-pole)	SB	Blinker "S"
K3	Cable connector (3-pole)	SD	Electrical jack (socket)
L	Generator	St	Parking light
		T	Speedometer lights

"S" : Sidecar

For sidecar operation, lead to sidecar blinker connected to K2 instead of the wiring to right-hand handlebar blinker!

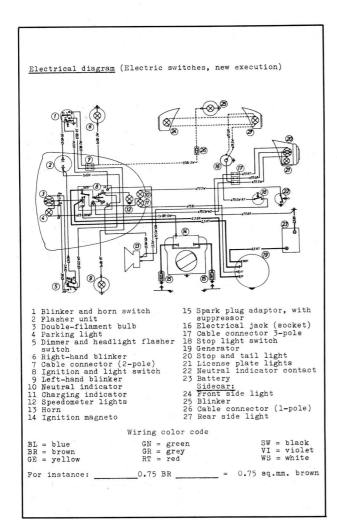

Electrical diagram (Electric switches, new execution)

1	Blinker and horn switch	15	Spark plug adaptor, with suppressor
2	Flasher unit	16	Electrical jack (socket)
3	Double-filament bulb	17	Cable connector 3-pole
4	Parking light	18	Stop light switch
5	Dimmer and headlight flasher switch	19	Generator
6	Right-hand blinker	20	Stop and tail light
7	Cable connector (2-pole)	21	License plate lights
8	Ignition and light switch	22	Neutral indicator contact
9	Left-hand blinker	23	Battery
10	Neutral indicator		**Sidecar:**
11	Charging indicator	24	Front side light
12	Speedometer lights	25	Blinker
13	Horn	26	Cable connector (1-pole)
14	Ignition magneto	27	Rear side light

Wiring color code

BL = blue		GN = green		SW = black	
BR = brown		GR = grey		VI = violet	
GE = yellow		RT = red		WS = white	

For instance: _____ 0.75 BR _____ = 0.75 sq.mm. brown

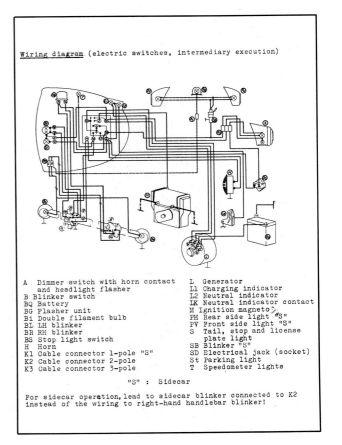

Wiring diagram (electric switches, intermediary execution)

A	Dimmer switch with horn contact and headlight flasher	L	Generator
B	Blinker switch	L1	Charging indicator
BQ	Battery	L2	Neutral indicator
BG	Flasher unit	IK	Neutral indicator contact
Bi	Double filament bulb	M	Ignition magneto
BL	LH blinker	PH	Rear side light "S"
BR	RH blinker	PV	Front side light "S"
BS	Stop light switch	S	Tail, stop and license plate light
H	Horn		
K1	Cable connector 1-pole "S"	SB	Blinker "S"
K2	Cable connector 2-pole	SD	Electrical jack (socket)
K3	Cable connector 3-pole	St	Parking light
		T	Speedometer lights

"S" : Sidecar

For sidecar operation, lead to sidecar blinker connected to K2 instead of the wiring to right-hand handlebar blinker!

Seats

Until the mid-1950s, all BMWs only came with separate solo saddles for the rider and the passenger, with the latter an optional accessory, usually mounted to the pressed steel pillion rack on the rear fender. The rider's saddle was most often made by either Pagusa or Denfeld, both old-line German manufacturers whose association with BMW goes back to the 1920s. A number of smaller firms, such as Bruninghaus, SFS, Drilastic, Norgus, and Dunlop, also made saddles for the BMW, or else just the replacement rubber tops. Some tops came with no maker's logo whatsoever, to help add to the confusion.

This section will only concern itself with the solo saddle for the rider, not the passenger. Passenger saddles are covered in Chapter 18.

The rider's saddle on the 1950–1954 machines was an elaborate affair, consisting of a pressed-steel Y-section, upon which was bolted a hard yet flexible rubber top that had its own internal framing to help maintain its shape. Up to 1955, most BMW twins were fitted with Pagusa brand-name rubber tops, and an absolutely correct restoration should have a Pagusa saddle.

The main seat frame was mounted to the motorcycle frame at the rear of the gas tank to a T-yoke, which had its own bushing, lubricated with a grease fitting. The saddle was suspended by a single horizontal steel coil spring, which was chrome plated and adjustable for tension by turning in the pivot bolt. Additionally, there were several mounting points on the seat frame, clearly marked with weight gradations, in kilograms. A rider, knowing his own weight, could easily set the seat for the correct tension and support.

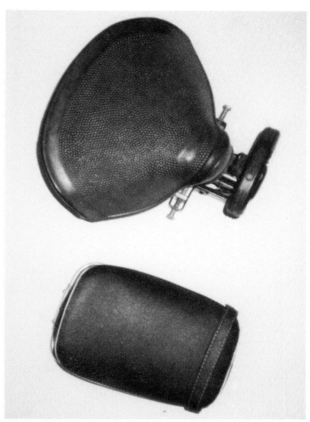

When running with a solo saddle, some provision had to be made for a passenger, and these two accessories were the most popular. At the bottom, the more common Denfeld bread loaf, which bolted to the top of the pressed-steel, flat, fender-top pillion rack. Above, a Denfeld pillion saddle, with hard rubber grab handle, which also fit the same rack.

The seat suspension spring most commonly found on a 1950–1954 BMW. Although this photo is of a seat on an R26 single, the seats were virtually identical with those of the 1950–1954 twins and many excellent restorations sport seats from the R26 or R27 BMW single. Note the three points of adjustment, one at the spring mount, and the other at three locations on the seat frame itself. *Craig Vechorik*

Not only did the seats look good on a BMW, they also provided a measure of comfort that the bench seats were never able to achieve. The fact that the seat swung on its own spring helped cancel out many road shocks, and allowed riders to spend many more hours "in the saddle" than their friends on other brands, and arrive relatively refreshed after a long journey.

Alas BMW, bowing to what was perceived as a desire on the part of prospective buyers for a more modern looking machine, soon made available a bench arrangement, first marketed by Schorsch Meier and carrying his famous signature on the tail. Soon Denfeld got the contract, and replaced the Meier trademark with its own logo on the same metal tag, riveted to the rear of the seat. The original seats were narrow and nice to look at, even when fitted to a pre-Earles fork machine. On a 1955–1969 BMW, however, they look much better. All had a tendency to dry out, and even one in perfect original condition will prove to be uncomfortable now that twenty-five or more years have

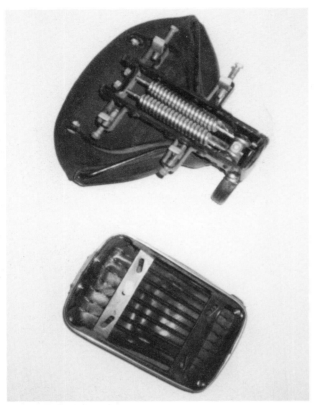

The view from below, showing the small coil springs under the leatherette top of the bread loaf pad, and the adjustable suspension coils of the pillion saddle. Both styles are still available, either as originals or reproductions.

passed. Once the covers are damaged, replacements will never look or fit as well as the originals. In most cases the white piping will not be the same or the aluminum trim will not fit. Restoring a bench seat can end up being much more expensive than buying a complete replacement solo seat with all the components.

To compound the problem of aesthetics, for the American market you could buy a BMW with a Denfeld extra wide dual seat, complete with little grab handles and extra supporting braces. The handles were either aluminum or chrome over steel, and the whole affair looked much too large for the bike. It completely covered the rear fender and was surprisingly uncomfortable, especially after the rubber pad underneath the cover hardened with age. Both the narrow and wide bench seats were suspended internally by the use of long, flat coil springs, much like those we remember from the bunk beds at boot camp. That's probably why most of us prefer the small, rubber solo saddle! Most Earles fork machines are now being restored with the bench seats, unless solo saddles are also favored, while 1950–1954 machines end up with solo saddles exclusively.

The 1955 through 1969 Earles and US-fork models originally also came with a variation of the earlier solo saddles, with rubber tops now made by Denfeld or one of the other manufacturers. The very early 1955 models had a short, vertical coil spring clamped in little concave cups, but soon thereafter all solo seats had what we now call the

An option to the solo saddle was either a narrow Schorsch Meier or Denfeld bench, seen here fitted to a 1955 R69 prototype, which still has the small EBER taillamp with three-screw rim and again, a front fender devoid of the production riveted-on flat, steel, center brace. *BMW Archives*

"silent bloc" seat suspension. This resembled a car engine motor mount, for it was a composition of rubber molded to angled metal brackets. Some adjustment of the silent bloc suspension is possible by moving the base to one of several mounting points on the frame plate of the seat frame T-section. All components are now being reproduced, including the rubber tops.

The Steiger Sanction

In 1983, when the small remaining stocks of original Denfeld saddles were rapidly drying up, an attempt was made to reproduce them. At that time, an American accessory manufacturer and fellow vintage motorcycle enthusiast, seeing the need for a replacement solo saddle for the Earles fork machines, contacted me and borrowed an original, unused Denfeld solo saddle, complete with frame and silent bloc. The aim was to have a complete reproduction made, changing only the name molded into the rubber top. Steiger, a suitable German-sounding name, was chosen, which fit nicely into the elongated oval that previously contained the word Denfeld. The original seat and all the specifications

If your tastes ran to the ultra-large, your BMW could be ordered with an extra-wide Denfeld bench, complete with grab handles for the passenger, which tended to overpower the rear fender. In both size and shape it was nowhere near as pretty as the narrow bench or the rubber solo saddle.

By 1955, all twins had solo saddles with a rubber silent-bloc suspension, though first series R50 and R69 models in 1955 had a single, vertical coil spring. This particular exam-

ple is a 1964 R69S with swinging pillion seat attached to the rear of the driver's saddle. *BMW Archives*

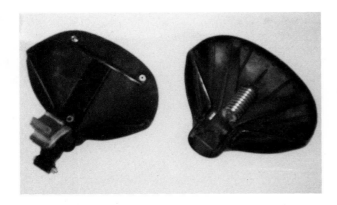

Two views of solo seats, one with coil spring and Y-frame for the 1950–1954 twins; the other with rubber block and T-frame for the 1955–1969 twins.

were sent to a firm in Asia, and soon several thousand Steiger seats, perfect copies of the then-unavailable Denfeld, were being manufactured.

The frame and silent bloc were perfectly executed, and in some ways were better than the original. The 1984 over-the-counter price of $129 was reasonable when compared to the asking price for leftover Denfeld originals. Even the various components could be purchased separately.

Unfortunately, the well-meaning Asian manufacturer, thinking he was improving on the Denfeld design, made the rubber top out of a compound much too soft than had been intended. He failed to realize that the rubber was meant to be hard from the outset, and thought instead that the example he had been given had hardened with age. Consequently, all those beautiful Steiger tops, with their perfectly formed internal metal frames, were much too soft and excruciatingly uncomfortable when sat upon. The rider's thighs immediately bottomed out on the internal framing! What had been an excellent concept was thus fatally flawed, and many of those sold were soon returned.

Happily for the rest of us, the seats were not scrapped and are still being sold today by a number of third parties, albeit at a regrettably higher price

than the originals. If you get a Steiger, the best solution is to replace the rubber top with a currently available Denfeld item. You'll end up with a virtual look-alike of the original German saddle at little more than half the cost. The extra Steiger top, while quite useless, can still be mounted on the framework of a rear pillion saddle, if your intent is to just show the bike with such an accessory, and not subject your passenger to the torture of a too soft rubber saddle. A number of BMW enthusiasts also have swapped the seat tops from rear to front, in retrospect a logical and cost effective solution.

Replacing a Rubber Top

Some years ago, Vintage BMW Club member Oscar Fricke in California decided to chronicle the steps needed to successfully remove and replace a Denfeld or Pagusa rubber top. As these tops are fitted over a tubular metal skeleton, it's a difficult process, worth sharing with you here.

The first step is to remove the seat or seats from the BMW and disassemble the old saddle, noting how all the pieces fit. If the old cover is damaged beyond repair, simply cut it off, and cut your frustration factor in half. If you plan to save or switch the top, the removal is the reverse of the assembly process that follows.

Fill your bathtub with hot, soapy water and let the new top (or the old seat) soak for a while. The heat will make the rubber more pliable. Get a friend to join you in the tub; the work will require two people, so you might as well have fun doing it.

To do the pillion seat, note that metal inserts come in two pieces. The rear metal piece, shaped like a small bow, is relatively easy to put in. The smaller front piece, also rather bow shaped, is also

A more detailed view of the 1955–1969 seat with its T-frame and internal tubing inside the rubber top. Denfeld was the brand most commonly used in the 1955–1969 era.

easy to insert. Make sure that the slightly curved ends protrude out and downward on either side. Try to bend the rubber into the shape that it will take when all is finished. Hook the seat onto the frame backwards and then turn it around so that all that needs to be done is match up the holes for the bolts.

Next is the hardest part, requiring the brute stretching power of two people. With everything in the tub, insert one bolt without the lock washer that normally goes between the seat frame and the rear metal piece. Then put in the other bolt with the lock washer. Now take out the first bolt and put it back in with its own lock washer.

The driver saddle is next. It's easiest to install the front metal piece backwards and upside-down, and then flip it down into the correct position. Next, insert the ends of the front metal piece into the ends of the rear metal piece. It is perhaps best to insert them both at the same time. When one is in, it doesn't seem possible to insert the other afterwards. Again, the strength of two is required. For more leverage, the T-shaped seat frame was bolted onto the rear metal piece backwards. With everything in the hot water, bend the rubber seat while the second person lines up the ends of the two pieces. When the ends are lined up, bend the seat in the other direction so that the pieces engage. You may want to use a hammer or rubber mallet to tap the ends in at this critical moment.

It's not as difficult as the directions seem to indicate. Having a seat in front of you will make it all clear. Don't forget to clean the tub afterwards!

Sidestands and Centerstands

What goes up should stay up, and BMW made certain of this with a strong and easy-to-use centerstand. The same could not be said for the sidestand, which was omitted from most of the model range between 1950 and 1969.

As for the centerstand, all the twins had basically the same design, which was not interchangeable between the 1950–1954 models and the 1955–1969 Earles-fork models that followed. The US-fork 1968-1969 twins had their own stand, and while it will fit the Earles fork twins, it was much taller and interfered with the mufflers. All centerstands had a piece of solid or hollow tubing welded to the left foot, intended as an aid to retracting the stand. It was soon knocked off if the machine ever went down, in spite of the fact that the tab was solidly welded to the stand. Once bent or misaligned, the tab no longer fit into the recess formed for it in the left muffler. Many owners cut them off once they became damaged, but for a proper restoration, your centerstand should have one.

All centerstands were held in the upright position by two short coil springs, which were hooked to the frame at their forward position. The stand

will remain retracted with only one spring, but it's a good idea to carry a spare. They're small and fit easily into the tool kit or can be taped or wired to the frame in some inconspicuous place. A good way to tell if the bike you're about to buy has had more miles than the odometer tells you is to look at the feet of the centerstand. If they're worn clean through, the machine has been up and down on its stand more times than you would care to imagine. If the curved bases are still fairly round, either the stand has been recently replaced, or the BMW is indeed a low mileage model. Contrary to popular belief, most stands were painted black, even on those BMWs delivered in colors other than black. A possible exception is the ex-Polizei machines, where virtually everything was painted green. Occasionally, white machines also had white stands.

Sidestands are another matter. It was not until October 1955 that BMW made provisions on the frame of the Earles-fork models for the fitment of a small pivoting sidestand. A mounting point was welded to the frame, starting with the R50 at frame number 552 530 into which screwed a round 12mm pivot pin. These early pins were of a too small diameter and often fractured. The sidestand, a short tubular affair with a small, half-dollar sized foot, was held in tension by a coil spring clipped to the metal oil pan, which had a small tab attached for that purpose. The stand leg had a triangular rubber block on one side to keep it from contacting the frame when retracted. The whole affair swung neatly out of the way when not in use.

Unfortunately, the leg was quite short, and extreme caution must be used when propping the bike up with just the sidestand. If the ground is too soft or not level, you run the risk of dropping the bike. Pay particular attention to the small cotter pin that keeps the leg on the pivot. If the pin falls out, or gets too worn or bent, the stand can slide down on its pivot, and has been known to pivot in the opposite direction, with disastrous results. Stick to using the centerstand whenever possible, and avoid propping the bike up by the sidestand when subjecting it to the stresses of kickstarting. The US-fork models of 1968–1969 had a longer leg when a sidestand was fitted.

Since prior to 1955 there were no official BMW sidestands, a number of manufacturers tried to make their own. The most famous one was the AKIPP stand, an ingenious design now ardently sought after by restorers of pre-1955 machines. Unfortunately, for all its beauty and utility, it was a most dangerous item, and numerous owners eventually fell victim to its one main flaw, a sudden tendency to drop down and contact the ground. This could be quite disconcerting, especially when cornering left with more than the usual exuberance!

The culprit was the little spring clip that held it up, and the fact that the AKIPP design made use

The exotic AKIPP folding sidestand, seen here fitted to an Earles-fork twin. The AKIPP was designed to fit the 1950–1954 plunger frames, which were a bit lower to the ground than the 1955–1969 twins. Note the spring clip that holds the stand under the footpeg when not in use. This is a new chrome-plated AKIPP currently being reproduced in Germany. *Craig Vechorik*

of the left footpeg. If the rider was not careful, his toe usually caused the stand to gradually drop down, until it finally snapped loose of the clip. The stands were quite effective otherwise, and look quite good when in good condition and properly chromed. Reproductions are just now being made. Again, if you have to have an AKIPP, use it with caution. While AKIPP stands and their mounting footpeg can easily be fitted to a 1955–1969 Earles or US-fork machine, they were really designed for the 1950–1954 plunger BMWs, which sat much lower to the ground. Mounting an AKIPP on a post-1954 machine will cause the bike to lean too far to the left.

Another solution to the sidestand dilemma was a fabrication one finds occasionally at flea markets, made with a piece of heavy steel plate and a readily available leg, usually from a British machine of the period. It was mounted between the engine and frame on the left side, and replaced both of the left side engine bolt spacers. It's sometimes amusing to see a 1955–1969 BMW with this stand mounted incorrectly, on the outside of the frame, after the owner has laboriously fabricated extra long bolts to accommodate the stand!

Finally, Swirin, an American firm, built an accessory stand for the 1955–1969 models that is still being made and is very effective. Unfortunately, it bolted to the frame with a U-bolt, behind the battery carrier on the left side. If not bolted solidly, it has a tendency to change its position, causing damage and rattling noises when the retraced leg contacts the left side muffler. The leg is extraordinarily long and could probably keep the bike upright in deep sand if necessary. The proper mounting of the Swirin stand is not to the lower frame tube between the foot shifter and kickstart bumper, but on the rear frame section near the passenger footpeg bracket. This prevents the mounting hardware from contacting or interfering with the transmission shift lever. The Swirin stand should not be used on a pre-1955 model, because it was not available at that time. It also will not work well if it is fitted, and looks out of place on these machines.

The AKIPP in its folded position, underneath the footpeg bracket which is part of the stand. In this photo, it can easily be understood why a rider's heel could accidentally unclip the stand, causing it to drop to the pavement, something to be avoided if the bike was being ridden at the time. *Craig Vechorik*

Chapter 15

Exhaust System

All BMWs have for decades been known for their silence, a reputation that's an outgrowth of a both a well-executed and effective exhaust system and the generally quiet mechanical design of the various drivetrain components. While other brands both annoy and impress their riders and bystanders with loud mechanical clatter and a raucous exhaust, BMWs were equally impressive by their silence.

A Complex Concept

All this was not without cost, however. Mufflers were filled with complex baffles, which were not only expensive to make, but which also provided numerous areas where moisture could be trapped. The resultant longevity of the mufflers was thereby severely compromised, especially on machines that received infrequent use. We've all heard the horror stories of mufflers rotting out while still in the wrappers. The best way to preserve your mufflers is not to ride the machine less, but ride it more often, in order to blow out the accumulated moisture on a regular basis.

Adding to the cost of BMW exhaust systems are several sets of non-interchangeable pipes, a fragile cross-over connector, a resonator for the early R69 instead of a cross-over, two styles of exhaust port clamps, four styles of mufflers (with separate exhaust diameter variations within those), and separate muffler shapes for the left and right sides! It's enough to make young men cower, and old men weep, especially when it comes time to find the right systems for your particular machine. To make matters worse, the German authorities in 1954 decreed that the old style finned mufflers were too loud, even for a BMW, which resulted in the scrapping of most old stocks, the hurried installation of tubular salami styles, and the use of S-pipe adapters on the pre-1954 models to make all these things fit. Happily, now that these older BMWs are all considered antiques, owners can once again fit the older style fishtails. To cater to the demand, a number of firms, both in the U.S. as well as Australia and Germany, are again manufacturing excellent examples in both chrome steel and stainless.

Mufflers: 1950–1954

The pre-1955 machines had three types of mufflers: two with fishtails and the later-required salami style. By 1954 all came with the tubular mufflers and S-bend adapters, or else with pipes with the S-bend built right in. The 1950 R51/2 and early R67 and R51/3 had fishtail mufflers on which the fishtails were of unequal length, with the lower one being longer. All very much prewar in design and nice to look at. By mid-1951, the lower fin was trimmed back to resemble the upper one, both for reasons of aesthetics and as a safety improvement; the longer, lower fin had gained a deserved reputation as an ankle-biter. The fishtails were dropped

The typical finned muffler setup seen in the early 1950s. In this example on a prewar R71, notice the longer lower fin used on the R51/2, early R67, and R51/3. By mid-1951, both upper and lower fins had been shortened and made the same length. *Rich Sheckler*

After September 1954, due to new German noise regulations, finned mufflers were no longer allowed and BMW, as well as other manufacturers, switched to longer and better baffled salami mufflers, as seen here on a 1954 R68. *BMW Archives*

bend adapter pipes had to be added, to which the new style mufflers were attached.

To further complicate things, the centerstand operating lever would now interfere with the mufflers, so it had to be cut off flush with the stand and a new lever, carrying the old BMW number 251 5 69 007 09, had to be welded on. All this in the interest of silence, for a motorcycle that, in all likelihood, was already the world's most silent! Now, forty years later, BMW owners of 1950–1954 machines are going to great lengths and greater expense to restore and retrofit those fishtail mufflers and those longer pipes that the German noise regulations of September 1954 eliminated.

All three styles of the 1950–1954 mufflers were extensively baffled, with a series of tubes and perforated plates, much like the inside of a locomotive boiler. These internal "foofy tubes" were excellent moisture traps, and most mufflers lasted no more than a few seasons before developing ripples and bulges, the first telltale signs of terminal internal rot.

There's little that could be done to save them once the rot ensued. Some stop-gap measures, such as pouring aluminum paint or Rustoleum through the mufflers, required removal of the mufflers, and only served to delay the inevitable. Pouring used oil through them also did little to preserve the muf-

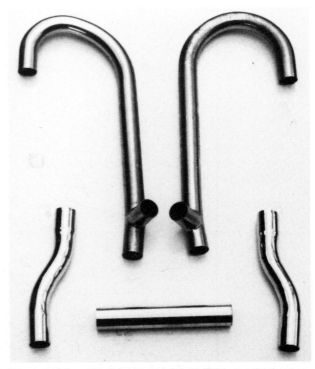

Fitment of the new tubular salami mufflers required extensive modifications to existing exhaust systems, which consisted of shortening the length and the fitting S-bend adapters. The system shown here is for an R68.

on all BMW motorcycles produced after September 1, 1954, per order of the German transportation authorities, to conform to the new anti-noise regulations, which limited output for all motorcycles over 250cc to 87 decibels.

Their replacement, the less pretty but still nice-to-look-at salami, or tubular styles, allowed only a moderate decibel level at the exhaust tip, an improvement over the earlier fishtails. To fit the new required mufflers, the ends of the exhaust pipes on the R68 had to be shortened to 2.75in, while the pipes on the other 1950–1964 twins had to be shortened to 3.2in, as measured from the center of the transverse connecting tube. Then, two S-

flers, although it probably helped keep down the mosquito population! Desperate owners were known to plug the salami mufflers with corks to keep out the moisture when the bikes were idle, an amusing tactic, especially when the bike was restarted with the corks still in place. The best solution is to replace the mufflers with stainless ones, which are now readily available, and not as expensive as one might think.

Exhaust Pipes

Pipes for the R51 and R67 series' were fixed to the cylinder head exhaust ports with threaded ring clamps, which were tightened or loosened with a hook wrench from the tool kit. This also holds true for the 1955–1969 R50 and R60 series. After enduring skinned knuckles and burned hands, smart owners usually purchased Matra tool 338/1, which was the dealer's version of the hook wrench, but more robust and with a longer handle. Others made up their own from factory drawings. Owners not so smart used a plumber's pipe wrench, which not only damaged the ring clamp, but was also notorious for compressing a balky ring and stripping the exhaust threads. Fracture of the exhaust port threaded stub was also a distinct possibility. If you have a plumber's wrench, keep it under the sink and away from your BMW. Keep it there next to the ViseGrips, another item from your tool kit that

should never come near your BMW.

At this time, it should be mentioned that the one item that is an absolute necessity when working on exhaust threads is a pipe joint compound called by various names such as NevaSeize. It's basically a petroleum-based silvery graphite paste, applied with a small brush. It and others under different names are available at any auto parts house or plumber's supply. Coat the exhaust port threads liberally each time you remove the exhaust system and you'll never run the risk of stripped exhaust threads. If you do have the misfortune of stripping your threads, a number of Vintage Club members now do excellent restoration work for reasonable fees. Their names are listed in the appendix.

If the ring clamp is so badly cross threaded that it cannot be removed, carefully cut across the clamp with a hacksaw until it is split, then remove it. New clamps are still being made, and can be refitted to the pipes on the R51 and R67 series, as well as the R50 and R60 and their /2 variants, by carefully softening the flanged end of the pipes and slipping them over. Judicious reheating of the pipe end and straightening everything out will make for an undetectable repair. If your ring clamp is scarred and pitted but still serviceable, cover it with an aftermarket finned aluminum accessory, which clamps over the ring and does much to dress up the machine. It looks identical to the finned ring

The standard system as seen on this R69S sported long, heavy, and extensively baffled tubular mufflers that did an excellent job of quieting the machine. They also were ex-cellent moisture traps and were prone to rust. *Richard Kahn, Butler & Smith,.*

clamp that actually did double duty as a pipe clamp on the R68, R69, R50S, and R69S models. Many a knowledgeable enthusiast has shown his ignorance when confronted with a lowly R50/2 fitted with accessory finned exhaust clamps by telling his companions that the machine is an S model!

The exhaust pipes on the sports R68, R69, R50S, and R69S models had slip rings and finned aluminum clamps, which could still be tightened by use of the hook wrench. A better way to work on them was to purchase the massive cast iron or aluminum clamping handle, Matra part number 338/2, which is still available from your dealer. It makes working on the machine a snap, but unfortunately the tool is too large to carry in your tool kit. They do fit easily into the trunk of a sidecar, and are handy for clubbing fish, mashing potatoes, and warding off angry dogs. Again, use NevaSeize liberally when working on your exhaust threads. Keeping an old screw-top aluminum 35mm film can full of the stuff in your tool box is also a good idea in case you need to do some exhaust work while on the road.

Mufflers: 1955–1969

By 1955, BMW had improved the size and shape of the mufflers, even though the engines and exhaust pipes had remained the same. Gone were the S-bend pipes, but now the mufflers were longer, fatter, and even more silent that their pre-1955 salami predecessors. They were also even more prone to rot out, and did so at an even faster rate. Again, exact look-alike replacements are available, either directly via your BMW dealer or as aftermarket improvements in stainless. Don't be dismayed if all you can get are the S mufflers, which

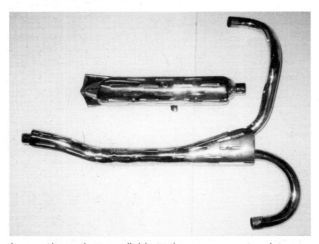

Among the options available to the racer were two-into-one systems made by Hoske for the BMW. This system is designed to fit a 1952 R68 ISDT machine, and still sports the short fin fishtail muffler. In Germany these are referred to as swallowtail mufflers.

have a larger diameter exhaust tip. In many cases, that's all that's available. You shouldn't be penalized in a concours for using them. Remember that the left and right version of all 1955–1969 mufflers are different, for the left has a small depression underneath to clear the centerstand pull up lever, while the right has a flat spot on the top to prevent interference with the foot brake assembly.

The Cross-Over

All side pipes from 1950 through 1969 were connected by a cross-over pipe that joined the left and right pipes transversely under the engine. Its purpose was to balance the exhaust pulses and to help quiet the exhaust noise at the muffler outlets. Amuse your friends by plugging up one muffler with the palm of your hand; the BMW will continue to run and won't even skip a beat! The pipe is hidden from view, quite inaccessible, and consequently forgotten until it rots out. Try to get underneath the machine on a regular basis and clean the outside of the pipe. Replacements are cheap, but to replace one requires the total removal of at least one side of your exhaust system. If the corrosion is allowed to go unchecked, it will eventually attack the side pipes as well, which will mean you'll soon be replacing more than just the cross-over pipe.

All cross-over pipes are the same for all models, but just to confuse the enthusiast, and to serve as an excellent trivia question and concours tie-breaker, the early R69 had a small resonator instead of a plain unbaffled cross-over pipe. Few if any R69 models are today fitted with this elusive bit of exhaust pipe trivia. Eventually someone will get around to making a reproduction, but since the application is so limited it may not warrant the investment. If you can find one sitting on some dusty dealer's shelf, snap it up, even if you don't have an R69. You should be able to trade it for something equally rare and desirable with a single ad in the classified section of the *Vintage BMW Bulletin*!

Exhaust System Variations

Sports mufflers, such as those made by Hoske, and special two-into-one high pipes, such as those fitted to ISDT machines, are nonstandard but very desirable and authentic period accessories. The Hoske mufflers were simple, long, thin, tapered megaphones, with a removable insert. They are rare to find as originals, but reproductions are being made. The two-into-one pipes are much rarer, and more complex, and consequently not yet being reproduced. Two versions exist, one for the pre-1955 machines, which had both finned and salami mufflers, all shrouded under some nice looking perforated heat shields. Again, Hoske made these for BMW and they were available on special order for the R68 and R69 for use on trials machines. The first prototype R68 was exhibited with such pipes,

Earles fork machines could also be fitted with custom systems, as seen here on this 1957 R69. Regretfully, I sold both the BMW and its exhaust system some years ago.

A pair of ersatz finned exhaust nuts, which look very nice over the regular ring clamps on a R50 or R60 or earlier models. Next to it, a BMW original for the R68, R69 and R69S series.

In competition, high pipes and a single muffler were required wear for ISDT competitors. Pictured is Sebastian Nachtmann on his R69S at the 1961 Six Days Trials in England. *Ulrich Schwab*

and several examples of this model have recently been restored in the U.S. in this configuration. There are also documented examples of such ISDT pipes being fitted to the R50 and R60 Earles-fork models. Naturally, the flanged ends replaced the slip rings on these versions. Again, if you run across a set for any of these models, buy it.

To Replate or Replace?

Finally, it should be noted that the plating on the original pipes, as well as the actual gauge of the metal, is thin, especially when compared to more contemporary machines. Running your BMW with a too lean carburetor setting will cause the pipes to discolor on the ends near the cylinder heads. If the pipes get rusted and pitted, there's little metal left to polish out and replate, so it may be better to just discard the old pipes and purchase new ones. Once they're dented, it's probably the only solution because the dents can never be effectively removed. Additionally, most plating shops will probably not want to contaminate their tanks with rusty old pipes, which will probably have all sorts of carbon and oil deposits still lurking inside. Save everyone a lot of aggravation, and yourself money in the long run, by getting new pipes. Nothing detracts more from an otherwise excellent restoration than a poorly restored exhaust system. Mufflers, incidentally, cannot be effectively restored at all, once internal rot has started, and most plating shops will show you the door if you come in with a set of used mufflers.

Chapter 16

Painting, Plating, Emblems, and Insignia

The Color of the Beast

"Any color as long as it's black" no longer holds true for the BMW, at least not since 1970. However, even prior to the modern era with its airbrushed "Silver Smoke R90S" and enough metal flake colors for the other models to put a rainbow to shame, BMWs were available in something other than the basic black. Tanks in the 1930s often had blue centers on the top. White, red, or green machines were used by police forces in Europe and elsewhere. The military had its own versions in gray, green, and desert tan. Nevertheless, most of the 1950–1969 BMWs you'll encounter today will be in black with white pinstriping and only a moderate use of chrome.

The Unpolished BMW

First, let's eliminate the polished and plated engine myth. BMW never polished or plated any part of their engines, transmissions, or rear drive cases. In fact, a factory bulletin was sent to all dealers in May 1952 specifically warning them about mirror polishing or plating portions of the engine and stating that no warranties would be honored if such a practice was embarked upon by any owners.

There is, of course, a sound reason for this. The original finish of the engine cases and other large castings is rough and irregular by design. This finish greatly increased the surface area for heat dissipation. Polishing or plating removes the finish, with the consequence of increased heat retention, which will hasten engine wear and eventual engine failure.

The only polished items on any BMW in the 1950–1969 era were aluminum wheel rims, aluminum control levers, the pre-1955 steering damper, hand-shift lever, and foot shifter, the kickstart lever (on the 1955–1969 models) and the gas cap. Chrome-plated items were limited to steel rims, foot shifters, and kick levers on the pre-1955 models; fender braces, grab handles, handlebars and risers, steering damper knobs, wheel spokes and nipples, headlamp rims, speedometer bezel, and taillamp rims for the 1955–1969 models. Exhaust pipes naturally were plated, as were the mufflers. Nuts and bolts visible to the owner were either cadmium plated or painted black, with only a few, such as the bolts for the handlebar risers, being plated. On the 1950–1954 models, the driveshaft and coupling pieces were plated, and the dome over the U-joint, if made of steel, was plated. Later, non-choke air cleaners, as used after 1962 on all the twins, were sometimes chrome plated, and that's about it.

Doing anything not seen in factory sales literature or press photos is inauthentic, will run you extra money, and will cost you points in any concours or show. Chrome or mirror polish for purely show reasons or ego gratification will not make for an authentic restoration, no matter how much it may please your own personal tastes, and will not make the bike go any faster or last any longer.

We've all seen BMWs where virtually everything, including the frame and fenders was plated. While this may be fine for a circus high-wire act, excessive plating only weakens the machine, again due to hydrogen embrittlement. To embark upon a restoration of a BMW once totally plated is a foolish endeavor, for every bit of plated material must first be painstakingly stripped before any restoration can begin. Highly polished parts, such as valve covers or other castings must first be unpolished by bead blasting. The list of tasks goes on and on. Better to start with a neglected but original machine than with a BMW polished to a high luster.

Painting and Prepping

The procedures involved in preparing and painting a motorcycle are not within the scope of this book. If you're an accomplished painter and have the equipment and facilities to prepare and paint your own machine, there's little more that I could teach you. For the amateur, I can only recommend that you clean the machine as much as possible, remove all the parts to be painted, and after all the sheet metal has been straightened and repaired, take it all to a competent painter who has a history of painting motorcycles. Ask your friends or anyone with a custom chopper at a gathering of motorcycles. Everyone has a favorite painter that they could recommend to others. Whatever your choice, don't embarrass yourself and the painter by bringing in oily and greasy parts. At the hourly rate the painter will charge you, you don't want him to spend half of his time cleaning parts you could have cleaned yourself with store bought solvents and some rags.

For minor touch-ups, or for those intent upon actually painting some small items themselves,

there are a few things you can do. Sanding off as much of the old paint with wet sandpaper and then steel wool will provide a good base. There's no need to strip the paint to bare metal. However, it's worth noting that many paints are incompatible, and unless you know what the original paint was, you're probably better off to strip to bare metal. Spray on a good quality sandable primer, and wet sand between coats; two or three coats should be sufficient. Then try a trick I learned years ago. Paint the parts with a brush! Not just any brush, but the best qual-

An R69S with the standard narrow bench seat, small tank, and non-choke air cleaner. The finish of the cast aluminum parts should be a slightly glossy but non-reflective pewter texture. A detail study for the restorer, painter, and striper—this is how a pre-1967 BMW should look. *Richard Kahn, Butler & Smith, Inc.*

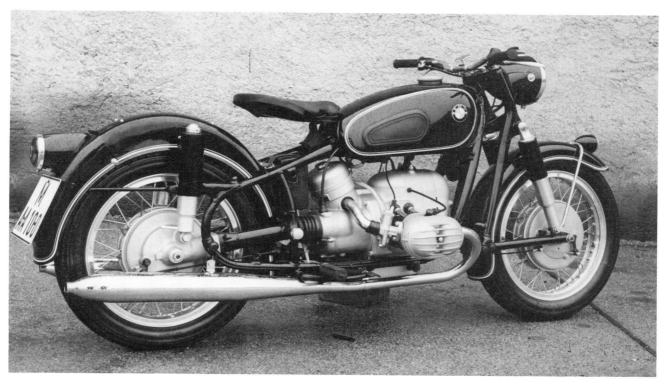

Never before seen, BMW's Earles fork 1955 R50 prototype, which serves as an excellent example of where the proper pinstriping should go. The front fender is missing its flat steel center brace, and the Hella taillamp is higher than on subsequent production models. The small front fender lamp was a styling exercise that thankfully was never put into production. *BMW Archives*

ity one inch sable brush you can find. In all cases, never use lacquer over enamel, as the lacquer will lift the old paint.

For paint, I've used Martin-Seynour No. 8000 Brilliant Black, an enamel, with great success. Brush it on unthinned out of the can and let it flow from the brush. Let it dry in a dust free environment, then wet sand with 600-grit sandpaper and brush paint again. After wet sanding the second coat, polish with a paste such as 3M Imperial Hand Glaze, No. 051131-05990, then wax. It will look like the original finish. I have painted an entire frame this way, with the engine still in place, after carefully cleaning off all traces of oil and grease and masking off the parts not to be painted. The results were so good that it was hard to convince people it was done with a brush. Fenders and large surfaces, such as tanks, are best left to the experts and sprayed with a gun. Small pieces, like stands, braces, seat brackets, and footpegs respond well to even the most shaky hand wielding a sable brush.

A Whiter Shade of Pale

On the subject of color, not every black is black. The Germans seem to have perfected the color, however. Go to your BMW dealer and buy a quart or pint of his black, and give it to your

Rear fender striping details on the 1955 prototype. Note that the brake rod and levers on both front and rear brakes were painted black. *BMW Archives*

A white R69S, now fitted with the Hella taillamp in the correct location, and a front fender with flat steel center strap. The extra-wide dual seat has grab handles and short vertical supporting braces. Both fenders and large sport tank have black striping. *Richard Kahn, Butler & Smith, Inc.*

Another white BMW, this time a 1965 R69S with large Heinrich tank striped to match the machine. The tank sports large aluminum BMW car emblems, which were standard on most Heinrich tanks of that era.

painter. Other colors are another story. While a white BMW may attract a lot of attention, once the paint starts to chip, especially at places where it has been worn off by the tightening of fasteners and bolts, rust bleeds will start, which will be an unsightly brown and will require constant attention.

There are also other reasons to stick with black. Most accessory items of the 1950–1969 era were made for black machines, including large tanks, saddle bags, sidestands, and fairings, as well as sidecars. Many of these will have to be repainted to match your newly restored non-black BMW. There were also several shades of white, from pure white to a creamy Dover white. As for other colors beyond white and black, some BMWs came in two variations of red, as well as a teal blue, and of course green. The modern equivalent of the original, much-sought-after "Bavarian Cream" is GM paint code #59 "Frost Beige," as used on the 1979–1985 Buick. It's still available both in bulk and in touch-up bottles.

If you're determined to paint your machine in a color other than black, be warned that the frames in some cases were still painted black, while others matched the color of the tanks, fenders, and headlight. The most pleasing is a machine where all the parts are the same color, but even here there are pitfalls. Tire pumps, which were manufactured by such German firms as SKS and never by BMW, only came in black. To paint one white or red is incorrect. Only police bikes in green ended up with green pumps, and that's probably because the entire machines were often repainted as a unit. Generally, white machines were all white, except for the centerstand and pump. Some came through with black frames, which was not as pleasing to the eye. Again, there are always some rare exceptions.

No matter what color you have painted the machine, striping will have to complement the base color. Black machines had white striping, which may eventually fade to a cream. White bikes were usually striped in black, blue machines in white or the occasional dark red, green machines in white.

All striping should be applied by hand. (Striping location and widths are discussed in Chapter 8.) Masking off the lines with tape is a common, inexpensive shortcut, one which is easily recognized by any competent judge and which will cost you points. The application of colored Mylar tape is another oft-seen amateur effort. Not only does it look unsightly, it soon puckers at the edges, and the width is often not the same as the original metric measurements. Use of Imron or other acrylics not available in the years the machine was produced will also count against you, since good quality lacquers and enamels are still readily available, as are competent hand stripers. Imron presents a glossy "wet" look, especially in black, even without polish-

ing. Use of Imron has declined due to its carcinogenic properties. Clear coating over striping or Mylar tape may give an exceptionally smooth finish and mirror-like appearance, but once the clear coat is dinged or chipped, it's virtually impossible to touch up or polish out. Some good results have recently been obtained by powder coating frames and small parts, but this seems to work well only on sections where no large flat surfaces are found. Fenders and tanks do not lend themselves well to powder coating.

Chrome Versus Stainless

Most chrome-plated items, such as wheel rims, should not be restored and then replated if factory original replacements can be found. In the long run, it's better to buy new items than to straighten, polish, and plate used ones. Not only will you save time and money, you'll also be able to recover part of your expenses by possibly selling the unrestored, original items to another enthusiast who may have neither the time nor the money to procure new parts. Many a derelict BMW has been made to run again quite reliably and successfully with used, but nevertheless usable parts. A number of firms and individuals are flourishing in the U.S. and Germany by providing inexpensive, reliable used parts to restorers of these older BMWs.

Stainless fasteners are another matter. Rusted old nuts and bolts can occasionally be brought back to their original state, though polishing them is difficult, especially where small items and fine threads are concerned. It may be better to purchase stainless equivalents for all those rusted fasteners. Most cadmium plated bolt heads will look just as good when replaced by stainless. Good selections of all sizes are usually found at marinas or shops catering to the sailing enthusiast. Some of the larger stepped washers with the chamfered edges are impossible to find in stainless, and these must either be restored or purchased new.

If you're determined to refinish your own small nuts and bolts, an electroless nickel process can often give you a finish similar to that of brushed stainless or cadmium plate. Try your local gunsmith or gun dealer; this plating process is popular with handgun owners. You can purchase an inexpensive kit that will replate virtually all the small parts found on the BMW. A mixture of salts and acids are used, and it can all be done in your garage, workshop, or kitchen.

Remember, don't plate what was originally painted. BMW probably had a good reason not to plate it, and in most cases it was for reasons of reliability, not cost, that a part was painted rather than plated or polished.

The Tank Emblem

All BMWs built prior to 1970 had fired cloi-

BMW always took pride in its distinctive logo, and still guards its use jealously, even though it has been seen in various forms for nearly eighty years. This early piece of 1930s advertising art shows the gold lettered serif style, just one of many variations in use over the past half century. *BMW Archives*

The famous postwar gold letter serif emblem, which should be used on all 1950–1966 BMWs. This example is the large, convex porcelain enamel dealer wall sign that can still be found in both original and reproduction form. Just the thing to dress up a workshop, office, or den.

Another serif emblem, executed in cloisonné enamel, and fitted to a 1938 BMW R12. Note that the letters are of a slightly different shape and more compressed near the top of the logo. This emblem briefly appeared on very early examples of the R51/2. *Rich Sheckler*

sonné enamel tank emblems, which were held on with two slotted, oval-headed screws. Only during World War II were certain machines fitted with stamped tin and painted emblems. Almost any BMW built prior to 1970 that you encounter today will have had its emblems repaired or replaced at one time or another. The success of that repair or replacement depended upon the knowledge of the owner. It's not uncommon to encounter a machine with mismatched emblems or emblems totally wrong for that particular model. The following will show you how to avoid the pitfalls.

From 1950 to mid-1966, the official factory authorized emblem in use on both BMW cars and motorcycles had serif letters, that is, letters with little tails on the tops, bottom, and ends. After mid-1966, the modern BMW letters were depicted in a sans-serif style, without the little styling tails. The letters after 1966 were silver on a black background, which surrounded the quartered circle of blue and white. Lines separated all the fields, also in silver or chrome. Prior to 1966, all silver letters and lines were either gold or silver, with a preponderance of the gold being found in the early 1950s.

Some early 1950 R51/2 models had prewar emblems, where the letters were squeezed together more at the top of the black circle than on the later postwar models. This was probably due to the factory using up leftover stocks of old emblems. All the original emblems, by the way, were crafted by the firm of Carl Dillenius, in Pfortzheim, Germany, and are marked so on the reverse side. Only recently have reproductions appeared. Prior to a few years ago, a damaged emblem was irreplaceable and had to be painstakingly restored.

Most emblems are damaged not by accident or by the ravages of time, but purely by the overzealous wielding of a screwdriver by a prior owner. It's always nice to give those screws just one more turn, or to try to line up the heads the way you imagined the factory lined them up (the factory never did, by the way). Invariably, the black enamel would fracture. Occasionally, an emblem would fall to the ground from a workbench, resulting in further damage, perhaps to the blue and white fields. Rarely, the blue colors would fade to a paler blue or turn an odd purple hue. Most likely, the original plating will start to flake away, which explains why so many previously silver lettered serif emblems have been polished down to their base layer of copper.

If a new or new-old-stock replacement cannot be found, repairs can be attempted. Incidentally, emblems should be replaced in pairs. There's nothing worse than a nice shiny new emblem on one side of the tank and a scratched and chipped one on the other. Always replace the emblems with a similar and correct style for that era. Serif lettering is incorrect for any post-1966 BMW. Modern sans-serif emblems look totally out of place on a pre-1966 machine for the same reason.

To repair a minor chip, clean the damaged area with a lacquer thinner, then fill in the spot with matching color lacquer. This works best in the black areas, but good results have been achieved with blue and white as well. You won't be able to fill in the damage all at once. It may take several applications. Since lacquer dries rapidly, this can be done in one evening. Polish off the excess with a good polishing compound such as Simichrome. Be careful not to rub the compound on the undamaged areas, as it might dull the porcelain finish.

If the damage is too great, and you can't buy a suitable replacement, you'll have to have the cloisonné enamel professionally restored. Seek out a firm that advertises in hobby journals such as *Hemmings Motor News* as doing such work for owners of vintage cars. The cost will not be cheap, and might run you more than the cost of a set of originals or quality reproductions.

Accessory items such as chrome trim rings that mounted under the emblems were popular in the 1950–1969 era, and are now being reproduced in polished stainless. They add much to the appearance of the tank, especially if used in conjunction with the large capacity models.

When the emblems are either restored or replaced, spring for a new set of screws. They're cheaper than trying to restore the old mangled and rusted originals. Put a drop of LocTite in the

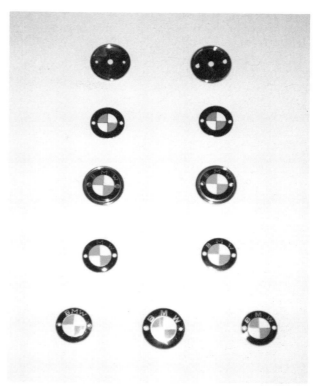

Not all BMW emblems are alike, and some people make a hobby of collecting the dozens of styles. In the top row, a pair of the reproduction stainless emblem trim rings, a popular 1960s accessory. The next row shows a pair of non-serif post-1966 tank emblems, in use in this size until 1969. The next row, a pair of serif emblems and their trim rings. Below that, just the serif emblems, with gold or polished copper trim and letters. In the row at the bottom, the left emblem is a serif style from a prewar twin, with the letters squeezed together near the top. The middle emblem is the large cloisonné enamel tank emblem first used on the 1970 /5 series, and the rightmost is the non-serif 1967–69 style.

threaded holes in the tank, use new rubber pads, and don't overtighten the screws.

Other Emblems and Insignia

Although a 1950 to 1969 BMW has numerous versions of its logo on the engines and frame (someone once counted nearly a dozen examples), there's little to differentiate one model from another. While nearly everyone can spot an R68 immediately, there's little to help us distinguish the R69 from the R69S, or the R50 and R60 series from the R50S.

Since the S models were the top of the line and BMW's flagships on the Autobahn and newly laid out American Interstates, something had to be done to give owners of the high-performance machines a little something extra to show for the extra dollars they had just spent. After all, when the motorcycles are parked all in a row, no amount of horsepower locked up in that engine will be visible to the passing observer.

Therefore, BMW decided somewhat belatedly to put little tags on the tails of its R69S and R50S. Early versions of the R69S had no such tags, nor did any but the very last of the 1,634 R50S models produced in 1961, it's only year. Those that did had little die-cast letters, chrome-plated, stuck into the rear fender just below the hinge. They invariably became pitted or were pried off by eager little hands with a penknife or screwdriver. Exact replacements are not being made. Originals can run into three figures if you find someone willing to part with one. Now and then, a few handmade ones appear, usually executed in sterling silver, but these are items too risky to be left out in the open, on a back fender of any motorcycle, BMW or other-wise. Some reproductions just now appearing out of eastern Europe have mis-shapen letters and are easy to spot; these are best avoided.

The best solution is to mail your pitted one, heavily insured, to a restoration shop specializing in restoring and replating pot-metal emblems. Be sure and warn them of the fragility of the item; once the tabs are broken off or the sharp edges of the letters and numbers are polished round, the emblem is worse than useless.

Tank emblems and other embellishments are the signature of your machine. To neglect them reflects badly on any restoration, and displays the machine in less than a good light. Your emblems will be the first thing a viewer notices; they should be the last thing he remembers.

Chapter 17

Sidecars

An owner or restorer of a 1950–1969 BMW eventually will think about mounting a sidecar to his vintage or classic BMW twin. Like all such endeavors, exercise caution from the outset to avoid disaster. We're not just talking about mechanical mayhem to your engine and drivetrain, we're talking a real threat to your safety and the safety of others. Leaping into the world of sidecars without so much as a careful study of the problems involved is a sure guarantee that something will go wrong.

True, all the 1950–1969 BMWs (with the exception of the R68 prior to frame number 650 924 and most of the 1968-1969 US-fork models) were designed from the outset to handle a sidecar. The frames came complete with welded on lugs and attaching points. Earles forks were designed with provisions for adjusting the trail when sidecars were mounted. BMW even provided supplemental gear sets in ratios ideally suited for sidecar work. VDO made specially geared speedometers. Springs and rims were available in an extra robust size to accommodate the extra loads. BMW even assembled certain models, such as the R67/3, directly with the sidecar attached, renaming the TR500 Steib product as their own Typ 284/3, usually referred to in the sales literature as the BMW Spezial. Owner's manuals had special sections on installing and running with a sidecar.

Nevertheless, it's a foolish owner indeed who simply mounts up a sidecar of his choice without first learning what is in store for him when he sets out on the Autobahn or Interstate on three wheels instead of two.

The Choices

First, a prospective sidecar owner should investigate what's available. While a number of sidecars are still being made today, most are of the plastic variety and ill suited, in both design and style, to a pre-1970 BMW. Older plastic concoctions, such as the British Watsonian, are robust and heavy. With their small road wheel, however, they don't look right on a BMW. Most plastic sidecars are too light to work well on any sort of motorcycle, BMW or otherwise.

Steel sidecars, on the other hand, are usually heavier, better made, and often complement the BMW styling of the 1950–1969 era. Unfortunately, most are by now as old the BMW you're restoring, and most have probably suffered more than the motorcycle in those intervening years. While it's quite easy to bring a motorcycle inside and out of the weather, sidecars, due to their bulk, are left outside

A very desirable combination of BMW R60/2 and BMW Spezial sidecar. When using the optional Hella bar-end signals, only one blinker was used in the handlebar; the other was mounted on a special base on the sidecar fender. *Richard Kahn, Butler & Smith, Inc.*

or covered with some sort of plastic, hastening their destruction. Steib sidecars, for all their strength and craftsmanship, were prone to rust out, like their other well-built and sophisticated German contemporaries, Mercedes and Porsche cars.

Steib has long since gone out of business, but a number of German entrepreneurs, as well as those in other countries, are producing some creditable copies. Out of India, we had the Globe, a solid Steib LS200 and S-350 look-alike, regrettably no longer being imported. Most came with smallish road wheels, but these could easily be upgraded to at least a 16in size. Out of China, we've seen a variety of military units, really quite crude, but almost exact duplicates of the military Steib sidecars fitted to BMW R12 and R75 models from the late 1930s up to 1945. From Russia, we've all seen the ubiquitous Ural sidecar, again a Steib military copy. Early versions of the Ural even had leaf springs, an opening trunk, and both 19in road and spare wheels, just like their true WW II Steib predecessors. If you find any of these for sale today, investigate them carefully. Many may have had a previous life as members of the military and could be hiding dozens of repairs and fractures. If the mounts have been altered so as to fit something other than a BMW, pass it up.

If you're lucky enough to be offered a true Steib, verify that fact by checking for the nameplate, usually riveted somewhere to the frame and easily visible. Inside the trunk, brazed to the floor, should be a little metal tag bearing the name Steib and some sort of body number. If it's a round nosed Steib, there should be a cast aluminum plate on the front with the Steib logo, although some Steibs were also manufactured with the logo of the motorcycle there instead. Wheel nuts should have the Steib logo as well, or else the motorcycle manufacturer's logo. Steib sidecars of the mid-1950s to the end of production were fitted with the characteris-

Another BMW Spezial, which is what they called a catalog Steib TR500 when it was delivered to the BMW factory and installed prior to delivery. In such instances, the Steib's distinctive cobra handle was deleted, or replaced with a Hella turn signal. The spare tire was a BMW road wheel and could be used as either a spare for the sidecar or the BMW. *Richard Kahn, Butler & Smith, Inc.*

If your didn't get a Spezial or a Steib TR500, perhaps the round nose Steib S500 was more to your liking. This is most commonly referred to as the cucumber or bullet nose Steib, and is seen here mounted to a Zündapp KS601. *Warren Mann*

Everyone got into the act for a while. This is a Globe from India, a nice knock-off of the long out-of-production Steib LS200. Regretfully, the Globe is also no longer being produced, but examples still turn up now and then. *David Braun*

From Holland, we were once able to get a close copy of the Steib TR500 called the Hollandia, but by the late 1960s even these had ceased being manufactured. Note the slightly different trunk shape, the absence of a spare tire, and the open fender, which distinguished the Hollandia from the Steib. *Richard Kahn, Butler & Smith, Inc.*

An interesting alternative to the Steib is this 1939 Stoye, mounted here on a postwar R51/3. Compare this German original to the modern postwar French Precision further on. *Jonathan Hayt*

156

tic cobra handle, a beautifully designed and executed running light-cum-grab handle that mounted to the top of the fender. Most Steibs were designed for European mounting on the right-hand side of the motorcycle. Those for the British market were provided with reversed frames and attachments, so the sidecars could be mounted on the left side as was British practice. Occasionally a left -hand Steib turns up in the U.S.. If you are offered one, buy it anyway. It can always be traded for one more appropriate to your BMW.

Whole books could be written about Steib sidecars alone, and a number of small booklets describing some of the hundreds of German and other European brands available during the 1930–1960 era are still in print in Germany. The most common European brands, other than the Steib, that one occasionally encounters in the U.S. are the Hollandia, Kali, Stoye, Stolz, Felber, and Bender and Nimbus. All are of steel, look similar, and look equally well when mounted on a BMW. The Dutch Hollandia, once imported exclusively by the former US BMW importer Butler and Smith, was ideally suited to the BMW, and looked much like its Steib TR500

In the early 1970s, an American living in Denmark got out the old Bender tooling and produced, for a brief time, this Bender-Florin copy of an early postwar Bender. They sold for under $800 and with the exception of using gaudy pink vinyl upholstery, were quite well made. Occasionally one turns up at flea markets, and all are worth considering. *John Remillard*

Out of France, as recently as the early 1990s, this Precision sidecar was a near exact copy of the prewar German Stoye.

It was available for a number of motorcycles, including the BMW. *L'Atelier Precision*

157

The original 1953 Bender SM, on which John Remillard's Bender-Florin was based. The Bender's trunk was a bit smaller than on the copy, but in most other respects it was the same. *Marie Lacko*

An Austrian "Felber" sidecar, manufactured after WW II but in a style reminiscent of pre-war models. An extraordinarily beautiful item, especially when fitted with the Richter "Kabine" top and windshields. The motorcycle is a postwar 494cc NSU "Konsul". *Marie Lacko*

counterpart. Some off brands, such as early examples of the Jawa or the lightweight aluminum Hungarian Duna occasionally turn up, along with some reproductions of earlier designs, like the Bender-Florin and Precision. Again, all look good on a BMW.

A Quick Tour of the Steibs

Since the sidecar of choice for a BMW is most often a Steib, I've provided a quick rundown on the various models that were once available. To aid you, I've reproduced a Steib sales catalog of the 1950s era.

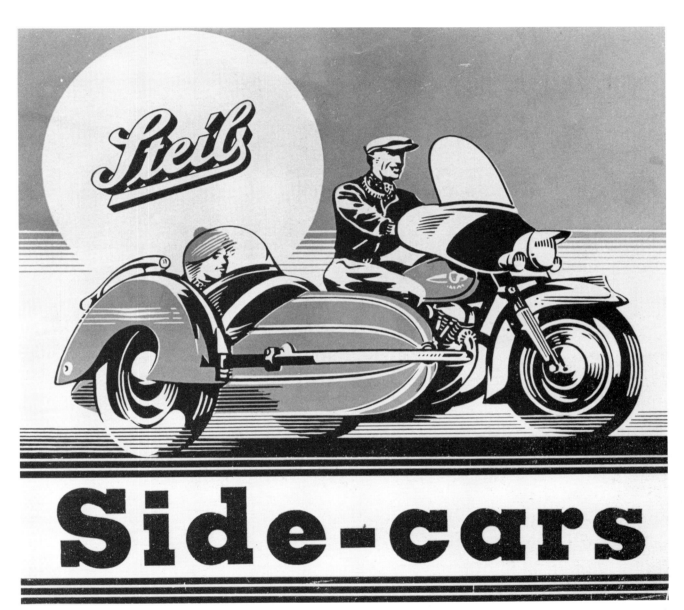

On this and the following pages are sections from an original 1954 Steib sales brochure, describing the various models and accessories available to the purchaser. Most every accessory is still available in reproduction form, even though the Steib factory has long since ceased producing sidecars.

159

Chassis made from high quality weldless steel tubing. Body is made from special high class sheet steel. Attachment of the chassis to the motorcycle frame is done by two quick detachable ball joints and two fork type fittings. The wheel spindle of this sidecar has **knee action suspension** and the wheel is quickly detachable. Back rest and seat is deeply sprung and upholstered with best quality leather cloth as well as the arm rests. The streamlined mudguard pivots at the rearside so as to facilitate wheel removal. The sidecar is enamelled in colours to match the motorcycle as required and is equipped with 19" rim suitable for 3.00" up to 3.50" tyres. This sidecar can also be delivered with spare wheel holder, windshield and coverall apron.

M O D E L   T R   5 0 0

Suitable for motorcycles of 500 cc and upwards.

No. 300z3
Coverall Apron
suitable for model LS 200,
S 350 and S 500

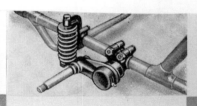

No. 600z1
Knee action suspension
suitable for model LS 200
and LT 200

160

The bumperbar chassis is made from high quality weldless steel tubing. The streamlined body is made from special high class sheet steel. Attachment of the chassis to the motorcycle frame is done by two quick detachable ball joints and two fork type fittings. The wheel spindle of this sidecar has **knee action suspension,** and the wheel is quickly detachable. The high polished luggage carrier is fitted to the body. The luggage room behind the back rest can be locked by safety lock. Seat is deeply sprung and upholstered with best quality leather cloth as well as the arm rests. The front part of the chassis as well as the hand rail are chromium plated. The streamlined mudguard pivots at the rearside so as to facilitate wheel removal. The sidecar is enamelled in colours to match the motorcycle as required and is equipped with 19" rim suitable for 3.00" up to 3.50" tyres.

M O D E L   S   3 5 0

Suitable for motorcycles of 350 up to 500 cc.

No. 600z23
Bumperbar
suitable for model LS 200
and LT 200

All sidecars can be supplied for attachment to left hand or right hand side of motorcycles.

Steib

The bumperbar chassis is made from high quality weldless steel tubing. The streamlined body is made from special high class sheet steel. Attachment to the chassis to the motorcycle frame is done by two quick detachable ball joints and two fork type fittings. The wheel spindle of this sidecar has **knee action suspension** and the wheel is quickly detachable. The spacious luggage locker has a yale type lock. Back rest and seat is deeply sprung and up-holstered with best quality leather cloth as well as the arm rests. The body is finished with highly polished stainless metal strips. The streamlined mudguard pivots at the rearside so as to facilitate wheel removal. The front part of the chassis as well as the hand rail are chromium plated. The sidecar is enamelled in colours to match the motorcycle as required and is equipped with 19" rim suitable for 3.00" up to 3.50" tyres.

MODE

the sa

S

However wit

wheel holder

The luggage

back rest can

safety-lock.

MODEL S 500 L

Suitable for motorcycles of 500 cc. and upwards.

**No. 300z6
Detachable Hood
w/o. windscreen 300z4,**
suitable for model LS 200,
S 350 and S 500

**No. 600z20
Luggage carrier**
pivoting, highly polis

Chassis is made from high quality weldless steel tubing. The box is made from special high quality sheet steel and the lid can be closed by two clip fasteners in addition a yale type lock is fitted. The dimensions of the box are 57 x 15 x 15". Capacity about 110 kos. Attachment of the chassis to the motorcycle frame is done by three patented detachable ball joints. The wheel is of the quick detachable type. The streamlined mudguard pivots at the rearside so as to facilitate wheel removal. The sidecar is enamelled in colours to match the motorcycle as required and is equipped with 19" rim suitable for 3.00" up to 3.50" tyres.

MODEL LT 200

Suitable for motorcycles up to 350 cc. for commercial purposes.

No. 300z4
Windscreen
suitable for model LS 200, S 350 and S 500

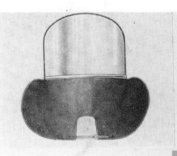

Windscreen for Motorcycle, suitable for all models

163

Chassis made from high quality weldless steel tubing. Body is made from special high class sheet steel. Attachment of the chassis to the motorcycle frame is done by three patented quick detachable ball joints. The wheel is of the quick detachable type and a high polished luggage carrier is fitted to the body. The luggage room behind the back rest can be locked by a safety lock. Seat is deeply sprung and upholstered with best quality leather cloth as well as the arm rests. The streamlined mudguard pivots at the rear side so as to facilitate wheel removal. The sidecar is enamelled in colours to match the motorcycle as required and is equipped with 19" rim suitable for 3.00" up to 3.50" tyres.

MODEL LS200
Suitable for motorcycles up to 250 cc.

the leading special factory for sidecars

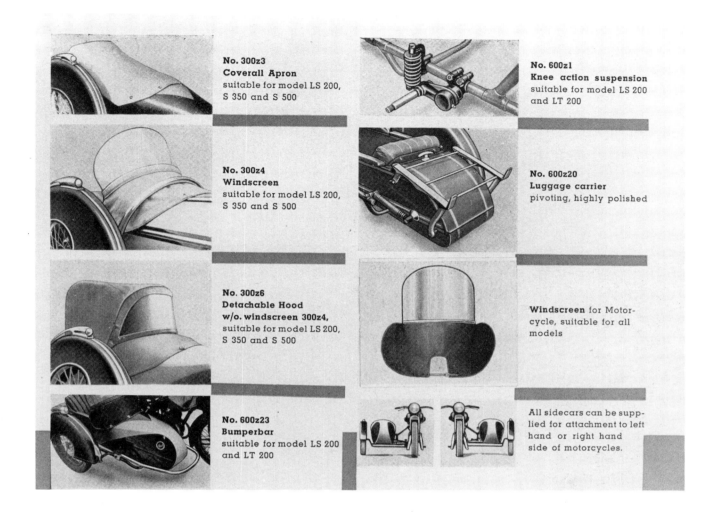

No. 300z3
Coverall Apron
suitable for model LS 200,
S 350 and S 500

No. 600z1
Knee action suspension
suitable for model LS 200
and LT 200

No. 300z4
Windscreen
suitable for model LS 200,
S 350 and S 500

No. 600z20
Luggage carrier
pivoting, highly polished

No. 300z6
Detachable Hood
w/o. windscreen 300z4,
suitable for model LS 200,
S 350 and S 500

Windscreen for Motor-
cycle, suitable for all
models

No. 600z23
Bumperbar
suitable for model LS 200
and LT 200

All sidecars can be supp-
lied for attachment to left
hand or right hand
side of motorcycles.

The smallest Steib was the LS200, a sweet little slab-sided affair looking very much like a canoe. It was ideally suited for mounting to a 250cc or less motorcycle, and most of the BMW sales brochures of the era show the LS200 fitted to a BMW single. When sold by the BMW factory, the distinctive cobra handle was deleted, and the name was changed from LS200 to Standard. Use of the LS200 on heavier and more powerful twins required the exercise of caution. Due to the sidecar's lightness, it was prone to lift on hard right-hand cornering. A commercial variation of the LS200 was the LT200, which replaced the passenger body with a cargo box, looking very much like a tin coffin. The LT200 is a desirable item and rare in the U.S., but of limited utility unless you actually plan to deliver newspapers or parcels with your BMW.

A similar sidecar produced during the mid-1960s was the Steib S-250, again primarily for use on an under 500cc motorcycle. It's not as pretty as the LS200 but quite rare and desirable. It could be found with either an enamel Steib or BMW logo on its nose.

The next size up was the round-nosed S-350. This small version of the larger bullet-nosed Steibs was also intended for use on a 500cc or less motorcycle. All the round-nosed Steibs, because of their body shapes and trim strips, are now generally referred to as the cucumber or Zeppelin models.

The upgrades from the S-350 were the S-500 and S-501. Both had larger, heavier bodies; extra mounting struts; and opening trunks. These worked best with machines of 500cc and larger capacity.

The flagship of the Steib line was the TR500, probably the most desirable Steib to be found today. In the BMW form it was called the Spezial, again with the cobra handle deleted. It was a heavy sidecar indeed, weighing in at 120kg (about 265lb), and was meant primarily for use with the R67 and R60 BMWs of the 1951–1969 period. Most BMW outfits sold to the German *Polizei* and military authorities came with the Steib TR500 sidecar fitted, suitably retagged with BMW's own ID plate on top near the opening trunk lid. A two-passenger version of the TR500, with clear bubble canopy and fore and aft

The Steib LT 200, a rare sight in the U.S., but common in Europe where it was used to deliver everything from newspapers to bottled beer. This one and the BMW to which it is attached occupies a place of honor at a BMW dealership in Maryland. *Bob Henig*

seating, was briefly marketed in England, but less than a dozen examples were made. One is known to be in the U.S., minus its Plexiglas canopy.

Accessories for Your Sidecar

Again, whole books could be written about what one could add to his BMW and sidecar. This will have to be a quick distillation of what was once available.

Wheels could be covered with a full width disc, a rarely seen item today. All but the TR500 Steibs could be had with a tight fitting and claustrophobic canvas top. All the Steibs, as well as the other brands, came with windshields, splash aprons, and tonneau covers. The German firm Richter made some exotic, enveloping aluminum and canvas tops for both the round-nosed and TR500 Steibs, which gave the sidecar a decided fighter cockpit appearance. Used Richter Kabine tops occasionally turn up, usually with discolored or broken plastic windows, which are quite difficult to repair.

The larger versions of most sidecars could be

A nice detail study of the trim and pinstriping on the nose of a Steib S500. It's little wonder these models are affectionately called the cucumber Steibs. *Dick Ekwall*

had with hydraulic brakes, which worked in conjunction with the BMW's rear mechanical foot brake. Setup instructions are quite complex, and once your brakes are properly balanced, they should be left alone.

Most owners eventually added some sort of auxiliary lights to the sidecar, with the Hella spotlamp mirror the most common choice. These look quite good and do cast some small amount of light off to the shoulder at night. All sidecars should have running lights as well, with a white light to the front and a red light to the rear. No brake lights were ever fitted to a sidecar, just a red running light.

Some Mounting Hints

The factory instructions, when followed carefully, should provide a suitably strong and properly aligned connection for your sidecar, regardless of the brand you're attaching. It should be remembered that the ball and claw mounts and the struts are your only insurance against disaster, so check them often. Some poorly made, untreated, and unhardened claw mounts occasionally turn up, which could spell disaster when you least expect it. Cheaply made struts and brackets have been known to bend and break, so, again, check everything often. Don't overload the sidecar, and try to avoid stunts like riding with the sidecar wheel up

in the air. The third wheel leaving the ground places unimaginable stresses on the BMW, especially the spokes, forks, and wheel splines. If you want to amuse the public, offer them rides, rather than clowning around with one wheel up in the air.

If you begin to notice unusual or excessive wear, especially on the sidecar tire, check the alignment. Keep tire pressures as high as the factory suggestions state. If you have a lightweight sidecar fitted to a particularly powerful BMW, such as the R69S, you can minimize the sidecar's tendency to lift on corners by keeping a filled, collapsible 5gal water container in the sidecar. The extra forty or so pounds will make for a better handling sidecar. Once you've added a passenger, the water can be dumped out and the container folded up. Many owners opt for a larger 6-volt battery, putting an industrial, car, or tractor battery in the trunk of the sidecar. Not only does this redistribute weight, but it also gives the BMW an increased electrical capacity.

Mounting Hardware

All 1950–1969 BMWs come with one ball permanently attached to the right side of the frame, at the rear near the back wheel. The only exceptions were the 1968–1969 US-fork models, and the early R68, which had the mounts deleted. Some of the early US models still came with the mounts, but in

No properly restored Steib is complete without its proper name tag. Fortunately for the restorer the tags, as well as the other accessories shown here, are now being reproduced and are available through several enthusiastic Vintage BMW Club members in the U.S. *Bob Henig*

The ultimate Steib accessory has to be the aluminum Richter Kabine top, which transformed the TR500 or BMW Spezial into a cozy weatherproof conveyance. These tops also turn up now and then at vintage BMW flea markets. *Richard Kahn, Butler & Smith, Inc.*

any event mounting a sidecar to a US-telescopic twin is not a wise idea.

The prospective owner of a sidecar additionally had to purchase two clevis bolts, for bolting through the frame holes near the seat and the front of the tank, again on the right-hand side of the BMW, and a ball which mounted to the front engine bolt. Most engine bolt balls came with the shaft firmly attached, which is what is recommended. Best to keep the original bolt in your set of spares, for when the time comes to sell the sidecar and return the BMW to its solo status. Struts and claws usually came with the sidecar. The lamp socket under the seat was used to plug in the running lights of the sidecar. As previously discussed, after 1951 BMW changed the size of the clevis bolt from 12mm to 13mm due to fractures, so be wary if you find some used hardware.

Changes to the BMW

Once you've decided to mount a sidecar, a number of major and expensive changes must be made to your BMW. First, try to avoid mounting any sort of sidecar unless it's the lightweight Steib LS200 or S-250, to any BMW with less than a 600cc engine. The R51/3, R50, and R50/2 machines are just not powerful enough. The ideal BMW is of course the R67 series, especially the R67/3, and the R60 and its variants.

The first thing to consider is a lower sidecar rear end ratio for your BMW. These are costly, however. You might want to do without, and simply regear your transmission. Putting in lower ratios in the gearbox is often a better solution. It not only saves you the expense of new rear end gears, but it also saves you the cost of regearing or purchasing a new VDO speedometer. Finding a wider section rear wheel rim is a necessary, but difficult task these days. Alloy wheel rims should be replaced with steel ones. An aluminum, extra-capacity oil pan should be installed, since your engine will be running hotter and working harder once it has to contend with the added stresses and weight of a sidecar. Sidecar springs should be fitted to the rear of the Earles fork BMWs, and your front end has to be adjusted for trail. All things to consider when contemplating a sidecar. Many BMW owners opt for two machines, one to keep as a solo bike, the other exclusively for sidecar use because once you've attached a sidecar, switching back and forth is out of the question.

Changes to Your Attitude

Riding a BMW with a sidecar is not the same as riding your BMW solo. In fact, you don't ride a sidecar bike, you drive it. The feeling at first is like piloting a powerful, but quiet, garden tractor. Changes in direction are accomplished by steering with the handlebars, especially at slow speeds. You can no longer rely upon just pressure from wrists alone to warp the bike around bends. Stopping all that extra weight requires careful use of both brakes, or all three if you're lucky enough to have a hydraulic brake on the sidecar.

Cornering, especially long, sweeping bends, such as on and off ramps on divided highways, often spells disaster for the novice or the unwary. No matter how heavy your sidecar, it will still want to lift on sharp right-hand turns. If you didn't pay attention in high school physics class, you'll soon find out why it lifts up. If you get yourself in such a predicament, putting on the brakes will only aggravate the condition. You must slam the sidecar wheel back down, and the only way to do this is by giving the bike more throttle, not less. Practice driving with your sidecar on wide empty parking lots. That way, you won't have to learn emergency procedures on the off ramp on a busy stretch of highway at 50mph in the rain. A school parking lot on a Sunday is the best, and all your mistakes can be made in relative privacy. If the surface is wet, so much the better. It could also be fun to slide around in circles, with no one around to see the panicked look on your face!

Tires, once not so important, will now wear much quicker. A good, hard, and reliable sidecar tire is the British Avon S-M, with its nice flat profile. It's still available in both 19in and 18in sizes. Oil should be changed more often, and spokes must regularly be tested for looseness and breaks. Tire pressures must be maintained, per the factory's recommendations.

Finally, as much fun as a sidecar can be, it has four major drawbacks. First, the BMW will now take up almost as much room as a car, and may actually displace your automobile in the garage. Second, all your friends with solo machines will want you to carry their excess baggage. Third, children and dogs will find the sidecar irresistible; the former wanting to be your passenger, the latter seeing it as an inviting and easily bitten target.

Fourth, toll booth attendants will try to charge you the going rate for multi-axle vehicles, higher than for cars or motorcycles. It's proper to discuss this with them and carry a copy of your state's motor vehicle regulations. Even though a BMW with a sidecar has only three wheels, most toll booth attendants will try to hit you with the 4-axle fee. The logic escapes us, and it's worth arguing the point. Usually, after a minute or two of irate honking from the cars behind you, the toll booth attendant gives in. If not, request a receipt, and ask to see the toll plaza supervisor. Eventually, you'll get a refund or an adjustment.

As a plus, the BMW with attached sidecar will be much harder to steal, and it's much more visible on the highway. Most motorists who would in all likelihood never see a solo machine will be drawn to one with a sidecar, and will probably give you a little extra room when passing. Most will consider you amusing and eccentric. Few will view you as a threat, since you can't do much lane splitting or passing with a sidecar.

On the other side of the coin, you're now an attractive nuisance and as such could be responsible for the accidents of others who might take their eyes of the road to gawk at you. I was probably the indirect cause of a nice three car fender bender on Route 128 near Boston a few years ago, thankfully at low speed, as several drivers craned their necks to look at the cute, funny old motorcycle (a 1954 BMW R67/2 with BMW Spezial sidecar) in the lane next to them. Amid the curses and the broken glass, your author chose discretion as the better part of valor and played the part of the inattentive innocent, and motored wisely on.

Chapter 18

Accessories

Nothing dresses up a BMW better than the proper and judicious use of accessories. Nothing destroys an otherwise perfect restoration faster than the use of nonstandard add-ons or the overuse of period accessories. If left unchecked, many an owner can spend almost as much on period accessories as was spent on the original restoration of the BMW!

The new enthusiast attending his first BMW concours, or visiting one of the several BMW shops in this country catering to the restoration of vintage BMW motorcycles, is soon confronted by a bewildering array of unusual, exotic, and often expensive accessories. All can break your heart if you don't have them and your bank book if you find you must have all that is available.

Gas Tanks

The most common accessory items the vintage BMW enthusiast usually considers first when planning an upgrade is a larger gas tank. While the beautifully shaped stock teardrop tanks on the 1950–1954 BMWs were a delight to behold, they held little in the way of fuel. The same holds true for the less graceful but equally small capacity 1955–1969 standard tanks. A larger tank makes sense, especially when hauling a sidecar or planning long, cross-country trips.

BMW anticipated such a need from the outset and made available in the pre-1955 era the Meier tank, a rounded, pleasantly shaped tank that held slightly more than 6gal. Not only was the tank named after the famed prewar ace Schorsch Meier, but it was also marketed and available through his BMW dealership in Munich. The tank is similar to the 1955–1969 sports tank, and is often confused with it. The knowledgeable enthusiast can spot the difference easily, however, because the Meier tank had long, narrow, tapered kneepads and usually a lipped toolbox cover, most often finished in polished chrome. While the Meier and the post-1954 sports tanks look alike, they are not interchangeable, and one from an Earles fork machine will not fit the pre-1955 plunger frame BMWs, and vice versa. The

front mounting flanges are shaped differently, and the two welded-in mounting holes underneath will not line up. Save yourself a lot of aggravation by testing the tanks for fit on a bare frame before you buy. Clever restorers have made the tanks work on the other frames, but not without the use of adapter plates and some careful bending and alteration of the front mounting brackets.

The same caveat holds true for accessory tanks made by the firms of Hoske and Heinrich. While some of their tanks may look similar externally, they were specifically made for either the pre-1955 plunger frames or the 1955–1969 Earles-fork and US-fork frames. Test before you buy.

Ernst Hoske, to aid the enthusiast, stamped his tanks underneath with several cryptic codes that indicated which frames the tanks were designed to fit. If the marks have not been obliterated, they can be found on the bottom, near the front on both sides. A tank stamped with a code contain-

Most commonly, the first accessory the BMW restorer and enthusiast considers is a larger tank, such as this 8gal Hoske seen here on a 1966 R50/2. The plastic pannier cases are the tall and narrow, top-opening Craven "Police Pursuit."

An even larger Hoske, this time mounted on, or should we say over, a 1951 R67. *Michael Gross*

ing R.51 on the right-hand bottom means it was meant for the pre-1955 plunger frames. Codes containing R.50 mean the tank was meant to fit the 1955–1969 frames. On the left were usually the maker's name, E.HOSKE, a manufacturing date, and the assembler's initials. Hoske also made a bewildering variety of tanks for other brands, such as Zündapp, NSU, and even Honda, so don't just snap up any Hoske tank on sight alone.

All Hoske tanks were made of steel, out of a number of small sections carefully formed and butt welded together. Over everything was spread a thin but solid layer of resin, cloth, and putty, much like fiberglass, giving the tank a smooth appearance. When restoring a Hoske tank, it's best to leave all this putty in place and patch the damaged areas.

All civilian Hoske tanks were rounded at the front, had slab sides at the rear, and gave the appearance of a keyhole when viewed from the top.

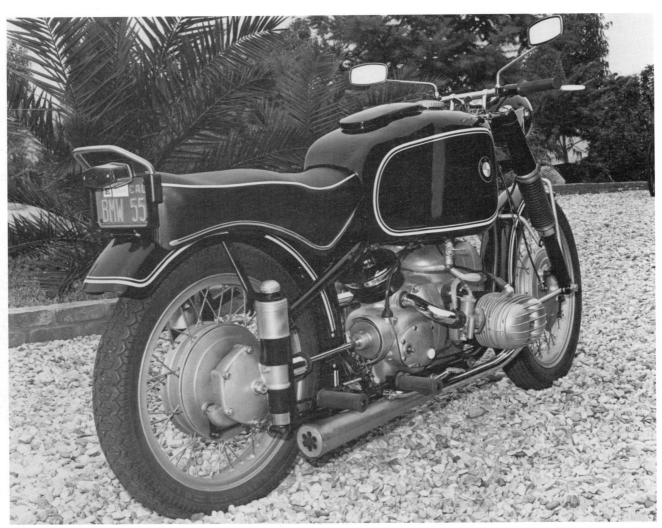

Large Hoske tanks did much to provide a custom BMW a unique flair, as can be seen on this 1954 R67/3. Note how the striping follows the contours of the tank. *Jurgen Amtmann*

172

Most had toolboxes set into the top surface. The lid was either chrome or painted black and was held shut with a non-locking knurled knob. Some had little square-headed Dzus type key mechanisms, similar to those found on the BMW sports tanks or on the tops of standard 1950–1954 tanks and R26 and R27 tanks. Some Hoske tanks had kneepads, some did not. Some pads were held on with metal brackets bolted to the tanks sides, some were glued on. Most of the striping followed the contours of the tank and conformed to the BMW striping scheme. A normal fuel filler opening was to be found on the top, in the center, in front of the toolbox lid if one was fitted.

Hoske tanks employed their own brand of Everbest fuel tap, which usually screwed directly into the tank rather than over a fine threaded boss. Many desperate owners, unable to find original Hoske-design taps, have often resorted to using bronze marine or industrial taps, British motorcycle taps ,or to the grafting on of salvaged BMW tank fittings, in order to use the more readily available and considerably less expensive BMW standard items.

Racing or Rennsport tanks were also once available, either over the counter or from firms such as Hoske. They were never made in large numbers, are quite rare, and came in a number of shapes and sizes tailored for the particular races in which the BMWs were competing. Enduro or trials tanks were tall and fat and held a lot of fuel. Others were short and narrow, with exaggerated cutouts for the knees. Most had a limited fuel capacity, since the weight of excess fuel, or the sloshing around of unused gas, was a decided handicap when racing a BMW.

Some Rennsport tanks had a second filler, either to let air out while fuel was hurriedly dumped in via the other, or to act as a filler for an auxiliary oil tank, something used only on all-out racing machines. A number of small Rennsport tanks were simply slab-sided versions of the larger capacity tanks, with small cutouts at the rear for the knees and no kneepads. Most of the racing tanks were devoid of toolboxes or had the toolbox hole filled with a removable leather or rubber chest pad, on which the rider could lie prone on those long straights, when every bit of wind resistance saved could be crucial. Most of the true racing tanks had no provision for the attachment of BMW emblems by means of screws, but used decals instead. Screws tended to vibrate loose, emblems were just added weight, and dropping things such as tank emblems on the track could be both a hazard as well as a means of getting one disqualified.

Hoske tanks, as well as those made by Heinrich, were often of such large capacity that deep cutouts had to be used on the right-hand side in order to allow access to the sidecar mounting brackets on the frames, and to clear the struts if a sidecar was fitted. If you plan to mount a sidecar on your BMW, finding a tank with the cutouts can

Two nice views of an early-1950s Hoske, which would look well on a pre-1955 plunger framed BMW. Note that this example has clip on rubber knee pads and a lipped toolbox

cover. The fuel taps are not original but are bronze marine items.

Some tanks never seem to stop growing. This is possibly a 10 or 11gal Hoske monster. Large tanks like this almost precluded their use on anything but a sidecar outfit. On a solo BMW, full tanks of this capacity have a decidedly negative effect on handling. I once had the misfortune of losing my balance and falling over at a gas pump after I had just filled my 10gal Hoske, much to the amusement of several onlookers.

save a lot of aggravation later on. Some tanks, especially the Hoskes, were also of such large capacity that depressions had to be inserted into the top, ahead of the fuel filler cap, to clear the handlebars.

I remember seeing a bright red Earles fork BMW twin, brought back by an acquaintance while he and I were returning from a cruise to Germany in 1964 on the steamship *Bremen*. The machine had a huge Hoske tank that was severely scalloped on top for just that reason. (If this book is read by someone with more information on either the bike or its owner, please contact the author.)

The other most commonly encountered tanks on pre-1970 BMWs were the ones made by the firm Karl Heinrich, located in the town of Maichingen near Stuttgart. Most Heinrich tanks were rounded on the top and sides, with cutouts for the knees. Most tanks were steel, although aluminum ones were also available. The majority of Heinrich tanks were made for the 1955–1969 BMW models. Most Heinrich tanks had a top-mounted toolbox, covered with a polished and locking aluminum lid, under

The ultimate Hoske in its Rennsport version, mounted here on an Amol Precision special, a factory Rennsport fitted with an R50S motor. Note the decal tank emblem, the large racing brakes, and original Earles fork pre-production design. On production BMWs, the fork legs were straight rather than curved. *Talbot Lovering*

which was a small fuel filler hole and cap. The lid was locked with a normal slotted key. Heinrich tanks are still being made and are available from various sources, albeit at considerable cost.

Most Heinrich tanks had a two-tone paint scheme, either black and white or all black or all silver. Striping was usually a matter of personal taste, but most stripes were similar to the BMW pattern or followed the major contours of the tank. Some Heinrich tanks utilized the large, pressed aluminum BMW car emblems, which were either glued on or pressed into recesses in the tank. Some Heinrich tanks had glued-on rubber kneepads, usually very thin and designed solely to keep the paint from being damaged by the riders' clothing. Most Heinrich tanks were of such a large capacity that they totally enveloped the engine, coming to rest just scant centimeters above the spark plugs. Consequently, fuel taps had to be severely angled to the rear. The taps, thankfully, were of the standard Everbest BMW design, and are still available.

Whichever tank you get, check it carefully for cracks and leaks. Sloshing the insides with a tank sealer is a good idea and cheap insurance. Having

Another Heinrich, this time in white, on an R69S with Steib TR500 and Richter Kabine.

As racy as the Hoske was, some versions of the Heinrich could make a BMW look fast even when standing still. Vintage BMW Club member Wilbur Clark from Ohio has a right to be proud of his R69S and its nice Heinrich tank. *Tracy Baker*

175

Heinrich tanks often came in a two-color paint scheme, which here nicely complement this R69S and Steib LS 200 outfit. *Marie Lacko*

Gas caps came in various flavors, but none were as unusual as this large plated item. This is a locking twist on cap that originally was used on BMW cars of the late 1930s and early 1950s. *Craig Vechorik*

10–12gal of volatile and explosive fuel between your legs, all of it resting in close proximity to hot exhaust pipes, high voltage plug wires, and arcing spark plugs can lead to disaster if your Heinrich or Hoske tank should spring a leak. Avoid plastic or fiberglass copies of these tanks. Some were made years ago in England and are occasionally still found at flea markets. Plastic tanks eventually develop stress fractures and can dump all their fuel without warning. There have been documented instances where such tanks suddenly sprung huge leaks while the bikes were idling at the curb or after an accident impact. The conflagrations that resulted were usually fatal.

There was once a nice tank meant to fit the Earles fork BMWs; it was made around 1969 by a Burt Mader of Massachusetts. Although it was plastic, it was well designed, beautifully executed, and usually custom painted by the designer to suit the buyer. Only a few dozen were made. If you find one, this is the exception to the rule. Buy it and restore it. It was a true BMW artifact of that era and one rarely seen today. Again, slosh the insides with a sealer, which can be found at most auto parts suppliers or, if you're desperate, at many small airports selling parts and accessories to the private pilot.

Gas Caps

While you're looking over that accessory tank, look into a gas cap or two. No postwar BMW tank as fitted to the standard catalog models ever came with a pop-off racing style cap, although they were common on certain prewar machines, and of course the norm on most of BMW's Italian and British competitors. The original BMW caps were slightly domed aluminum twist-on items, made by the German firm BLAU. Once dinged, they are impossible to repair. All BLAU caps were edge vented via a series of small holes under the crimped-on cover. None of the original caps were locking. All are impossible to find today. Owners have resorted to using automobile caps that fit, with mixed results.

This author once found some nice, plated brass American automobile gas caps from the 1940s and 1950s that looked amazingly similar to the aluminum BLAU items, except for a small center vent hole. Careful polishing will turn such a mundane item as a 1949 Buick gas cap into a nicely polished brass accessory. Not enough to get you a first at a concours, but nice enough for everyday use.

The original caps came with round cork gaskets, which eventually dried out and allowed fuel to spill onto the tank. While the cork gaskets are still available, a good, inexpensive replacement that will do in an emergency is a Kawasaki cap gasket, part number 51059-007 (the old Kawasaki number was 51059-003). Regardless of which one you get, it's a good idea to keep one in your toolbox. Because it's made of synthetic rubber, it should last much longer in there than the more fragile BMW cork item.

Sometimes you'll come across a BLAU cap similar to the BMW original, but embossed with some German wording such "MobilMix TT." These were for two-stroke bikes of that era and while they look nice on a BMW, they were never intended to be used as such. Again, a nice period item, but one that will count against you at a concours.

The alternative to an original BLAU is a locking gas cap made by a number of manufacturers in Germany as over-the-counter accessories. Most are readily available and still inexpensive. Ones made by the firm Hama were the most common, and came with little BMW logos embossed on the tops, next to a swinging cover for the key slot. The keys are usually lost by the time you find a cap at a flea market, but that shouldn't stop you from buying the cap. Simply drill a small hole into the mechanism right through the key way, and insert a suitable Allen wrench. The wrench will 'lock' the internal rotating parts, allowing you to tighten or loosen the entire cap. Remove the wrench, and the cap's

outer cover again spins freely, making it a locking cap once more! Only you know the difference.

These Hama caps had two styles of BMW logos, one with serif letters, one without. Use the serif letter style on any pre-1966 BMW to be absolutely correct. Other Hama caps had plain tops, and they also came with several styles of finger notches.

Another style of BLAU aluminum cap often seen today has deep finger notches rather than the fine thin vertical line knurling found on the originals. These were never available during the 1950–1969 era, but that's all that is available today. Eventually, that's all we'll be seeing, so it's probably all right to use them if no others are to be had. There were also some chrome steel abominations, with long ears, similar to fake knock off hubs such as fitted to Chrysler Imperials and DeSoto cars, and just about as pretty to look at. They're period accessories, to be sure, but rather dangerous if you

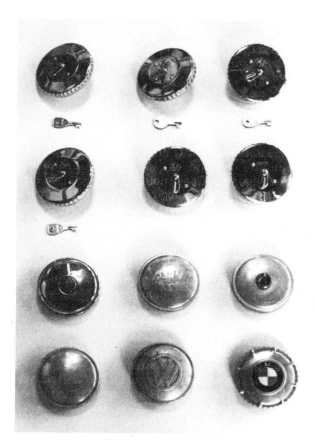

A nice collection of locking and non-locking BMW gas caps. The plated locking ones were made by Hama, and were usually embossed with serif and non-serif BMW logos. In the bottom row, the cap at left is an original BLAU cap, while the center one is a Volkswagen cap. Next to it, a similar Volkswagen item, also made by BLAU, on which has been glued a nicely painted aluminum BMW hubcap emblem, thereby disguising its more mundane Wolfsburg application.

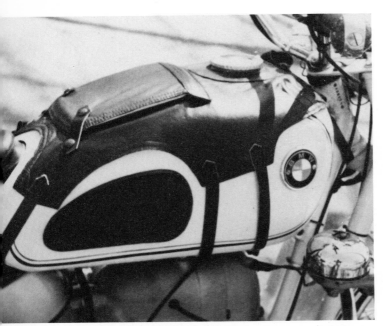

Popular accessories of the 1960s, now once again being reproduced, were these leather tank covers. This one is for a 6.5gal sport tank. The top flap unsnapped to allow access to the toolbox. Covers were also available for the smaller 4gal standard tank.

ever slide across a tank top in an accident.

A clever alternative, if you can still find one, is the BLAU aluminum cap made for the Volkswagen, in particular the 1950s era Beetles, transporters, and minibuses. The cap is large, may have a knurled edge with finger notches, and a raised area on top bearing the VW logo in a circle. The circle is a little over 50mm in diameter, an ideal size for gluing on a small enamel badge, such as the 45mm colored slightly convex aluminum BMW logo used as the center on hubcaps on the 2002 and 320i car models. You can also use a German 5 DM piece, Maria Theresa Thaler, or whatever suits you. Pester your old time VW dealer; he may have a box full of the old caps that he's just dying to get rid of!

Covering the Tank

While there were no official tank covers available for the 1950–1954 standard or Meier tanks, nor any for the various styles of Hoske or Heinrich, the 1955–1969 tanks could be protected to some degree by the fitment of two clever leather and felt covers. Both covers are now being reproduced, using originals as patterns, and are available from several sources in this country as noted in the appendix. They look nice on either the standard or sport tank on the Earles and US-fork twins and, if properly cared for, can be a useful addition and an asset in a concours competition.

They do have several disadvantages, however. First, they can be damaged by gasoline spills. Grit,

once trapped under the green felt cover, can badly damage the finish on the tank. They can also be easily stolen, as there's no effective way to secure them. If the bike is caught in the rain, the cover must be removed and carefully dried. Original colors were black, red, or white, but these days all I have seen are the black ones.

Some of the nice accessories available in the late 1960s from the importer of BMW motorcycles. Along with tank covers, you could outfit your BMW with leather muffs for the hands and a leather lap apron, which attached to the tank and stayed with the machine when the rider dismounted. *Richard Kahn, Butler & Smith, Inc.*

Mirrors and Lamps

All motorcycles need at least one mirror, and BMWs are no exception. Unfortunately, the style and number of mirrors available to the restorer of a 1950–1969 BMW is enough to test your will power and your bank book. BMW bought their mirrors from the German firm Albert, and no proper BMW is properly restored without at least one correct Albert mirror or a matched pair. Albert mirrors are again being reproduced, and although the quality and execution is not quite as good as the originals, it's much better than anything found up to now. Other accessory mirrors available during the 1950–1969 era were made by Hagus, Bumm, and Talbot, all old-line German firms. Like Albert, all had their names pressed into the mirror head. If you're determined to find the correct Albert head, or lenses and other trim items, try some of the older, established Volkswagen or Mercedes-Benz dealers in your area. Albert and Talbot mirrors made for these cars and were virtually identical, although the stalks were naturally different.

Mirrors came in several variations: handlebar mount, bar end mount, and headlamp mount. Some of the best looking were the graceful Albert bar end versions with their aluminum posts that screwed into the end of the left handlebar. Rubber grips would need to have holes cut onto the end to accommodate them, but Magura grips with the holes already molded in were also available then, as well as now. Contrary to popular belief, Albert bar end mirrors did not interchange left to right. If Albert did indeed make a right-hand bar end version, I have yet to see one.

Headlamp mirrors were also a popular option and look quite nice, especially when used in conjunction with the low Europa bars. The arms should angle downward, not up, and the left and right sides, at least on the Albert versions, did not interchange, since the left and right heads were of a different shape. Hagus headlamp mirrors did interchange, having identical heads left and right, but the arms, again, should angle downward.

Most mirror heads were teardrop in shape, especially on the ones made by Albert and Hagus. Albert also made some round ones. A company making round ones, with an added twist, was the Berlin firm Talbot. Their mirrors could be either plain or streamlined (for Porsche and Mercedes-Benz cars). For the Volkswagen and motorcycle trade, the round heads were fitted with clever little turn signals built into the mirror head. Finding a pair of

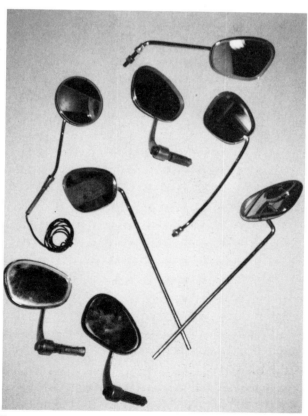

Front and back views of several German accessory mirrors from the 1950s to the late 1960s. Most are Albert or Bumm bar end or headlamp mount, while the long ones are for

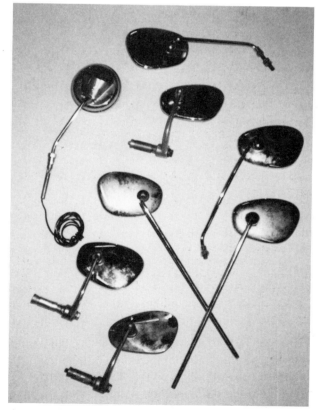

clamp-on handlebar applications. The odd one with a wire attached is a Talbot mirror, made in Berlin, fitted with a small semicircular orange turn signal lens.

179

The ultimate Hella accessory has to be a pair of Hella spot-lamps, complete with rotating mirror heads and brackets for the Earls fork tops. A pair of these, in original condition, will set you back a bundle. Unfortunately, no one is yet reproducing these items.

these today is akin to finding an uncanceled Hindenburg Air Mail. Door-hinge mounted ones for Volkswagen beetles and minibuses are virtually identical, and their stems can be rethreaded to allow their use as headlamp mirrors.

Handlebar clamp-on mirrors are another alternative, and the Albert version, with its long, straight stem is the one most often seen, with both round and teardrop heads. They are usually mounted in pairs. Screw-in mirrors, again made by Albert, again with the two styles of heads, were only available for the left side, and were only made to screw into the 1960–1969 left side clutch control casting. A word to the wise: The threads are left-handed, and in most cases the threads in the casting will have been stripped. If you use the Hella bar

end turn signals, you will be limited to using only bar clamp mirrors or headlamp mirrors.

The ultimate mirror accessory is the Hella spotlamp mirror, and it's by far the most expensive and the most elusive. Small fortunes have been made selling a perfect pair, with their ultrarare fork top brackets, which may have been squirreled away in some private stock for decades. Finding a pair complete in their original cardboard boxes is every BMW restorer's dream, although the boxes themselves have little utility!

If the spotlamp mirrors don't have the pressed-steel fork top brackets, they will have to be mounted on the bars using the standard pinch clamps. The fork tops brackets were usually made only for the Earles fork tops, but a few brackets have been spotted that were made for the 1950–1954 telescopic forks. If you can borrow a set, note that the lefts and rights are not interchangeable. They should be easy enough to duplicate. Finding a pair to borrow will be the hard part. Most owners of just a single Hella spotlamp mount it on the grab rail of a Steib sidecar, or salt it away until a mate can be found.

Early versions of the Hella lamp, usually in a prewar design, have also been seen. Many were intended for windshield use on German touring cars and trucks of the prewar era, but all look equally good on the BMW. Like all Hellas, they had the unique feature of having the mirror head rotate in order to turn the spotlamp on and off.

The actual utility of the lamp was marginal, since most of the bulbs were too small to cast much light, limited as they were by the power available

Inside and outside views of two versions of the aluminum oil pan that will fit on all 1951–69 BMW twins. The pan on the left, with the thinner, shallower fins, is what is still readily available today, and is a copy of the 1960s Bowman product. It increases the capacity by half a quart. It has a place at the rear for inserting an oil temperature gauge if desired and requires use of an oil pickup extension. The pan with the larger, deeper fins is a rare BMW item, which does not increase the oil capacity, but does allow for effective cleaning without removing the pan, by means of a deep sediment trap and a large drain hole. Finding either one of these at a flea market is cause for celebration.

A pair of Bosch lamps, probably used as running lights on either cars, trucks, or sidecars in the late 1930s. These have a red lens to the rear and look nice when mounted to a fender on a sidecar. The Stoye in the sidecar section had one of these fitted to the fender top.

from the 6-volt electrical system of the BMW. All Hella spotlamps, being mounted way out in the open as they are, are extremely prone to damage, and as such are probably best kept on the parts shelves in most BMW owners' basements. Because of their complexity, no one is yet making reproductions, which is another reason Hella spotlamps command such a high premium. Lenses were available in clear, blue, or red, the latter two for police use generally. Lenses in all of the three colors are still easy to find.

Oil Pans

A practical, sturdy accessory for your BMW is a large, finned oil pan. Executed in aluminum, it's a definite enhancement to the looks of a BMW. Indeed, the pressed-tin pan it replaces is distinctly shabby in appearance when placed next to a finely cast and finished alloy pan. Aluminum pans were made to fit the 1951–1969 BMW twins, and since all the blocks were the same, all will interchange. No alloy pan was ever made (or at least never imported into the U.S.) for the 1950 R51/2, which employed both a different block casting and a different steel oil pan pressing.

When buying a new or used aluminum pan, ascertain whether it's of the increased capacity type, such as once made by Bowman, or simply a finned alloy version of the original capacity steel one. If the former, you'll need a pickup screen extension. If you don't use the extension, all the increased capacity is wasted because you'll never get at the extra air cooled oil in the bottom of the pan. The normal capacity pan is easily recognizable; it doesn't have as deep an area inside for the oil. If it's like the original Bowman design or a German original, it will have a narrow, deep clean-out well and a large diameter drain plug hole, ideal as a sediment trap and for getting a bristle brush in there and cleaning it all out. One major drawback to at least one of the pans is that the added capacity is a mere half quart, leaving you with a half empty container of oil to contend with after an oil change.

Whichever pan you find, it's a useful and inexpensive accessory, one that is almost a requirement when hauling a sidecar, since every bit of help your now hard-working engine can get will increase its longevity. In all cases, use a magnetic drain plug, and to be absolutely safe, drill a small hole across the flats of the hex head and safety wire the drain plug to the pan. A good attaching point for the safety wire is the little tab for the sidestand spring, which both versions of the pan came with.

Tachometers

The 1951–1969 BMW engine can be easily fitted with one of several versions of a mechanical tachometer made for the BMW by the German firm VDO. Unfortunately, due to the type of engine design unique to the R51/2, with its twin camshafts and front mounted coil and distributor, fitting of the camshaft driven VDO instrument is impossible.

Up until mid-1966, only the earlier version of the VDO camshaft driven tachometer could be used, but by late-1966 all BMW twin-cylinder motors had a modified timing chest casting, which accommodated a removable triangular oil pump cover. This cover could be replaced with an oil pump driven tachometer gearbox, to which the tachometer drive cable attached. The easy change to an oil pump driven tachometer was finally implemented in June 1967 on the R69S (with engine number 661 445), when the gears were extended sufficiently to allow rapid installation of the gearbox without further disassembly. Earlier engines starting with number 640 296 on the R50/2, number 628 250 on the R60/2, and number 660 144 on the R69S could also be fitted with the new tachometer, but disassembly of the oil pump gears was required.

When inspecting the instrument heads, look underneath the case. If the case is stamped 4:1, the head will only work with the camshaft driven gearbox, which is mounted externally via a hole drilled into the front engine cover. If the ratio stamped

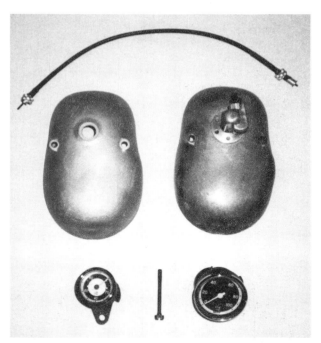

A camshaft-driven VDO tachometer outfit which will fit on all 1951–1969 BMW twins. Mounting is straightforward, and requires the installation of a slotted magneto rotor bolt and a special drilled out front electrical cover. While the right angle gearbox was similar during 1951–1969, several mounting methods were available, as can be seen here. The instrument head on the left is the standard unit which mounted on top of the handlebars, while the larger one at right drops into the headlight shell.

onto the gauge body is 2:1, the instrument head is for the late-1966-on oil-pump-driven gearbox. To confound the restorer, the external camshaft drive tachometer gearbox, VDO part number 63/16/1, is stamped with a 2:1 ratio! It also shows the date of manufacture and can easily be disassembled when it's time to repack it with grease. Some clever owners drill and tap a hole in the side of the box and thread in a grease fitting for that purpose.

All VDO instrument heads should be painted black, with a crimped-on chrome bezel and flat glass. The overall size is 2-1/2in high and 2-3/8in in diameter, with a welded-on bracket on the base having a mounting slot. The slot was meant to allow fitment via the hex nut on the right-hand side of the Earles fork triple clamp, although mounting one on either side is possible. The face should be a two-tone black and beige, or black and white, similar to the face markings on the BMW speedometer of the period. The needle is white and rotates in a clockwise direction, with zero at one o'clock and a face reading to 8000rpm. None were illuminated.

The oil-pump-driven instrument used a longer cable than the camshaft-driven instrument. Addi-tionally, use of the camshaft-driven gearbox required the relocation of the horn to the right-hand side of the gas tank, and the intricacies of fitting the earlier camshaft driven gearbox are spelled out in service bulletin 1/63 (201) of May 21, 1963, which is reproduced in this chapter. A major shortcoming of the camshaft-driven gearbox was the flexible, slotted key coupling to the camshaft, which demanded diligent attention and frequent lubrication. Failure to keep it well greased soon resulted in erratic readings and eventual shearing or destruction of the key. To help the installation of the camshaft gearbox, BMW did spare the prospective owner the agony of drilling out the front cover, and made available a predrilled cover as an option.

Other VDO tachometers, whether oil-pump- or camshaft-driven, were of a size identical to the speedometer head, and could be mounted in place of the speedometer in the headlamp bucket. They spun clockwise, their all black or all white faces read to 10,000rpm (zero was at seven o'clock), and they were edge-lit via an internal bulb. These are rare and were used primarily on racing BMWs.

Fortunately for the restorer, reproductions of

A top view of a small fortune in accessories. Along with the Hella bar-end signals, is an Albert clutch mount mirror, a single Hella spotlamp mirror, and a VDO tachometer.

BAYERISCHE MOTOREN WERKE
AKTIENGESELLSCHAFT

Rundschreiben der Abteilung   Kundendienst

Motorcycles: Group Motor Nr. 1/63 (201) eng.

München, May 21, 1963
KV2 er/wi-pi

Re: Installation of a Revolution Counter (Tachometer)
    on Models R 69 S and R 50 S

As a special equipment for the above mentioned motorcycle types
the spare parts department delivers a revolution counter which
can be mounted subsequently on models equipped with vibration
damper.

Parts required:

1 Revolution counter	80 80 150
1 Flexible drive shaft	80 80 154
1 Angle drive for revolution counter	80 80 152
1 Mounting bracket	80 80 155
1 Cylindrical screw with driving slot	80 04 101
1 Wire tape	40 66 130
1 Front end cover	00 02 183
1 Lockwasher	99 32 110

Abolished parts:

1 Support clip	80 46 137
1 Screw	99 13 825
1 Nut M 10	99 22 111
1 Lockwasher B 10	99 33 108
1 Allen head screw	30 36 184
1 Flat washer	20 00 345
1 Front end cover	00 02 179

Installation:

1. Attach new mounting bracket for horn 80 80 155 on top engine
mount. After it, unscrew horn with leaf spring assembly from
support clip, carry it through between frame and engine to the
left and refit it on the previously attached mounting bracket
by means of stop plate with the former screw M 8. Remove support clip from frame.

2. Unscrew hydraulic steering damper from rear attachment and
push in piston rod completely. Remove front end cover from engine. Exchange hexagon allen-head screw of magneto rotor attachment against a cylindrical screw with slot 80 04 101.

This new cylindrical screw must be tightened to a torque of 14.5 ft/lbs. by torque wrench and commercial-type socket wrench supplement for slot-head screw. When tightening put the gears in fourth position and brake the rear wheel, lest engine joins in rotation. After that check ignition timing adjustment.

3. On fork prong above, on the right, unscrew fastening screw and attach the revolution counter with it. Instead of flat washer use the new lockwasher 99 32 110. Connect flexible drive shaft on the instrument, carry it through between headlamp and its holder downwards, going by in front of the lower fork guide and install it on the inside of the right frame tube.

4. Install the new front end cover 00 02 183 with nuts and lockwashers of the former front end cover on the engine. Remove the first nut from angle drive for revolution counter and screw the second nut entirely onto the thread. Introduce angle drive for revolution counter into the bore until the drive take-off member joins onto the slot-ground of the cylindrical screw. Screw the nut from thread end provisionally onto the contact surface on front end cover, thereafter screw two thirds turns further, by which the end clearance of 1 mm (.04") between angle drive for revolution counter and the slot ground of the cylindrical screw is adjusted.

Caution! Do not alter this adjustment during the following operations.

Thereafter take out the drive of revolution counter and remove the front end cover again. Reinstall the angle drive of revolution counter into the front end cover and tighten it with counter nut from inside just slightly. Seen in driving direction, output should be directed sloping upward to the right.

Finally mount front end cover. Start engine and accelerate up to approx. 1000 r.p.m. Loosen somewhat the nut of the angle drive for revolution counter at the outside of the front end cover and displace the angle drive for revolution counter with-in the hole, which is larger in its diameter about 1 mm (.04") than the thread, until the most possible running silence, sensible in the hand, is found. Finally tighten the nut and stop engine.

5. Connect flexible drive shaft to the angle drive for revolution counter and attach it on the frame tube by wire tape above the side-car mounting eye. Rubber grommet on the flexible drive shaft should be located below the wire tape.

Connect steering damper again. Finally undertake function test.

With kind regards
BAYERISCHE MOTOREN WERKE
Aktiengesellschaft

ppa. *Herbstreit*   i. V. *Makowitzki*

both the oil-pump-driven gearbox and either of the smaller instrument heads are currently available, along with cables in both lengths. As of the early 1990s, the camshaft-driven gearbox is not being reproduced. There are even similar VDO instruments, in 2:1 and 4:1 ratios, still being made for such non-BMW applications as Honda, Harley-Davidson, and Bultaco. These tachometers can occasionally be found at swap meets and flea markets at reasonable prices. They differ only from the black painted originals in having chrome plated cases, all black or all white faces, and bright red needles. They generally read to 10,000rpm, something your pre-1970 will never see. As an added benefit, they rotate in the same clockwise direction (but zero is at seven o'clock, not one o'clock) and all are lit internally via a small bulb. If you spot one, buy it, and check out the aforementioned dealers of the other brands to see if they've got any old ones lying forgotten on their shelves. If you want, you can paint them black; they are always good trade material at a swap meet.

Bags and Racks

All BMWs from 1950 through 1969 allowed for the fitment of at least a rudimentary parcel rack, which we generally call a pillion rack. It was a simple pressed-steel affair, riveted and welded together, and mounted to the top and sides of the rear fender. Most 1950–1954 BMWs came with the racks already fitted. Naturally, if the BMW had a long bench or dual seat, the rack was superfluous and could in fact not be used. If the owner chose not to mount a rack at all, the four holes in the top of the fender were plugged with little rubber plugs, which are again being reproduced. For a while, the little plugs were not available anywhere, and owners had to resort to rubber grommets or other nonstandard solutions. The pillion racks also served as

Bags in the 1960s came in all shapes and sizes. Here is a set of streamlined Denfelds with plastic trim, sold through the BMW importer Butler & Smith. *Joe Hazzard*

a base for a number of pillion or passenger saddles or cushions.

Happily, reproductions of the rack, in kit or welded up form, are now available at reasonable prices. The rack for the plunger framed twins had longer tabs than the one for the 1955–1969 models, but the remaining portions were the same. The rack for the 1950 R51/2, again since it was a prewar design, was slightly different, in having two mounting holes rather than four for attaching to the top of the fender. It cannot be adapted to the 1951–1954 twins, due to the mounting holes' interference with the fender wiring harness conduit.

If you wanted to carry more luggage, you had to use a folding luggage carrier that overhung the taillight and looked awkward, especially when loaded with gear. The carriers were made by both Denfeld and other manufacturers, and usually were chrome plated, although some of the early ones were painted black.

The Denfeld carriers had neat little red, black, or gray rubber inserts in their rails on some versions, and came with clever but totally useless gray rubber straps bearing the Denfeld logo. (Remem-

ber, this was before the ubiquitous bungee cord.) The original gray Denfeld straps were nice to look at and look great when showing your bike. To use them to secure anything other than a rolled up beach towel is to invite disaster. If the folding rack is mismounted, or if too much luggage is carried, the owner runs the very real risk of permanently damaging the rear fender, as both rack and luggage collapse onto that nice painted sheet metal. Damage of the taillamp housing is also a possibility.

Denfeld and Hoske also made some nice chrome-plated headlamp and taillamp guards, beautiful to look at but of dubious utility. To lift the bike via these guards usually damaged the rear fender, and the front headlight guard did little if anything to protect the rim in case of a spill. Like the eyebrow Hella headlamp rim, it was an accessory whose beauty was usually only in the eye of the beholder. Both versions of the lamp guards are currently being reproduced.

If you really wanted to carry things, saddlebags were the only solution. Again, Denfeld made some nice leather bags in several styles during the 1950–1969 era. All were military looking; large,

Original old-style Denfelds on an R60/2 owned by the author from 1973 until 1980. These were tall brown bags, very military in looks, were favored by the German *Polizei*. If properly cared for, they were moderately weatherproof and lasted a long time. For the accessory enthusiast, this BMW also had matching Denfeld solo and pillion saddles, a VDO tachometer, large sport tank, and an Albert bar-end mirror. The sidecar was a Ural acquired in Germany in 1974.

deep, and lockable with a padlock (as well as any leather case can be locked). All were prone to dry out once exposed to the weather, were not particularly watertight, were easily damaged in an accident, and were frequently stolen. Mounting them required special racks and brackets, which looked awkward when the bags weren't mounted. Bags came in green, brown, or black, with green most often reserved for the police. Their design and shape mirrored the bags Denfeld was making for the Wehrmacht during the 1939-1945 era, and as such are still in great demand by restorers of German military motorcycles.

If you didn't like the Denfelds, there are always bags from England, such as the ones made by Craven. The early Craven bags, called Silver Arrows, were fragile, glued-together affairs made of a phenolic-like plastic and wood, with wide aluminum bands and rivets, soon to become a Craven trademark. They are highly desirable today, and like all Craven bags, their insides smell like old

This white R69 has streamlined matching Enduro bags, another popular accessory from the 1960s. *Marie Lacko*

Craven bags looked perhaps the best on a BMW, with their understated black finish and plain aluminum trim. These British items were called the Golden Arrows, and although the lids were locking and relatively waterproof, they occa-sionally popped open, spilling the bags' contents all over the highway. The handlebar fairing is a Flanders accessory, made in California. *Richard Kahn, Butler & Smith, Inc.*

socks at the bottom of the laundry basket. Unfortunately, unlike their later counterparts, these early Cravens were not at all watertight and in fact leaked like sieves. The bracket portions were a nightmare to assemble, but did provide a stable platform for both the bags and the wide, robust rack that usually was part of the assembly. Once mounted, the brackets were usually left in place.

Craven bags most often seen on 1955–1969 BMWs are the Golden Arrows, with their sideways or swing-down non-removable lids, or the Dolomites, with their detachable lids that usually popped off while on the road, only to be noted as missing after many miles had passed. Several of the Craven styles are being reproduced today in the standard colors of either all white or all black, with the usual straps and keys. All Craven keys fit all the other Craven cases, so having a locking case is probably effective only for keeping out the honest man!

Americans, if they didn't favor the Craven cases or leather Denfeld bags, could opt for an American made accessory, the Enduro bag, which gave the BMW a distinctly unique appearance. Like the Craven bags, Enduros were made of plastic, although somewhat less expensively, and with a rough rather than the smooth glossy finish of the British product. Like the Craven bags, Enduros had hinged lids which, like the Cravens, were prone to blow off. The Enduros, however, seemed to fit onto the BMW without any visible brackets whatsoever, being clamped to the rear shock towers of the 1955–1969 Earles and US-fork machines. The bags fit so tightly to the frame, and the shape of the Enduros was such that from certain angles, especially from the rear, a BMW fitted with them was often mistaken for a Vespa scooter.

The original Connecticut manufacturer went out of business some years ago, but a fellow vintage BMW enthusiast purchased the molds and is now turning out reproductions for all that want them. Enduros also added somewhat to the safety of a BMW, since provisions were made from the outset to accommodate small accessory running lights at the rear of the bags. Often these lights were converted into turn signals, with mixed results.

Another pair of Craven bags, along with matching small top box. Completing the picture is another fine British product, an Avon Avonaire frame-mounted fairing, which gave this

R69US a totally different look. *Richard Kahn, Butler & Smith, Inc.*

Turn Signals

No 1950–1969 BMW ever came with turn signals as we know them today, mounted on flimsy stalks and looking totally out of place on anything but a tractor or a powerboat. Hella, to its credit, solved the dilemma of the safety conscious. They produced some clever and rugged little signals in beautiful polished castings, which fit into the ends of the handlebars. Magura went along with the concept by marketing rubber grips with the ends open, so that the signals could better be fitted. A 6-volt flasher from Bosch or Hella went into the headlight bucket, and a non-canceling accessory switch, similar to the standard Hella dip and horn switch assembly, was clamped to the handlebar. Magura also started to make its bars with the small hole for the wiring predrilled, or else the owner could drill his own.

The turn signals are still available, and the 6-volt Hella flasher is marked 91M1E1x21cp-6V. If you are using different sized or rated bulbs, ask for Hella number 91M1E1x15W-6V or 91M1E1x18W-6V. Installation is a snap, as only two lamps were required. Lenses were orange, and the whole thing looked so good that the Japanese started making copies, with a slightly different shape so that naturally none of the parts interchange. Japanese copies had longer bodies and red lenses, but functioned the same. Domiracer, a major vintage parts accessory house in Cincinnati, Ohio, has also started selling excellent Hella look-alikes at reasonable cost. The look-alikes are made out of a highly polished and plated zinc alloy with the same orange Hella-style lenses.

If you have a good battery, and if the night is particularly dark, the Hella signals are effective. In daylight, they serve to amuse the onlooker at best. They're usually left on for endless miles, unless the BMW owner is astute and clever enough to wire a small beeper into the system, something Hella, in all their wisdom, overlooked. Or maybe German

For seats and racks, you only have to turn to your local vintage BMW club member and supplier, of which there are quite a number both in Germany and the U.S.. Pictured here are two styles of Denfeld "breadloaf" pads, one Denfeld rubber pillion saddle, a Denfeld riders saddle with rubber silent bloc, plus a flat swinging pillion with white piping for an R69. The flat pressed steel rack without the side braces is for an R26 or R27 single. *Bob Henig*

BMW owners were thought to be more attentive from the outset than their American counterparts. We'll never know.

Pads and Saddles

The rear passenger was usually considered an afterthought, even by BMW, and few provisions were made by the motorcycle manufacturer for the carrying of an extra person, until the advent of the bench seat. It was up to the owner to purchase something for the passenger to sit on, and among the solutions were rubber swinging pillion saddles or foam and leatherette pads.

If the seat was to be a sprung rubber pillion saddle, the buyer had a multitude of choices. First, he could delete the flat, pressed steel rack, and mount a curved-base Denfeld or Pagusa, or one of any number of brands, straight to the top curve of the rear fender. All well and good, until you wanted

A detail shot of the Hella bar end signal, still available today as aluminum originals or plated and polished die-cast reproductions. *Craig Vechorik Photo*

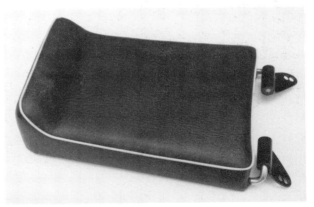

A similar swinging pillion pad, but note that the mounting hardware is a bit different. This one is made to fit a 1952–1954 R68. *Bob Henig*

to carry luggage instead. Worse, if your passenger was particularly robust, you ran the risk of denting the fender! If you find a curved base pillion saddle at a swap meet, or even in a dealer's stock, make certain it has four mounting holes, and not three or two. The latter will not fit a BMW and were made for other brands, such DKW or NSU. It's best to test fit one to a fender before you buy. To alter it later is difficult. Some dealers may not even know the difference, and often receive a shipment from Germany with some of the others mixed in.

If you elect to keep the flat rack, you'll have to get a pillion saddle with a flat base, which should have either three mounting holes conforming to the holes in the rack or expanding screw clamps. The best made pillion saddles were from Denfeld and Pagusa, and all provided some sort of adjustment to the spring tension to allow for varying loads. Early pillion saddles had hard rubber grab rings that provided a measure of security for the passenger. Again, the German safety authorities soon deemed these rings to be dangerous in a collision, which was probably the case. They soon forced

their replacement with either soft rubber rings, leather straps, or no hand holds at all. Pre-1955 BMWs should have the hard rubber handle variety.

A third option for the passenger was to perch precariously, and no more comfortably, on little pillion pads, commonly termed "breadloafs" today! They looked much like a flat loaf of bread, were usually made by Denfeld, and in fact could be mistaken for the cut off back end of a bench seat, which they greatly resembled. These items are sought after today and command a high price. Several styles were available, either mounting directly onto the fender curve or attaching to the top of the flat pillion rack.

Owners of the R68 and R69 sports models, if desiring an absolutely correct restoration, should mount only the accessory "flat swinging pillion," which was hinged at its front to the rear of the rider's solo saddle, and pivoted at its own rear on little flat spring-cum-brackets mounted to the sides of the rear fender. Originals were made of leather and finding one is again a task for the truly driven. While the pads look the same for the R68 and R69,

An excellent study of a mid-1960s German R50/2, fitted with two-piece curved crashbars, Hella bar end signals, and narrow Denfeld bench seat. Note that the brake rod and levers are now cadmium plated rather than black. *Kurt von Schwanewede*

A one-piece crashbar on this 1954 R67/2, which was the first motorcycle to pass through a tollgate on the New York Thruway after it was reopened to allow motorcyclists access. The BMW is fitted with a German Aero handlebar fairing, which attached to the headlamp with a strap and by bolts to the handlebar ends. In a stiff crosswind, it must have made handling quite exciting. *Richard Kahn, Butler & Smith, Inc.*

Heinrich fairings were usually handlebar mounted, either of aluminum or plastic, with the lower legshield portion attached to both the tank and frame. Two-tone colors of white and black were the most common, though solid colors in black or silver were also available. *Karl Heinrich*

the rear brackets are not identical. Reproductions of both the pads and the hardware are now available, but at considerable cost.

Crashbars and Fairings

In spite of the BMW's engine design that projects both cylinders out into the airstream, the heads and cylinders on the BMW twin are extremely well designed and strong enough to survive all but the most catastrophic of crashes. Naturally, the aluminum valve covers tend to suffer the most, and with the price of originals and reproduction valve covers now nearing the $100 mark, many owners consider the fitment of crashbars.

It should be noted that crashbars will have to be mounted securely to the frame, which will in all likelihood result in damage to the finish. They will be tubular or flat spring steel, heavily chrome-plated, and once scratched, scuffed, or damaged, will

Another Avon fairing, on an R69S, which sports a large tank, folding Denfeld luggage carrier, and the larger outlet BMW mufflers. The round oval license plate is the export "Zoll" plate you received when you picked up a bike or car in Germany. It allowed you to leave the country without having to pay the heavy value-added tax.

192

have to be removed in order to repair or refinish them. In hard crashes, crashbars have been known to save the heads and barrels from damage, at the expense of bending or warping the frame. Whether you choose to go to the effort to mount one and suffer the risks mentioned is up to you. Original style crashbars are expensive to restore, and in my opinion, detract from the inherent beauty of the BMW. Additionally, if you plan to mount one of the period fairings, such as the Avon, Peel, or Heinrich, crashbars will in all likelihood interfere with the mounting. The fairings themselves may have to be modified in order to accommodate the crashbar.

Crashbars were of three general types: tubular, one-piece frame-mounted; spring-steel frame-mounted; and tubular two-piece frame-mounted. The latter two are no longer being made and are hard to come by.

Fairings, on the other hand, tend to enhance the looks of a BMW, especially when painted to match the bike or when mounted in such a way as

to not smother the BMW's inherent good looks. Fortunately for us, we won't have to suffer such abominations as the plastic shroud that covered the Vincent Series D Black Prince and Black Knight, but some of the earlier American fairings come mighty close in that department.

Common fairings available in the 1950s and 1960s were the handlebar mounted Aero, a clear plastic and aluminum item mounted to the handlebars, and quite large to look at. It was probably the only large fairing available in the early 1950s that looked halfway decent on a BMW. Other handlebar fairings were solid plastic with clear screens made by Flanders or Wixom. The latter also provided some enveloping frame mounted lowers, which gave the BMW the appearance of a speedboat. The British-made Avon Avonaire fairings were one-piece frame-mounted designs, nice to look at, with cutouts for the cylinders. They, and the Peel, are desirable today. An attempt was made some years ago to reproduce the Peel and examples are still to be

In this 1967 photo of Tad Adamowski, head of shipping operations for UNICEF, we see the Heinrich lowers and an

Aero fairing, with its rubber strap under the headlight lens. *Richard Kahn, Butler & Smith, Inc.*

193

found today.

On the German side, Heinrich had perhaps the most extensive line of fairings designed for the BMW. Heinrich fairing were made in steel, aluminum, or plastic, and were usually handlebar mounted, with legshields attached to both the frame and over the gas tank. The attachment of a complete set of Heinrich uppers and lowers was complex, but once properly fitted they gave excellent protection to the rider. Most of the handlebar fairings were painted to match the BMW color scheme, with a two-tone white and black the most popular. Police in both Germany and other countries favored the Heinrich, and many shots of police BMWs show the full set of Heinrich accessories fitted.

When contemplating any sort of fairing, the prospective buyer again must consider the additional cost to restore the various components, and the additional costs one would have to bear should the BMW meet with an accident. Damage to a Heinrich or any of the others can be quite extensive, even if the bike just suffers a simple fall while parked at the curb. Another factor not considered until it's too late is that once a faring is mounted, all those previously unheard engine noises will now be captured, amplified, and reflected right back at the rider. Once a fairing is fitted, your previously silent BMW will suddenly turn into a noisy bit of machinery.

Mixed in with this mouthwatering collection of period prewar accessories are such niceties as a clip-on inspection lamp and plug, locking and non-locking gas caps, emblems and trim rings, several styles of handlebar posts, a pre-1955 plastic headed ignition key, and removable fork lock. All these items are currently available from several vintage BMW enthusiasts in the U.S. *Bob Henig*

The Last Bits and Pieces

There's really little else any one of us would want to mount on a 1950–1969 BMW. The electrical system is just too primitive for radios, CBs, and high-powered horns or lights. Besides, these things just don't belong on a BMW, unless yours is a police bike and still on active duty. Chrome-plated geegaws, reflectors, and foxtails may look cute and clever on some of the other brands, but not on a BMW, thank you.

If you want to make your BMW a little different, consider a set of tank emblem surrounds, once popular accessories that have recently been reproduced by a vintage club member in California. They're now in stainless, versus the original chrome plated tin, and therefore will never rust and peel like the originals.

A final item with which to amaze your friends is the seldom seen 6-volt accessory trouble light, which plugs into the accessory socket under the seat, an item usually sitting idle on a pre-1969 BMW. The trouble light dates back to the early 1930s, when all BMWs had them, and can still be found today, still being made by the same company to the same 1930s pattern. If your BMW dealer hasn't got one, try an old time Mercedes-Benz dealer. Their cars from the 1950s and 1960s used the same lamp, which plugged into the same BMW-type socket under the hood. If you need just the plug and want to adapt your own 6-volt lamp, the plug can be ordered under Hella number 8JA 002 262-002.

A nice inexpensive accessory item for the 1950–1969 BMW is a pair of finned exhaust ring covers, which fit all twins except the R68, R69, and the S models. Not only can they hide a pair of damaged and discolored exhaust rings, they also provide some additional cooling to the cylinder head near the exhaust port. The vented metal exhaust pipe shields, also period accessories, helped hide rusted and dented pipes, and protected you somewhat from getting accidentally burned. *Craig Vechorik*

Chapter 19

Getting Help

No book can possibly tell you all there is to know about restoring a motorcycle, and books about BMWs are no exception. No amount of personal experience or expertise can take the place of professional help. No matter how many BMWs you've owned, and how many you've restored, you will eventually have to seek the advice of others.

Once you've admitted to yourself that you just can't go any further without help, one or two courses are available to you. You can either farm out everything that's left to professionals, or you can seek the advice of experts and continue to go it alone. In most cases, you've already exhausted the possibilities in the second choice, and now find yourself at an impasse.

However, even though you'll now be bringing

An example of a well-intended but flawed restoration. My first vintage BMW, restored in the early 1970s, done at a time when few sources of original parts had been developed. The 1950 R51/2 is fitted with a 1951 R51/3 engine, disguised somewhat with split valve covers from an R27 sin-gle! Except for the rubber fork boots, all else is pretty much correct for a 1950 R51/2, including the external wiring harness on the rear fender. The machine is now in California. *Marie Lacko*

the remaining parts of your BMW to a commercial shop or mechanic, you can minimize your expenses, speed up the work, and probably end up with a better BMW in the end, if you elect to do some of the legwork yourself.

The appendix includes a list of firms specializing in the restoration of vintage and classic motorcycles, as well as firms catering exclusively to the remanufacture or resale of spare parts and accessories. You can save yourself some money and time by purchasing the parts beforehand, and bringing them to your mechanic. Make sure you discuss this with your mechanic ahead of time; some may prefer to purchase the parts themselves, or may already have them in stock. If you already have spares of your own, by all means stress this fact to your mechanic or restoration shop.

Painters and Platers

With only two exceptions, I've tried to avoid mentioning painters in the appendix. Painting is an art that's practiced by many, and mastered by few. There are bound to be excellent painters in your area who have done, or are capable of doing, BMW motorcycle fenders, tanks, and frames. To ship your parts halfway across the country increases the risk of damage, and increases the cost of your restoration by adding in the costs of shipping and crating. Better to cart the parts across town to a local painter than to mail them away. Besides, with a local professional, you can visit your parts often and make enough of a nuisance of yourself that the work will eventually get done in the time originally estimated. You can also take the painted parts quickly to a local striper, and watch and give advice while the striping is being done, unless the painter can also do that work himself. Arm yourself with dimensional data and factory photos to show the striper where the lines should go.

Plating, by the same token, is best done locally, especially if you can find a plater with a good reputation. A word of caution is required here, how-

Your local painter won't be able to provide this sort of service, but you might want to show him how it used to be done. Pictured is the tank and wheel paint shop at the BMW factory where 1951–1954 tanks and wheels underwent an infrared baking, suspended from an overhead conveyer. The steel wheels have already been treated to their silver center section. *Dr. George Kruse*

ever. Some chrome-plating shops do shoddy work and can ruin some expensive and irreplaceable items. If you come armed with a neatly typed list of everything you'll be leaving with them, along with photographs, you can accomplish several things at once. First, the plater will see that you're conscientious about your restoration. Second, if he sees that you've already prepared the evidence in the way of photographs, he'll probably take better care of the part, and not risk a lawsuit later on should some of them get lost or ruined.

In your list of items, describe the pieces in layman's terms that a plater possibly unfamiliar with the BMW would understand. "Magura risers" may have little meaning; "curved motorcycle handlebar posts" describes the items better. Thankfully, there are only a few items on a BMW that might require plating or polishing. Ask the plater to initial the list of parts you've provided and leave him a copy. If he refuses, go elsewhere.

Mechanical Work

Again, local mechanics and machinists are the best choice, but here I have been able to come up with a number of reliable shops in the U.S. that have built a good reputation over the years when it comes to restoring and rebuilding vintage and classic motorcycles. If in doubt, ask your local BMW dealer where he gets his work done. If he offers to do the work himself, ask the names of any local customers that have BMWs similar to yours. Not only can you check on the quality of the dealer's work, you'll also probably meet some more like-minded BMW enthusiasts with whom you can share your common passion.

Bits and Pieces

A good number of BMW dealers and private parties now either import reproduction or original parts for vintage and classic BMWs or manufacture their own. Again, ask around and find out how other customers have been treated. Just because their prices may seem high, it's no reason to avoid them. In many cases, they will be your only source of parts and may be the only ones who are willing to look for your particular item on their next trip to Germany. It's like having your own import agent traveling to the German flea markets for you. All you have to provide is money. Most of the part suppliers are also vintage BMW enthusiasts and probably have some nice old machines of their own or one just like the one you're restoring.

As a last resort, you can try ordering direct from overseas, but this could spell disaster for the unwary. In all likelihood, you will have to correspond in the seller's own language, which may be fine if his language is German, but which may be

Three-way surface machining of 1951–1954 transmission cases at the BMW factory in Munich. *BMW Archives*

more difficult if he speaks Greek or Hungarian. You'll usually have to prepay, probably in the seller's currency, which will mean the added expense of purchasing a foreign currency bank draft from your bank. Add to that long months of waiting and more delays if the items arrive damaged or get tied up in customs until you pay Uncle Sam his pound of flesh. Better to leave all these hassles to the parts importer, who makes a living at this and has probably found ways to avoid all the pitfalls that can snare the novice.

Recommendations

Not only would it be unfair and impolite to recommend one dealer over another, it could also be misleading. Shops and firms come and go regularly, and even as this manuscript is being written, more individuals are entering the marketplace as parts importers and restoration shop owners. Some have begun a career as agents for overseas dealers, specializing in ferreting out BMWs long hidden and inaccessible behind the former Iron Curtain.

Wouldn't it be nice to find a shop like this today? Perhaps the engine from your R68 is in this picture, taken in 1954 at the BMW factory. Note the little bin full of white rubber timing hole plugs next to the engine conveyer belt. Back then knickers and knee socks were still considered proper attire, even on BMW's assembly line. Considering how few of the R68 were built, this photo must represent an entire month's production in 1954. *BMW Archives*

Where having the resources, skill, and contacts pays off. This is the real thing, a 1950 R51/2 restored by Vintage Club member Arlen Anderson, absolutely correct in all respects except for the 1955–69 style tire pump! Note the subtle differences in valve covers from the R27 items in the previous photo. *Marie Lacko*

Chapter 20

Preparing for the Show

If this book has been any help at all, and if you were successful in the first place and found a nice 1950–1969 BMW ready for restoration, you're now ready to wrap it all up and either ride and enjoy your bike to its fullest or prepare to send it on its first show outing.

In spite of the thrill of collecting trophies, plaques, and ribbons and of having others marvel at your machine for its beauty—and at you for your cleverness—there's nothing that can compare to the thrill of actually riding something you've either brought back from the brink of extinction, or refined to a reflection of its former glory. In either case, the BMW was meant to be used, ridden, and enjoyed. To restore a machine and never ride it is like undergoing a successful heart transplant, and then electing to never leave the recovery room. Why restore an old Stearman and then not fly it?

The same holds true for the BMW, which ranks right up there with all the other classics enthusiasts are now restoring and riding. Vincent and Velocette owners ride most of their restored machines, so do owners of ancient Harleys and Indians. A "plastic bagger" who trailers his machine in sterile wrappings to a meet, never starting the motor, and never so much as spoiling the tank or engine by adding fluids to them, is looked upon with disdain by most organizations. No matter how perfect your machine, the proof of the pudding is in the starting, so to speak, and an engine that doesn't run, or a bike that cannot be ridden, is usually judged more harshly in a concours competition.

Do yourself and the BMW a favor by at least starting the machine occasionally and giving it some needed exercise. I'm not demanding that you ride your precious jewel cross-country in all sorts of weather, to all sorts of events. Just ride it now and then, even if you don't plan to ride it as daily transportation.

Restored or Original?

Throughout this book we've tried to assist you in restoring your BMW. This is not to say that every

While not all vintage BMW meets will have posters as handsome as this 1985 Dennis Simon original, most events will be well publicized in several of the major BMW club magazines in the U.S., such as *On the Level*, the *BMW Owners News*, or the *Vintage BMW Bulletin. Dennis Simon*

199

Vintage events usually choose sites that complement the character of the machines, such as this setting at Soper Field in Brookline, New Hampshire, in 1974. Most of the machines and their proud owners are still among the ranks of the Vintage BMW Club, some twenty years later. *Richard Pogue*

A gathering of BMW riders in the mid-1960s in California. Handlebar fairings of the Wixom variety, along with the Wixom frame mounted lowers, were quite popular. *Richard Kahn, Butler & Smith, Inc.*

BMW should be restored. Many a fine, unrestored example of a pre-1970 BMW is still to be found, often in the hands of its original owner. To strip and refinish a machine that has no marks against it other than the passage of years is often counterproductive, and in some cases decreases the value of the machine. All things being equal, a finely maintained and cleanly presented original, unrestored BMW will defeat a restored one at a concours. If you find a clean original, try to keep it in its original state. Internal repairs and renovations are of course permissible, but if the chrome and sheet metal are good, it's best to leave them alone. Not only do you save money in the long run, many prospective buyers are willing to pay more for an unrestored original BMW than for an equivalent restored one.

Getting to the Meet

If the BMW is particularly old or fragile, or if the owner fits that category, by all means trailer the bike to a meet. If the meet is many days away, you could do some serious cosmetic damage to a pristine restored machine by riding it, especially if the roads are rough and the weather less than ideal.

At a vintage BMW event in Andover, Massachusetts, some years ago, an exhibitor treated us to what was perhaps the ultimate in enthusiasm. He flew his restored 1932 BMW R16 up from Virginia in his private plane and rode it from the local airport to the meet. He also rode it over several of the adjoining counties. By the meet's end, the rare and irreplaceable machine had covered hundreds of miles, suffered a major magneto failure, been repaired in the parking lot, and still managed to run away with all the awards! It was then ridden back to the airport and flown home.

Trailering is best if an enclosed trailer is used, since open trailers will do little to protect the machine from road grit, dust, and dirt. They also won't

Most meets will be of the casual, unstructured variety, such as this Vintage BMW Club event in Andover, Massachu- setts. Expect to answer many questions whenever you park your machine. *Marie Lacko*

There's always time to learn something new or to discuss the fine points of a restoration, as is being done by these Vintage Club members in Washington state. *Dave Kaechele*

protect the BMW much when parked at night at the back of some distant motel, or while you're in the restaurant getting dinner. If you do decide to ride it, bring along enough spares to ensure your successful arrival and bring along enough cleaning materials, polish, and rags to be able to prepare your BMW for the show.

Detailing

When getting ready to prepare your BMW for judging, you'll need to present a clean machine. Rags will be needed to wipe off excess oil; use softer rags for polishing the chrome and paint. Armorall is best for rubber items, but may leave an oily film on painted surfaces. Use of 3M Hand Glaze on the paintwork gives good results, but tends to remove all traces of protective wax. It's usually good only for one showing, but does present a nicely finished tank and fenders in their best light. Simichrome is good for polishing chrome and the few polished aluminum items on a BMW.

Engine cases and other castings that have a rough, non-polished finish can best be cleaned and kept looking like new by lightly rubbing them with 0000-grade steel wool and kerosene. Lightly spraying with WD-40 after the rubbing is done, and then wiping it all off with a rag will present the judge with a nice, dry casting, looking for all the world like it just came out of BMW's foundry. Wheels are cleaned with rags and WD-40, tires with Armorall. Get in the tread pattern with an old toothbrush and

Q-Tips. Don't forget to wipe under the engine and transmission. Polish dried fuel stains from the carburetors with the same steel wool and kerosene. If you've brought along some touch-up paint, go over all the stone chips carefully. Don't forget some touch-up paint to match the pinstriping. If you brought along some silver paint, go over the braided fuel lines. Wipe off the battery and any accumulated corrosion near the terminals. If the rubber strap holding down the battery is cracked, replace it or at least reverse it, to hide the cracks.

Ancillary Matter

If you have a tool kit and manual, you may want to lay it out next to the bike on the knitted red and white BMW shop rag. If you're the original owner, advertise the fact. Some go so far as bringing along, under glass and frame, the original sales documents and title, especially if the BMW is particularly old. It's all known as provenance and certainly helps present your pride and joy in a better light. It certainly can't hurt, and although most judges won't award you extra points for a nice display, it does make it all the more interesting for the spectator. Replacement tool kits and tire pumps are still available, as are reprint manuals. You can even still get, in reprint form, copies of the original tie-on dealer price tags from the late 1960s, at least for the R50/2, R60/2, and R69S models.

Entering the Machine

You're now at the meet, you see a bunch of bikes lining up, your machine is relatively presentable, so you decide to go see what's going on. To your delight, you find it's a bike judging for all sorts of BMWs, possibly even for other makes as well. Some of those entered are already being cleaned furiously by their owners, and some, to tell the truth, don't look half as good as yours. Why not enter and perhaps go home with a ribbon or trophy?

Prepare yourself for a rude awakening. Not only will you be up against BMWs far better than yours (which are probably being polished within the confines of their enclosed trailers) you'll also be up against owners for whom winning isn't everything, it's the only thing. If you can stand the strain, eavesdrop as they berate the judges after the meet, if for some inexplicable reason their BMW didn't win. Try to enter an event without feeling that winning is a life and death affair. Many

Although this is a BMW R25/3, displaying your complete tool kit and original tire patch tin with your 1950–1969 BMW twin will certainly add appeal to your machine when entered in a concours competition. *BMW Archives*

friendships have been destroyed and club memberships canceled over something as foolish as a little blue ribbon. If you feel you really need to have a trophy, it's infinitely easier and cheaper to just go out and purchase one, engraving it any way you chose.

In spite of all these caveats, you decide to exhibit your BMW anyway. While in the midst of cleaning and polishing, a judge walks over and asks you what class you're in. If you don't know, now is the time to find out and make a commitment. Try to enter the class your machine would have the most success in. A conscientious judge will usually give you some good advice, and may even steer you to a class for which your machine is better suited. His aim, after all, is to see that everyone has fun, that all will want to come back next year, and to level the playing field as much as possible.

If yours is a pre-1955 BMW, it should go into a class with its contemporaries. If it has a sidecar attached, perhaps it will do best in the sidecar class. If it's a one-off special, a racer, or a trials bike, you may have to enter it in the custom class. A pre-1970 BMW should not have to compete against the more modern versions of the BMW, but it will have to compete against better restored, and better maintained unrestored machines in its own class, unless the meet is large enough, and the awards extensive enough, to accommodate separate restored and unrestored categories in all the classes.

Surviving the Inquisitor

Once your bike is parked where it will be judged, the judge will hand you a judging sheet, usually with places to enter pertinent data about yourself and your machine. Remember, not all judges may be familiar with your particular model, although all will know as much as the average enthusiast about the BMW. Most will have judged before; none are being paid for this, and most are doing it because they enjoy it. Making their job a little easier and not hassling them for a minor oversight may even get you asked to be a judge next year.

The entry and score sheet should have a place for your information, at the least your name, your town, and the license tag of your bike. Most awards will be handed out at the meet, so a full mailing address isn't required. Most owners prefer it that way. You will, however, be asked many things about your BMW, such as the year, model, the model of sidecar, its year of manufacture, and the name of the owner if it's different from the exhibitor. Some sheets also ask if you previously won at a major event. Being a previous winner shouldn't count against you. Some judges just like to know such information, and may mention it when they call you up to collect your "fourteenth consecutive first place award."

A properly designed form should also ask you

Some owners bring their entire collection to share with others. This is a view of one Vintage BMW Club member's BMWs, among them a 1955 R69, a 1928 R52, a 1954 R25/3, and a 1953 R51/3, as displayed at a California meet some years ago. *Duane Ausherman*

When it's time for the judging, get ready for some intense scrutiny. This post-1966 R69S (identified by the non-serif tank emblems) is getting more than just a simple once over by these judges.

to record the year the bike was restored, if that is the case, or whether it's all original and unrestored. There should also be a place for the serial number, which will be used as a tie breaker for awards such as oldest BMW. If you rode the bike to the meet, the form should ask you the distance you rode. Again, in cases of a tie on points, the judges may decide to give the award to the bike that was ridden, rather than trailered.

Judging Guidelines

The following judges' guidelines are an extract from a Judging Entry and Score Sheet devised by Vintage BMW club member Larry Sparber, who has been judging BMW competitions for both the BMW Owners of America and The BMW Riders of America, the two largest clubs in the U.S., as well as events hosted by the Vintage BMW Motorcycle Owners, Ltd. The form is based on over fifteen years of such participation, and was constructed using Sparber's past experience as a judge for the Rolls-Royce Owners Club, as a Master Senior Judge for the AACA, and from his lengthy stints as Guest Judge at the BMW of North America spon-

sored Lime Rock Vintage Fall Festivals. As such, the form is comprehensive in both scope and detail, and serves as an excellent checkoff sheet for both judge and exhibitor alike.

Some of the more pertinent points are restated here for you to note when preparing a bike for a show, or when planning to judge a number of such machines at a meet you might be attending. In the form, it's stated that judges and entrants are to keep in mind that each machine will be judged on its individual visual merits, rather than against like models in its respective class. The judge's task should be to showcase outstanding examples in each class of entrant, using a point system to judge each entrant equally, by quality, not the personality of the machine or owner.

The judge and the exhibitor should keep in mind that while one machine may have been trailered to the meet and another ridden, or while one may exhibit fresh or recent restorative qualities, it will not necessarily automatically acquire more points than a well-preserved, original condition model of a similar type.

It's the owner's responsibility to prepare his

machine to a basic condition of cleanliness, wiping off apparently visible dirt, grease, rust, and oil, except as would logically be present, such as on a grease fitting or inside a muffler tip. Chrome and paint should be polished for maximum effect, as compared to having an obvious layer of dust and road dirt, as may be apparent to sight and touch. Over polishing and plating are to be considered grounds for points deduction, as are any fitments not in character with the machine or in conflict with the intent of the manufacturer. Judges should look for an overall balanced machine in terms of condition, appearance, and originality, combined with logic and common sense in the judge's point scoring decisions.

In the judging of stock (unmodified) machines, an entry exhibited with an engine of newer design (i.e., an electric start post -1970 motor in a pre-1970 frame) than was engineered for that series BMW will be subject to the maximum point deduction for that category. This also holds true for conversions, such as VW engines fitted to BMW frames. Such converted or modified machines should be judged and entered in the custom or modified classes. Similar point deductions should be considered when confronted with nonstandard engines inserted in otherwise standard frames, such as the use of an R67/2 motor in a frame obviously from an R51/3, and still stamped and tagged as such. Alterations of original numbers will also account for maximum point deductions, as will the obliteration of serial numbers and other factory supplied data.

Accessories should be of the factory authorized variety or a recognized aftermarket offering designated for, and designed to be used on, the particular BMW being displayed. An example of nonstandard accessories would be plastic saddlebags from the 1970-1980 series of BMW, fitted to a pre-1970 BMW. Point deductions in such cases would be the rule.

Tires should be of an appropriate size, pattern, and design for the particular era, with oversized tires marked down accordingly. It should be noted that although most German brands are now again available in patterns appropriate for earlier BMWs, in the interests of safety, brands other than German originals will be permitted. Regardless of brand, tires should be of a safe and roadworthy condition. Use of age-dried tires or marginal treads are grounds for point deductions. In cases of ties in all categories, the judges have the option of using condition of tires, as well as brand name and type, as a tie breaker.

Sidecars will be judged using the appropriate criteria from the categories defined for the motorcycles, with the obvious deletion of engine and drivetrain categories.

Entries will be scored using a deductive system, whereby all entries will begin with the maximum number of points. Deductions are at the rate of one to five points per component per occurrence in each section, based on condition and appearance. In the case of a total deviation, such as the absence of a required part (e.g., tire pump or taillight) or the use of an engine incorrect for that particular model, the maximum number of points may be deducted, at the judges discretion.

If the judges or team of judges cannot resolve a particular deduction, the chief judge will assist in the re-evaluation of the issue, and make the final decision. All judges will complete and total the points on the scoring sheet, giving the sheets to the chief judge at the end of the competition, prior to the announcement of awards.

In fairness to all, and since the intent of any restoration is to bring the motorcycle back as close as possible to its original state, any BMW in contention for an award may be required to be started and ridden for some distance in view of the judges on the judging field. Failure to start will result in a penalty, and motorcycles with incomplete engines or engines missing internal parts will be immediately disqualified. Additionally, while those judging should not be prevented from entering and displaying their own machines, judges will not be allowed to judge motorcycles in a class in which their own machines are entered.

Class Breakdowns

In the interest of expediency, BMW motorcycles will be broken down into components for the purpose of judging. Each component or category will be worth twenty points before the judging begins, for a total of 100. Points will then be deducted by the judges for shortcomings within each category, for a maximum deduction of twenty points in each category. The five categories are as follows:
• Main "Body" and Its Components: including the tank and cap, fenders, kneepads, license bracket, seat(s), fairing/windshields, bags, cases, racks as applicable.
• Chassis Components: including frame, suspension, battery holder, center/side stands, foot rests, handlebar/control assemblies, gauges, brakes, wheels, cables, and tires and spokes. Tool kits and manuals will only be considered if displayed. Failure to show such items does not imply their absence and no marks will be deducted.
• Drivetrain: including the engine and all its components, such as carburetors, air tubes and air cleaner, transmission and shift and kick levers, rear drive, and the complete exhaust system.
• Electrics: including lights, headlight shell, horn, switches, wiring, taillight, and battery.
• Painting and Plating: including considerations of the correct type and color for the model; location, quality, and condition of striping; and appropriate-

ness and condition of emblems and other related insignia.

Once the judging starts, owners must stop cleaning and polishing, but should stay close to their machines to answer any questions the judges might have. Often a point of confusion or disagreement can only be clarified by the owner. No judge should be expected to be an expert on every possible aspect of every BMW ever built.

Awards should not differentiate between a first, second, or third. It's better to give one Award of Excellence to the best motorcycle in its class. If several tie for such an award, additional ones can be given out, without offending the other winners or causing any ruffled feathers. By giving out a first over a second place, the recipient of the latter will in all likelihood want to know why his machine was deemed less worthy than the first place winner's bike.

All entrants should be given their own score sheets at the end of the meet, so that areas in which they lost points can be understood and remedied for a future event. Under no circumstances should judges allow competitors to see another entrant's score sheet. If the entrants want to compare scores later on, that is their business. Judges must be willing to discuss the scoring with any competitor that has questions about how his own score was tabulated.

Remember, a motorcycle judging is a place where everyone should have fun, and where all owners should be able to take pleasure in displaying both their restored and unrestored machines, without fear of penalty or prejudice.

Awards can be simple yet memorable, like these cloisonné enamel medals and ribbons won by my 1936 BMW R12 in three consecutive years at the BMW of North America sponsored Vintage Fall Festival at Lime Rock Park, Connecticut.

When the judging is over, nothing can match the thrill of the awards ceremony, as evidenced by Vintage BMW Club member Lockwood Doensch, who couldn't be happier with the award he and his R69US just won at a vintage meet in Ohio. *Rich Scheckler*

Appendices

Component Parts Required for 12-Volt/ 100-Watt Generator System for /2 BMW

Quantity	Description of Part	Part No.
1 ea	Generator, 12v/100W	12 31 8002 033
2 ea	Fillister head screw M 6x75	07 11 9919 960
1 ea	Vibration damper R 50s, R 69s	11 23 0070 141
1 ea	Allen head hex screw, 100W Generator	11 23 0070 148
1 ea	Spring Washer B8	07 11 9932 090
1 ea	Regulator switch 12v	12 31 8002 325
1 ea	Retaining plate	65 12 8002 325
1 ea	Protection cap	12 31 8008 115
1 ea	Hex head screw M 5x12	07 11 9913 231
1 ea	Hex head screw M 5x15	07 11 9913 235
2 ea	Washer 5, 8	07 11 9931 404
1 ea	Kickstarter lever, 12 volt	23 51 1056 122
2 ea	Battery, 6-volt 12-amp hr (clear Housing)	61 21 8042 030
2 ea	Battery tension strap	61 21 8042 140
2 ea	Rubber pad for battery	61 21 8042 111
2 ea	Rubber ring for battery	61 21 8042 181
1 ea	Battery holder	61 21 8042 230
1 ea	Fillister head screw AM 6x12	07 11 9919 463
1 ea	Shakeproof washer J 6, 4	07 11 9919 136
1 ea	Hex nut M 6	07 11 9922 053
2 ea	Hex head screw M 6x12	07 11 9913 441
2 ea	Shakeproof washer J6, 4	07 11 9936 136
2 ea	Hex nut M 6	07 11 9922 053
1 ea	Signal horn 12-volt KLAXON	61 33 8046 040
1 ea	Flasher 12-volt	61 31 8048 146
	Miscellaneous bulbs for lights on motorcycle. Can also use automotive flasher to operate more than one turn signal.	
1 ea	Wiring harness, 12-volt, unscreened or Wiring harness, 12-volt screened	61 11 8066 045 / 61 11 8066 046
1 ea	Cable for wiring batteries together B 2, 5 x 260	07 11 9976 520
2 ea	Kabelschuhe (Cable shoe)	61 13 8070 138
2 ea	Rubber sockets	61 13 8070 220
1 ea	Interference condenser 12-volt	65 12 8002 267
1 ea	Interference condenser 12-volt on frame	65 31 8002 265
1 ea	Retaining plate	65 31 8002 277
1 ea	Retaining angle	65 31 8002 278
1 ea	Tension jib for battery support	61 21 8042 234

Bearing and Seal Cross References

Craig Vechorik (Technical Editor of the *Vintage BMW Bulletin* when this book was written), recently compiled a useful list of inexpensive, readily available replacement seals and bearings which can be found at most bearing supply houses or auto parts discounters.

Unless otherwise noted, these components will fit the following 1955–1969 twins, and their /2 variants : R50, R60, R69, R69S, as well as some late R68, R51/3, and R67/2 BMWs.

All of the dimensions are in millimeters, and these part numbers are for Chicago Rawhide CR brand seals, which can be cross referenced easily at any auto parts store. The prices of bearings and seals vary wildly from store to store, so shop around! A brief discussion of seal lip compounds is also in order.

Nitrile. The most common seal material, and what all of the original BMW seals were made of. Nitrile is used in applications of temperatures of -65 to 225deg F. It will stand short exposures to temperatures up to 250deg F.

Viton. A superior seal material, good for temperatures from -40 to 400deg F. This material has extreme resistance to abrasion (dirt) and superior wear characteristics. It is more expensive than Nitrile but worth it.

Axle seals, outside (25x35x7)	CR # 9705 Nitrile CR # 9706 Viton
Axles seals, inside (25x38x6)	CR # 9701 Nitrile
Wheel bearings	#30204 (The stock number for the equivalent at Auto Zone, a major US retail chain, is #765891.)
Rear swing arm bearings	#30203 (these are the same as /5 & /6 wheel bearings)
Rear swing arm seal (22x40x6.35)	CR #8550 Nitrile CR #8552 Viton
Camshaft seal (25x35 x7)	CR #9705 Nitrile CR #9706 Viton
or Camshaft seal (28x40x7)	CR #10930 Nitrile CR #10932 Viton
Crankshaft, front (20x35x7)	CR #9715 Nitrile CR #9716 Viton
or Crankshaft, front (20x32x7)	CR #9710 Nitrile
Rear Main Seal (52x72x8)	CR #20440 Nitrile CR #20441 Viton
Cardan Seal, Rear end (65x85x10)	CR #25420 Nitrile CR #25421 Viton

Main Bearings (ex. R69S)	#207K Fafnir	
Cam Bearings	#6203 SKF	

Exhaust pipe crush washers are the same as for the 900 Kawasaki (part # 11001906). Another source is Vesrah part # VX4005, from the major supplier of aftermarket Japanese parts.

The tapered steering head bearings are of Japanese manufacture and can be bought through *any* bike shop that deals with the motorcycle wholesaler Dixie Cycle Supply. Dixie's part number for the kit is SSW #300, and the manufacturer's number is SSW 055.

Color coding makes work easier when carrying out repairs and troubleshooting. In the DIN standard there are eight basic colors which have the following meanings:

Green = GN	leads from ignition coils to contact brakers	
Red = RT	leads from batt. to generators and to light & ignition switches	

Black = SW   leads from batt. to starter as well as from light & ignition switches to ignition coil, starting syst., day-light consumers

Brown = BR	earth leads (ground)	
Lt. Blu = BL	leads to generator, oil pressure, generator indicator light etc.	
White = WS	leads to headlamp HI-beam	
Yellow = GE	leads to headlamp LO-beam	
Grey = GR	leads for tail & parking light, license plate light etc.	

There are also additional code colors in the form of colored stripes on the insulation. For example, the markings for the following leads are:

Red/Blue = left turn signals, Black/Blue = right turn signals

Black/Green = hot horn lead, etc., etc., etc.

Wiring Diagram Checklist

Terminal

marking	Wire leading from	to
1	Ignition Coil	Contact breaker
2	Magnet	Ignition switch(short circuiting switch)
4	Ignition Coil	Spark Plug (Distributor)
15	Ignition Switch	Ignition Coil
15/54	Main Switch	Ignition Coil
30	Battery, positive	Starter, main switch, ignition switch
30/51	Battery or Generator	Relay switch
31	Battery, negative	Earth (to engine or transmission block)
49	Ignition switch	Flasher unit
49a	Flasher unit	Flasher switch
50	Starter switch	Starter soleniod switch
51	Generator regulator	Battery, starter, main switch.
54	Main switch(see also15/54)	Day consumer, horn, turn indic, switch
56	Light switch	Dipswitch (dimmer switch)
56a	Dip switch	Headlamp(Hi-beam)
56b	Dip switch	Headlamp(Lo-beam)
57	Light switch	Parking light
58	Light switch	Taillight, lic.plate light, side-car
61	Generator regulator	Generator tell-tale lamp
85	Relay	Earth (ground)
86	Relay	Battery (via switch or direct)
87	Relay w/normally-open contact	to accessory, like foglamps, etc.
87a	Relay w/normally-closed contact	to accessory
87b	Relay w/2 normally-open contact	to accessory
L	Turn indicator switch	Left-hand turn indicator
R	Turn indicator switch	Right-hand turn indicator
D+	Generator, positive	Regulator, positive
D-	Generator, negative	Regulator, negative
DF	Generator exciter winding	Regulator
B+	Regulator	Battery
X	American type flasher	to Power (hot lead), day consumers
P	American type flasher	to Pilot indicator light
L	American type flasher	to switch operating lamps to be flashed

This illustrated list shows the minimum number of indispensable tools that a responsible agent should have in his workshop.

283	296	338/1
284	297	355
285	299	357
286	311	422A
289	319	467
290	326	494

Special Tools for BMW Motorcycles

Matra Order No. and Illustration	Description
289	Replacer, for seal ring in rear wheel drive. To insert seal ring slide 289 over splined portion of final coupling flange.
290	Replacer, for seal ring in rear wheel drive. To install ring gear slide 290 over splined portion of final coupling flange.
292	Locking Fixture, for flywheel. To loosen and tighten crankshaft nut lock clutch bolts and casing screws with 292. Same fixture with 3 screwed-on holder bushings V 5032 (shop-made tool).
293 1	Crank Web Support for horse-shoe plate, for crankshaft disassembly. Screw 293.1 upon 293/2. Support crankshaft with 331/1 in 293/2/1, press out crankpin, together with centre web, using 293/5 and press.
293/2/3	Horse-shoe Plate 293/2 with crank web support 293 3 for crankshaft disassembly. Support crankshaft with 331/1 in 293/2/3, press out crankpin with centre web using 293/5 and press.
293/4	Intermediate Plate for crankshaft assembly. Support crankpin with 331/1 on 293/4, press outer crank web on crankpin, using plate of 293/5 and press.
293/5	Drift Punch for crankshaft. Application see 293/1 2'3 and 293 4.
294	Valve Seat Cutter, 45 deg., 36 mm dia. For cutting fit on cutter guide shank 431.
295	Valve reseating cutter, 15 deg., 36 mm dia. For refacing seats to valve head diameter. Fit on cutter guide shank 431.
296	Ratchet Wrench, for loosening and tightening nut on rear wheel drive pinion.
297	Replacer Bushings for oil seal of driving shaft. Slide 297/1 over splines to install shaft with drift bushing W 5023 (shop-made tool). 297/2 serves to remove and replace the oil seal (Simmerring).
298	Graduated Dial, for adjustment of ignition timing. Insert 298 in bore of centered clutch plate and clamp with upper nut. Reset dial after spigot nut has been loosened.
299	Puller, for ball bearing 6204 and sprocket; for sprocket R 51/2 with extension arbour, shop-made tool W 5001.
311	Puller, for flywheel with 2 sets of screws Flange of 311 with 2 screws 24 mm long, or with 2 screws 20 mm long is screwed on flywheel. Press off flywheel.

Special Tools for BMW Motorcycles

Matra Order No. and Illustration	Description
316	Spanner, open end 41 mm for adjustment of fork steering column.
316A	Spanner, double open end 41mm for adjustment of fork steering column.
319	Assembly Tool, transmission drive shaft. Slide 319/2 on shaft without kickstarter gear, press on in vice and remove circlip. Press circlip with 319/2 over cone 319/3 on shaft. Use 319/1 to press on ball bearing 6204.
326	Tensioner, for kickstarter Spring. Grasp cover for starter shaft with 326. Give spring initial tension by turning 180° – 270° anticlockwise and insert 2 countersunk screws.
331/1	Steel Bushing for press operations under hydraulic press; see 281/1/2/3/4, 288/1/2, 293/1/2/3/4 and 385/5.
331/2	Cover for 331/1 with slit and bore. Application see 331/7A, 385/5, 281/3, 281/4, 385/5.
331/3	Cover for 331/1 to be used as flat press plate.

Matra Order No. and Illustration	Description
331/7A	Bushing, split, for pressing shock absorber flange off propeller shaft. Support shock absorber hub on 331/7A and 331/2. Use arbour 281/1 to press out propeller shaft in 331/1.
338/1	Hook Spanner, 49 mm dia. for exhaust nut.
353A	Device, for centering of crankshaft, consisting of one base plate, 2 longitudinally slideable prismatic supports, and adjustable support for rotation test.
353B	Gauge Support with stand; used with 353A for dial gauge adjustment in all directions.
353C	Dial Gauge with .01 mm scale for 353B.
355	Puller for camshaft. Loosen bearing screws behind camshaft gear, screw spindle into camshaft and withdraw shaft by means of puller clamp V 5033 (shop-made tool).

Special Tools for BMW Motorcycles

Matra Order No. and Illustration	Description	Matra Order No. and Illustration	Description
356	Puller, for ball bearing in rear wheel drive. For ball bearing 6205, with pressure plate 29 mm dia., 3 mm thickness (shop-made) for ball bearing 6206.	368	Holder, used for grinding-in valves with 7 mm stem dia.
357	Clamping screws for clutch assembly. Compress clutch evenly with 3 items 357, then replace them progressively by clutch screws.	385/5	Bushing, split, for pressing on final coupling flange; to be applied on propeller shaft together with 331/2 and 331/1.
359	Remover for Speedometer Bushing. Apply 359 on bushing collar and withdraw bushing.	422A	Puller, for coupling flange on transmission.
360	Replacer Bushings for lock ring on driven shaft. Slide lock ring over cone 360/1 and press it in seat on shaft by means of 360/2.	431	Cutter Shank 7 mm dia. for cutters 294 and 295.
361	Wooden Plate for valve removal and re-installation; used to retain valves when tensioning valve springs. Use with valve spring lifter V 5034 (shop-made tool).	442	Valve Guide Reamer, 7 mm dia.
362	Wooden Clamping Blocks for front wheel fork, (one set) used to clamp fork in Vice.	451	Replacer tool, for leather seal in rear wheel drive casing. When installing final coupling flange, place 451 upon flange.
365	Puller for cover of rear wheel drive casing	467	Puller, for bearing cover of crank shaft front bearing. Clamp 467 with set screws, and remove cover with bearing.

Special Tools for BMW Motorcycles

Matra Order No. and Illustration	Description
281 (see 281/1 – 281/4)	Press tools, for removing and replacing shock absorber flange on propeller shaft, consisting of 281/1, 281/2, 281/3 and 281/4.
281/1	Remover, shock absorber flange on propeller shaft. Support flange hub in 331/1 using 331/7A and 331/2, insert remover 281/1 in bore of propeller shaft, press out shaft.
281/2	Replacer, shock absorber flange on propeller shaft. Support shaft collar on 281/3 and 281/4 in 331/2 and 331/1, and press on flange using replacer and press. Observe correct flange distance: 31±1 mm.
281/3	Support Bushing, split, 15 mm bore, R=5 mm, for replacing shock absorber flange. Application see 281/2.
281/4	Support Bushing, split, 14 mm bore, R=3 mm, for replacing shock absorber flange. Application see 281/2.
282	Puller, rear ball bearing of crankshaft. Apply 282/1 with 282/3 on crankshaft journal, grasp ball bearing and collar of 282/1 with 282/4, slide 282/5 over 282/4 and pull off ball bearing with 282/2.
283	Pin Spanner, 52/55 mm dia., for threaded ring on rear wheel drive housing.
284	Pin Spanner, 58/62 dia., round pin 5 mm for bell-shaped cover on propeller shaft.
285	Pin Spanner, 54 mm dia., round pin 5 mm, for spigot nut on fork end pieces. Oppose with 286.
286	Pin Spanner, 45 mm dia., round pin 5 mm, for spring retainer on front wheel fork. Oppose with 285.
287	Valve Insert Extractor. Use set of taps (3 items) and guide to cut thread in valve insert. Heat cylinder head to approx. 390 deg. F. Turn spindle and guide into valve insert and withdraw insert.
288/1	Fixture for removing drive shaft ball bearing. Support drive shaft (snap ring removed) on top speed gear in 288/1 and 331/1, press out shaft, using 288/3.
288/2	Fixture for removing drive shaft roller bearing inner race. Close 282/2 on low speed gear placed in tooth notches, support on 331/1 and press out shaft with 288/3.
288/3	Drift Punch, for drive shaft. Application see 288/1 and 288/2.

Special Tools for BMW Motorcycles

Matra Order No. and Illustration	Description
493 (see 493/1 – 493/5)	Press Tools for disassembly and assembly of crankshaft R 24 and R 25 consisting of 493/1 – 493/4.
493/1	Support for press operations on crankshaft
493/2	Support Plate for R 24. Support crankshaft at connecting rod with 493/1 in 493/2, secure with 493/4 and use 293/5 to press out crankpin together with rear web.
493/3	Support Plate for R 25 Support crankshaft at connecting rod with 493/1 in 493/3, secure with 493/4 and use 293/5 to press out crankpin together with rear web.
493/4	Locking Tool for support plates 493/2 and 493/3 used to secure crankshaft in support.
494	Holding Fixture with key for nut of transmission driven shaft. Apply 494 in pins of shock absorber flange, resp. against nose on transmission housing.
495	Drift Punch for crankshaft, used for assembly of crankshaft halves.

Matra Order No. and Illustration	Description
498	Locking Fixture for Flywheel to loosen and tighten crankshaft nut, lock clutch bolts and casing screws with 498.
499 (see 499/1 – 6)	Multi-Purpose Puller Device for engines R 51/3 and R 67.
499/1/2	Grasp gear on crankshaft with 2 puller jaws 499/2, bolt jaws to puller and spindle assembly 499/1 and pull gear.
499/3-6	Use Puller 499/1 with screwed-in hook screws 499/3 for oil pump drive gear, collar screws 499/4 for gearcase cover, 499/5 screws 8 x 72 mm for front bearing cover, 499/6 screws 8 x 33 mm for camshaft gear.
348747-10	Torque Wrench 0 - 6 mkg with square extension for tightening cylinder head screws with a torque of 3 – 3.5 mkg using 14 mm double hexagon sockets and magneto rotor screw with torque of 2 mkg using 11 mm socket. (1 mkg = 7.22 ft. lb.)

Addendum to "Special Tools for BMW Motorcycles," Edition of 3.52

The following Matra and shop-made tools, designed for use with the R51/2, R51/3, and R67 series can also be used to service the below-listed models of the R68, R50, R60, R69, and R69S motorcycle:

Special Tool No.	R68	R50	Application R60	R69	R69S
286	X	X	X	X	X
292	X	X	X	X	X
297/1	X	X	X	X	X
297/2	X	X	X	X	X
299	X	X	X	X	X
311	X	X	X	X	X
319/1	X	X	X	X	X
319/2	X	X	X	X	X

215

Special Tool No.	R68	R50	Application R60	R69	R69S
319/3	X	X	X	X	X
338/1		X	X		
338/2	X			X	X
355	X	X	X	X	X
W5003	X	X	X	X	X
W5009	X				
W5013	X				
V5014	X	X	X	X	
V5017	X	X	X	X	
V5020	X	X	X	X	
W5021	X	X	X	X	X
W5026	X				
V5030	X	X	X	X	X
V5031	X				
V5033	X	X	X	X	
V5034	X	X	X	X	X
V5035	X	X	X	X	X
L5036	X	X	X	X	X
W5038	X	X	X	X	X
W5039	X	X	X	X	X
V5040	X	X	X	X	X
V5041	X	X	X	X	X
V5042	X				
V5043		X	X	X	X

A complete set of tool drawings of these shop-made tools is available from the author through the "Vintage BMW Bulletin". See address in the appendices.

Total Production of BMW Motorcycles (Singles and Twins) 1950-69

Year	Production
1950	17,061
1951	25,101
1952	28,310
1953	27,704
1954	29,699
1955	23,531
1956	15,500
1957	5,429
1958	7,156
1959	8,412
1960	9,473
1961	9,460
1962	4,302
1963	6,043
1964	9,043
1965	7,118
1966	9,071
1967	7,896
1968	5,074
1969	4,701

Specifications of BMW twin-cylinder motorcycles 1950-69

Years	Model	Cylinders	Bore x stroke	CC	Hp/rpm	Production
1950-51	R51/2	2	68 x 68	494	24/5800	5,000
1951-54	R51/3	2	68 x 68	494	24/5800	18,420
1951	R67	2	72 x 73	594	26/5500	1,470
1952-54	R67/2	2	72 x 73	594	28/5600	4,234
1955-56	R67/3	2	72 x 73	594	28/5600	700
1952-54	R68	2	72 x 73	594	35/7000	1,452
1955-60	R50	2	68 x 68	494	26/5800	13,510
1960-69	R50/2	2	68 x 68	494	26/5800	19,036
1955-60	R69	2	72 x 73	594	35/6800	2,956
1956-60	R60	2	72 x 73	594	28/5600	3,530
1960-69	R60/2	2	72 x 73	594	30/5800	17,306

Engine numbers of BMW twin-cylinder motorcycles 1950-69

Years	Model	Engine numbers	Remarks
1950-51	R51/2	516001-521005	First postwar twin
1951-54	R51/3	522001-540950	
1951	R67	610001-611449	First postwar 600cc
1952-54	R67/2	6120001-616226	
1955-56	R67/3	617001-617700	
1952-54	R68	650001-651453	First sport BMW
1955-60	R50	550001-563515	First swing-arm twin
1960-69	R50/2	630001-649037	
1967-69	R50US	(Within above)	US telescopics
1960-62	R50S	564005-565639	Hot 500 cc
1956-60	R60	618001-621530	First swingarm 600
1960-69	R60/2	622001-629999	
1967-69	R60US	(Within-above) also 1810000-1819307	US telescopics
1955-60	R69	652001-654955	Hot 600 cc
1960-69	R69S	655004-666320	Raised compression
1968-69	R69US	(Within above)	US telescopics

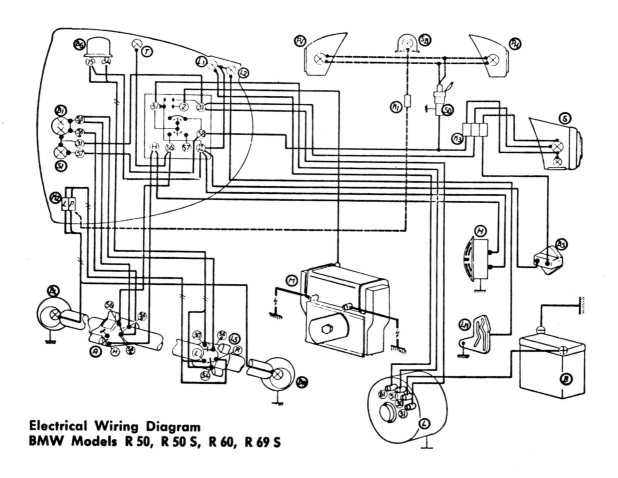

Electrical Wiring Diagram
BMW Models R 50, R 50 S, R 60, R 69 S

Key to Electrical Wiring Diagram: BMW Models R 50, R 50 S, R 60, R 69 S

A = Dimming switch	L2 = Neutral indicator
B = Battery	LK = Neutral indicator contact
BG = Flasher unit	LS = Blinker and headlight flasher switch
Bi = Double-filament bulb	
BL = Left blinker	M = Magneto
BR = Right blinker	PH = Rear side light "S" *)
BS = Stoplight switch	PV = Front side light "S" *)
H = Horn	S = Stop, and license plate lights
K1 = Cable connector (1-pole)	
K2 = Cable connector (2-pole)	SB = Blinker "S" *)
K3 = Cable connector (3-pole)	SD = Electrical jack (socket)
L = Generator (dynamo)	St = Parking light
L1 = Charging indicator	T = Speedometer light

*) "S" = Sidecar

BMW R50/2-R69S U.S.-1961-1969 6-Volt Only

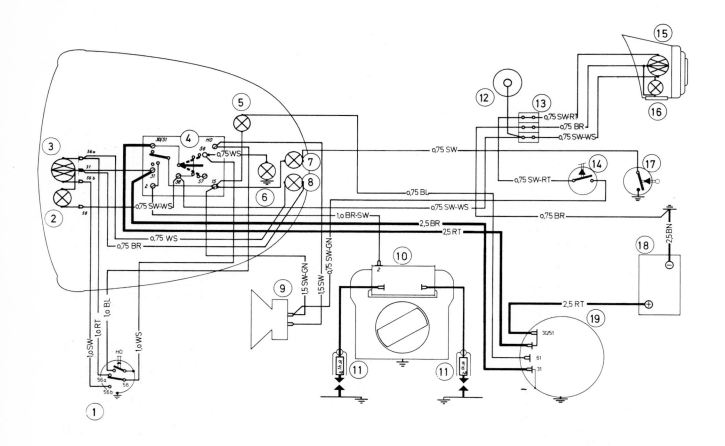

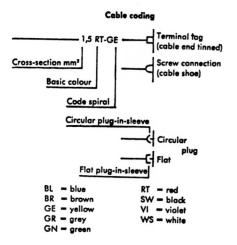

1 Horn and Dimmer switch
2 Parking lamp
3 Headlight
4 Combination Ignition/light switch
5 Charge indicator lamp
6 Speedometer illumination lamp
7 Neutral indicator lamp
8 High beam indicator lamp
9 Horn
10 Ignition coil
11 Spark plug
12 Attachment for sidecar running lamp
13 Terminal connection
14 Brake lamp switch
15 Taillamp and stop light
16 License plate illumination
17 Neutral switch
18 Battery
19 Generator

Key to wiring diagram

Cable coding

1,5 RT-GE — Terminal tag (cable end tinned)

Cross-section mm² — Screw connection (cable shoe)

Basic colour

Code spiral

Circular plug-in-sleeve — Circular plug

— Flat

Flat plug-in-sleeve

BL = blue   RT = red
BR = brown   SW = black
GE = yellow   VI = violet
GR = grey   WS = white
GN = green

BMW R51/3, R67, R67/2, R68-1951-54

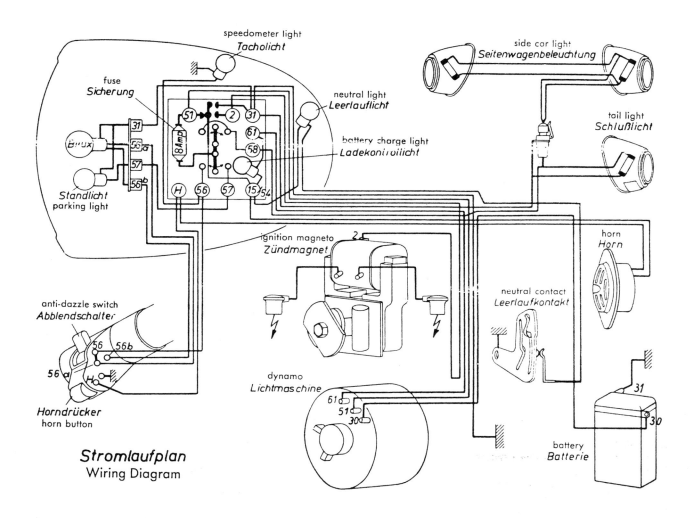

speedometer light
Tacholicht

fuse
Sicherung

neutral light
Leerlauflicht

battery charge light
Ladekontrollicht

side car light
Seitenwagenbeleuchtung

tail light
Schlußlicht

Standlicht
parking light

ignition magneto
Zündmagnet

horn
Horn

anti-dazzle switch
Abblendschalter

neutral contact
Leerlaufkontakt

dynamo
Lichtmaschine

Horndrücker
horn button

battery
Batterie

Stromlaufplan
Wiring Diagram

BMW and related motorcycle publications

Some of the major and most popular publications which deal specifically with BMW motorcycles, as well as those which, on a regular basis, devote time and space to the restoration and repair of BMWs and other classics are listed here.

The Antique Motorcycle, published quarterly by the Antique Motorcycle Club of America, Inc., Richard J. Schunk, editor. Beautiful color magazine, with excellent classified ads. To join the AMC, write Dick Winger, P.O. Box 333 Sweetser, IN 46987.

BMW Owners News, published monthly by BMW Motorcycle Owners of America, Inc. Devoted to the BMW, rally, and touring enthusiast, with classified ads for BMWs, sidecars, and other makes. To join BMWMOA, contact BMW Motorcycle Owners of America, Inc., P.O. Box 489, Chesterfield, MO 63006-0489.

Classic Bike, The Classic Motorcycle, Classic Mechanics, and *Classic Racer,* all British magazines of excellent quality and content, with detailed advertisements. Distributed in the U.S. by *Motorsport,* 550 Honey Locust Rd., Jonesburg, MO 63351-9600.

Hack'D, a periodical concerned with sidecars and the hobby, Jim Dodson, editor. Available from P.O. Box 813, Buckhannon, WV 26201

Hemmings Motor News, published monthly, at Box 100, Bennington, VT 05201. Large, comprehensive classified advertising magazine dealing primarily with automobiles, but which now has a motorcycle section.

Old Bike Journal, published monthly, at P.O. Box 391, Mt. Morris, IL 61054-7906. New magazine with classified ads arranged by country of manufacture, and also featuring technical and racing articles and extensive photography.

On the Level, published monthly by BMW Riders Association, Robert Hellman, editor. Main emphasis is the riding, enjoyment, and use of BMW motorcycles, with considerable coverage of technical features and future BMW developments, provided by sources close to the factory. To join BMWRA, contact BMW Riders Association, P.O. Box 510309, Melbourne Beach, FL 32951.

Rider. Slick newsstand publication, which covers all brands as well as BMW. To subscribe, contact P.O. Box 51901, Boulder, CO 80321-1901.

Road Rider. The original touring and camping magazine, with considerable BMW emphasis and excellent, free classifieds. Contact P.O. Box 488, Mt. Morris, IL 61054-0488.

Sidecarist,, published by the United Sidecar Association. The magazine is concerned with the use and fitment of sidecars to all brands of motorcycles, and has comprehensive classified ads. To join, contact United Sidecar Association, Inc. 130 S Michigan Ave Villa Park, IL 60181

Vintage BMW Bulletin, published bimonthly by Vintage BMW Motorcycle Owners, Ltd., Roland Slabon, editor. An illustrated magazine devoted to the preservation, enjoyment, and use of pre-1970 BMW motorcycles. Classified advertising is free to members and covers all years of BMW production, sidecars, and other classic makes. To join VBMWMO, Ltd., write to P.O.Box 67, Exeter, NH 03833.

Walneck's Classic Cycle Trader, an illustrated newspaper featuring classified ads and road tests, Buzz Walneck, publisher. Contact 7923 Janes Ave., Woodridge, IL 60517.

German motorcycle magazines

Markt fur Klassische Automobile und Motorrader. Huttenstrasse 10, D-6200 Wiesbaden, West Germany, or in the U.S. contact the Deutsches Motorrad Register, 8663 Grover Place, Shreveport, LA 71115.

Das Motorrad and *Motorrad Classic.* Leuschner Strasse 1, D-7000 Struttgart 1, Germany.

Part Sources

The following is a brief list of U.S. sources for new, used, or reproduction BMW parts and accessories, as well as sidecars and restoration services. This list is current as of spring 1994. I realize that this list is far from complete, and apologize for any omissions. The latest sources for parts and suppliers will always be listed in the publications of the U.S. BMW clubs. I have omitted the dozens of major German and European suppliers, but these can be found in the advertising sections of the German and British magazines.

Accessory Mart, Inc.
P.O. Box 26116
Cincinnatti, OH 45226

Excellent source of new, used, obsolete British and German parts, complete machines and sidecars. A comprehensive illustrated catalog is published periodically.

American Jawa, Ltd.
185 Express St.
Plainview, NY 11803
    Importer of Jawa, Velorex sidecars, and accessories.

BING Agency International
824 South Broad St.
Fremont, NE 68025
    U.S. distributor of German BING carburetors and repair parts.

Bley Vintage Engineering
700 Chase
Elk Grove, IL 60007
    Emphasis on vintage racing, as well as quality machine-shop work and complete restorations.

Blue Moon Cycle
20 Skin Alley
Norcross, GA 30071
    Seller of new and used BMW parts.

BMW Motorrad St. Louis/Sidecar
Restorations
4011 Forest Park Blvd.
St. Louis, MO 63108
    Importer of EML sidecars. Also sells vintage sidecars, parts, accessories, and BMW motorcycles.

Bob's BMW
10630 Riggs Hill Rd., Unit Y
Jessup, MD 20794
    Importer of new, used, obsolete, and reproduction BMW parts and accessories, sidecars, and the occasional prewar BMW motorcycle. BMW books, artwork.

Buchanan Frame
629 East Garvey
Monterey Park, CA 91754
    Quality spoke and wheel service, with reproduction spokes in stainless steel the specialty.

California BMW
2490 Old Middlefield Way
Mt. View, CA 94043
    BMW dealer, provider of excellent parts and service for most postwar BMWs.

Capital Cycle Corporation
21580 Beaumeade Circle #170
Ashburn, VA 22011
    Catalog sales and service for most post-1955 BMWs and the parts required to keep them running.

Classic Motorcycles Inc.
2114 East Vollmer Ave
Milwaukee, WI 53207
    Importer of new/NOS 1950–1969 BMW parts and accessories.

Craig Vechorik
P.O. Box 5130
MSU, MS 39762
    Fabricates stainless steel axles for any year BMW.

David Quinn Motorcycles
335 Litchfield Turnpike
Bethany, CT 06525
    Importer and distributor for Craven bags, Belstaff clothing, and Avon fairings.

Dick Tatem
523 North Main St.
Newport, NH 03773
    Halogen 6V headlight conversions.

Ed Korn
170 Jackson St.
Madison, WI 53704
    Fabricates virtually all special repair tool for postwar BMWs. Has produced three excellent repair videos dealing with pre-1970 BMWs. Also provides BMW books and service Bulletin Reprints.

EPCO, Inc.
RR 4 Box 179
Germantown, OH 45327
    Manufacturer of stainless steel BMW exhaust pipes.

Frank's Maintenance and Engineering
945 Pitner Ave
Evanston, IL 60602
    Manufacturer of fork tubes.

Gary VanderEyk
P.O. Box 67
Clinton, Ontario N0M 1L0
Canada
    Rebuilder of 1955–1969 Everbest petcocks.

Holt BMW Ducati
15530 US 50 E at 690
Athens, OH 95701
    Custom and original painting and striping of any year BMW.

Irv's Speedometer Hospital
3810 Collier Rd.
Randallstown, MD 21133
    Repairs speedometers and tachometers.

Jim Hosking/Hosking Book Works
136 Hosking Lane
Accord, NY 12404
    Motorcycle books and literature, shop and owners manual reprints.

Jim Young
Box 537
North Pembroke, MA 02358
    Importer of custom-made replica exhaust pipes and mufflers in stainless steel for virtually any old or new BMW or other classic.

Motorrad Elektrik
Rt. 12, Box 53
Gadsden, AL 35901
    Repairs, rebuilds, and offers 6-volt to 12-volt conversions for older BMWs.

Palo Alto Speedometer
718 Emerson
Palo Alto, CA 94301
    Quality speedometer and tachometer repairs, and instrument face restorations.

Paul Sturges
1906 Birch Lane
Newberg, OR 97132
    Restoration of cyclinder head exhaust threads.

Peel TT Touring
Ian M. MacKintosh
33931 Diana Dr.
Dana Point, CA 92629
    Manufacturer and distributor of a quality vintage Peel fairing replica for pre-1970 BMW motorcycles.

Pentacomm Inc.
1105 Marine St.
Clearwater, FL 34615
    Manufacturer of improved replacement point plate and components for 1951–1969 BMW twins.

Bob Wark/The Wark Shop
Rt.1, Box 292
Marietta, OH 45705
    BMW painting services.

Watsonian Sidecars
c/o Doug Bingham/Sidestrider, Inc.
15838 Arminta St., Unit 25
Van Nuys, CA 91406
    Importer and distributor of British Watsonian sidecars and accessories.

American BMW clubs

The following are some of the more prominent clubs and organizations in the U.S. devoted wholly or in part to the use and enjoyment of BMW motorcycles. While some also concern themselves with all brands of motorcycles, or just limit themselves to what we now consider antiques, all can be excellent sources of assistance, information, camaraderie, and an excellent way to find, through the classifieds in their various publications, that BMW you've always wanted.

Antique Motorcycle Club of America, Inc.
P.O. Box 333
Sweetser, IN 46987
    Devoted to all brands of antique and classic motorcycles. They publish an excellent quality color magazine, *The Antique Motorcycle*. The AMC has numerous national chapters and events.

BMW Motorcycle Owners of America, Inc.
P.O. Box 489
Chesterfield, MO 63006-0489
    Founded 1971, and concerned primarily with touring and rallies. Their magazine, *BMW Owners News,* has an extensive classified section. BMWMOA has many national chapters and events.

BMW Riders Association
P.O. Box 510309
Melbourne, Fl 32951
    Founded 1971, and devoted primarily to the riding and enjoyment of BMW motorcycles, with considerable emphasis on technical and future BMW development. The BMWRA publication is *On the Level*. BMWRA has numerous regional chapters and national events.

Deutsches Motorrad Register
8663 Grover Place
Shreveport, LA 71115
    Founded in 1982, and concerned with the dissemination of information on all German motorcycles. An excellent source of contact for members with unusual or limited-production machines. The club is U.S. distributor for *Markt fur Klassische Automobile und Motorrader,* an excellent German-language magazine dealing with vintage vehicles with an illustrated classifieds section.

United Sidecar Association, Inc.
130 S Michigan Ave
Villa Park, IL 60181
    Concerned with sidecars and their history. Classified ads in the U.S. publication, *The Sidecarist.*

Vintage BMW Motorcycle Owners, Ltd.
P.O. Box 67
Exeter, NH 03833
    Founded 1972, and devoted to the preservation, enjoyment, and use of antique (1923-1945), and vintage (1948-1954), classic (1955-1969), and contemporary (post 1970) BMW motorcycles. Members worldwide, with several annual rallies and events in the U.S. Their publication, *Vintage BMW Bulletin*, is a bimonthly, illustrated magazine covering historical, technical, and rally features, with a classified section for BMWs.

BMW Factory and European BMW clubs
BMW of North America, Inc.
Public Relations
P.O. Box 1227
Westwood, NJ 07675

Bayerische Motoren Werke AG
Postfach 40 02 40
D-8000 Munchen 50
Germany

BMW Motorrad GmbH
Triebstr. 32
D-8000 Munchen 50
Germany

BMW Clubs Europa e. V.
Herrn Wolfgang Marx
Petuelring 130
D-8000 Munchen 40
Germany

BMW Veteranen Club Deutschland
Im Breiten Feld 19
D-5910 Kreuztal-Kredenbach
West Germany

Intern. Verband der BMW Clubs
Lierberg 7-A
D-4330 Muelheim/R
West Germany

The BMW Club
Peter Kyle
1 Barrowsfield
South Croydon, Surrey CR2 9EA
England

The Vintage Motor Cycle Club, Ltd.
138 Derby Street
Burton-on-Trent
Staffs. DE14 2LF
England

Index